FORZA
ITALIA

For Dindy and Róisín

FORZA ITALIA

PADDY AGNEW

A JOURNEY IN SEARCH OF ITALY
AND ITS FOOTBALL

EBURY
PRESS

1 3 5 7 9 10 8 6 4 2

Copyright © 2006 Paddy Agnew

First published 2006 by Ebury Press,
an imprint of Random House,
20 Vauxhall Bridge Road, London SW1V 2SA

Random House Australia (Pty) Limited
20 Alfred Street, Milsons Point, Sydney, New South Wales 2061, Australia

Random House New Zealand Limited
18 Poland Road, Glenfield, Auckland 10, New Zealand

Random House (Pty) Limited
Isle of Houghton, Corner of Boundary Road and Carse O'Gowrie,
Houghton 2198, South Africa

The Random House Group Limited Reg. No. 954009

www.randomhouse.co.uk

Printed and bound in Great Britain by
Mackays of Chatham plc, Chatham, Kent

A CIP catalogue record for this book is available from the British Library

Cover design by Two Associates
Interior design by seagulls.net

Picture section images © Empics and © Getty Images where stated.
All other images used courtesy of the author.

9780091905613 (after Jan 2007)
ISBN 0 091905613

CONTENTS

ACKNOWLEDGEMENTS

Anyone who has ever written a book knows that there are many, too many friends, colleagues and loved ones to whom gratitude is due for encouragement, ideas and inspiration. First thanks are obviously due to my wife, Dindy, and to my daughter, Róisín, and not just for unfailing solidarity in the face of writer tantrums. Writing about and commentating on football means being out of the family home every weekend, Saturday and Sunday, for nine to ten months of the year. In practice, Róisín has grown up without the faintest idea of what exactly a 'family weekend' might entail. For this I am sorry but persuading FIFA, UEFA and others to play football on a Monday-to-Friday basis only has so far proved beyond me. I will keep on trying.

Thanks also to family friend, Colm Toibin, for advice and support.

Further thanks go to Andrew Goodfellow at Ebury who was foolhardy enough to ask me to write this book in the first place and then patiently allowed me to shift the emphasis from the objective to the subjective and from purely football to football-as-politics. Thanks are also due to his colleague Alex Hazle for searching out the photographs and overall help with production.

I owe a debt of gratitude to Italian colleagues and Italian news organisations, too numerous to mention here but acknowledged in the text. Yet, I would specially like to thank Giuseppe Smorto, Corrado Sannucci, Gianni Mura, Fulvio Bianchi and Eugenio Capodacqua of Rome daily, *La Repubblica* for their help, friendship and writing over the years.

I am especially grateful to Geraldine Kennedy, editor of the *Irish Times*, for allowing me a six month leave of absence. In the same context, my thanks go to *Irish Times* foreign editor Paddy Smyth for his patience. In relation to football, thanks are also due to *Irish Times* sports editor, Malachy Logan, since for most of the last 20 years his pages have provided the first testing ground for many of the ideas, stories and observations in this book.

A special thanks goes to Italian football historian Mario Pennacchia who, as an act of kindness and at his own behest, did some painstaking research for the short history chapter. Finally, my thanks to Dublin journalist and publisher Vincent Browne who gave me my first break in journalism many moons ago.

INTRODUCTION
ROTTERDAM REFLECTIONS

Twenty seconds, 20 miserable seconds ... Along with the 22 million Italians gathered around their TV sets back in the *bel paese*, I am unlikely ever to forget Italy's dramatic last-gasp defeat by France in the European Championship final in Rotterdam on Sunday, 2 July 2000.

Just when Italy stood on the brink of a remarkable, not widely expected success, the redoubtable French side of Zidane, Deschamps, Thuram et al pulled it out of the fire, first with an equaliser from Sylvain Wiltord in stoppage time and then with David Trezeguet's winning golden goal.

Having lived and worked in Italy for the last 20 years, I often find myself accredited as 'Italian Media' at big tournaments. Therefore, on that mild Rotterdam night, I found myself in the Italian section of the press box. As Wiltord's equaliser went in, it met with a collective groan of despair all around me. The chorus at La Scala could not have been more in unison, with all of us immediately suspecting that from here on, there could be only one winner and it would not be Italy.

That groan was prompted by two considerations. Firstly, there was the straightforward, chauvinistic disappointment at the dawning realisation that the boys in blue, the *azzurri*, were not going to pull it off, after all. Secondly, there was the more prosaic consideration that, with newspaper deadlines looming, we journalists were in trouble.

One of the least noble of football-writing trade secrets concerns deadlines. With so many night-time games these days, the football writer is often in the awkward position of knowing that his poised, carefully reasoned match analysis needs to be filed right on the final whistle. As a result, the stressed reporter starts writing at half-time and then spends the entire second half in a schizophrenic limbo, caught between his computer screen, his observations and the ongoing match. Inevitably, this necessary business of writing a match report while the game is still in progress can be fraught with pitfalls.

That press box groan was motivated by the realisation that hundreds of carefully written, deeply analytical pieces explaining a splendid Italian triumph were now out the window. After all, the pendulum swing from 'Magnificent Italian Triumph' to 'French Fight Back to Win Title' is about as big a story turnaround as you get, and, what is more, you get it in just 20 seconds.

If you are the old dog for the hard road, then in tight matches like this one, you write two 'intros' or opening paragraphs. Thus, when the Wiltord goal went in, I was not especially worried as I already had Report B on file. The ease with which one moved from an enthusiastic celebration of the Italian triumph to laudatory admiration for the French comeback speaks volumes about the whorish nature of the sports writer's world.

For all that, I felt genuinely sorry and disappointed that Italy had not won. Italy had done pretty well throughout the tournament (drawing a veil over their absurd semi-final win against host country the Netherlands) and had certainly played better than France in the final. On football grounds, Italy would have stolen nothing in lifting the title. Then, too, I simply had wanted Italy to win, wanted Italy and Italians to have something to celebrate and feel good about, even if only for a few days.

My own sense of disappointment surprised me. At previous tournaments, I had been much more removed, feeling only a mild sympathy for Italy's fate. Indeed, when Roberto Baggio missed his famous penalty in the 1994 World Cup final shoot-out in Pasadena, Los Angeles, I had positively exulted, partly because I had not relished the thought of newly installed Prime Minister Silvio Berlusconi laying claim to part of the success. (Berlusconi was the man who discovered Italy's coach at USA '94, Arrigo Sacchi.)

This time was different. I felt linked to Italy's fate, and not just for the obvious professional reason of being someone who lives, at least in part, by writing about Italian football. Earlier in the day, as I sat in the press centre close to the de Kuip stadium just hours before the kick-off, my wife, Dympna (Dindy), had called me on my mobile phone. She was ringing from our home in Trevignano Romano, just north of Rome.

After the usual exchange of gossip, not to mention the daily *bollettino* of 'things that have gone wrong/broken down since you left' (dishwashers, car tyre punctures, fugitive family dogs etc.), our (then) eleven-year-old daughter Róisín came on the line. Almost immediately, she nutmegged me with a question that in any other context would seem both banal and obvious: 'Do you think we can win today, Daddy?'

It was the 'we' that set me thinking. Róisín was and is, of course, entitled to use the first person plural when referring to the Italian football team. After all, even though both her parents are bona fide Irish, she was born and has lived all her life in Italy. It is, for better or for worse, her homeland, albeit one shared at a distance with her parents' native green sod.

By the standards of Italian eleven-year-olds, however, Róisín's interest in football was sporadic. Just about every Italian child picks a team at an early age, opting to become a *juventino, milanista, interista, laziale* or *romanista*, often before learning to read or write, and more often than not because of strictly observed family tradition.

Róisín, however, is not such a child. Furthermore, as she has moved from childhood to adolescence she has tended to feel much more Irish than Italian, for what that is worth. Her concern about how 'we' would get on against France, however, had reminded me that part of me, somewhere, somehow, felt intimately linked to Italy.

If you live and work in a country for 20 years, and if you get married, have a child, build a house, take out your first mortgage and buy your first car in that same country, then you have put down some roots, be they sentimental or of the reinforced concrete foundation kind. The expatriate can spend a lot of life in a never-never land, an outsider in their adopted country and a stranger in their native land. For me, watching an Italian football team play, be it a club or the national team, gets me out of never-never land and straight into the Italian mainstream. Curiously, watching the Italian national team play can tend to have the same effect on Italians themselves, since one of the oft-repeated clichés of modern Italian living is that Italy and Italians only really assume a national identity when the *azzurri* line up to do battle at either the World Cup or the European Championship.

Listening to 25,000 Italian fans sing – and for once sing passably well – 'Fratelli d'Italia' prior to the Rotterdam kick-off, I wanted Italy to win. Victory in a football match generates a transient emotion but one which, for all that, can be intensely positive; call it the feel-good factor, if you like. Modern Italians, too, badly need a positive and winning version of the national image to contrast with their daily diet of Mafia killings, political chicanery, traffic jams, strikes and infrastructural shortcomings. Not for nothing is a popular morning radio programme called *How To Survive in Italy Today Without Dying of Rage*.

Four days prior to the Rotterdam final, I had been sitting in the press room at the Arena Stadium in Amsterdam, minutes before the semi-final clash between the Netherlands and Italy, when colleague Simon Kuper told me that 'for the good of football' (or words to that effect) the Netherlands had better win. Simon is an outstanding, thoughtful and original football writer, and his words probably reflected the feelings of many of our colleagues. Italian teams, national or club, do not always enjoy a good international press. There are many commentators who feel that the traditionally defensive Italian game is not only dull and boring but also quintessentially negative and cynical, with a tendency to the dishonest.

Even if I understand that a majority of fans would prefer to see the Netherlands or France win a tournament like Euro 2000, I still wanted – and want – Italy to win. Not for its football virtues, even if Italian football has those too. No, it is more about decent, ordinary and sometimes extraordinary Italians.

I might be thinking of Carmine Mancuso, a police inspector (later a politician) when I first met him in Palermo, Sicily in December 1986. I had gone to Palermo to write a magazine piece on the ongoing *Maxi Processo*, a collective Mafia trial in which 344 mafiosi received heavy sentences, 19 of them getting life for a variety of crimes ranging from multiple murder to drug trafficking to racketeering. On the Saturday afternoon that I talked to Carmine in his apartment, he had to cut short the interview because his wife had to go to the dentist. The point was that, if she went to the dentist, so too did he and his police escort. It is a funny world when your wife requires a police escort to the dentist. Yet, Mancuso, his wife and his family lived every day with the threat of Mafia violence. Years earlier, Carmine's father, Lenin, also a policeman, had been killed by the Mafia while on escort duty.

I might also be thinking of Paola Passalacqua, head of an all-women team of restorers whom I met in Assisi as they set about re-assembling a thirteenth-century Cimabué fresco, which had been violently dislodged from its normal resting place when an earthquake hit the Basilica of San Francesco on 26 September 1997. Without the help of sophisticated or computerised technology, and working in the open in front of the Basilica, the team was trying to put together 90 square metres of fresco that had collapsed into pieces as small as those in a child's jigsaw puzzle. She and her team had to examine each small piece of smashed plaster, deducing, sometimes just from the shade of blue or green, whether it belonged to the face or some other part of the original fresco. Working out in the open, she told me that the work required patience and that was why women were best at it. For their skill, dedication and professionalism, the majority of the team received miserly State salaries of less than £300 per month.

I could be thinking about Rosaria Schifani. On a blisteringly hot July day in 1992, I was again down in Palermo, this time to attend the funeral of the Mafia-investigating magistrate Paolo Borsellino, killed by Cosa Nostra just as his good friend and colleague Giovanni Falcone had been killed two months earlier, both of them 'taken out' by massive explosions. Outside the cathedral of Maria Assunta, the air was tense. Angry young Palermitans, shut out of the cathedral, refused to let reporters through and shouted furious chants of 'Justice, Justice' at the Italian Prime Minister of the day, Giuliano Amato, as he was frog-marched into the cathedral by his worried escort. Inside the cathedral, the tension and anger was, if anything, even worse. The Cardinal of Palermo, Salvatore Pappalardo, who was presiding over the ceremony, was stopped in mid-sentence as a tall, dark-haired, handsome woman in black burst up the crowded aisle and straight onto the altar. This woman was 22-year-old widow Rosaria Schifani. Her husband, Vito, had been one of three escort policemen killed in the explosion that had killed Judge Falcone two months earlier. Visibly distressed, she took the pulpit microphone from the Cardinal and reproached him. 'You should not say that, you should not talk about hope,' she said. 'There is no hope here.'

In tears and unable to say anything else, she went back down to her seat in the church. I was standing at the top of the cathedral, close to the altar, and as she passed by me, she whimpered to herself in utter despair: '*Vito, ti voglio ... Vito mio*' (I want you, Vito, my own Vito).

Or there are those ordinary half a million Italians, mainly Romans, who, on a bright November morning in 2003, came out to honour Italy's dead, in a lavish and moving state funeral for the 19 Italians who, a week earlier, had been killed in a suicide bomb attack on an Italian military base in the southern Iraqi city of Nasiriya. Unlike their US counterparts, the Italian military dead were not flown back in the dark of the night, ignored by those who had sent them out to die in the first place. Italy and Italians paid their dues to a central part of the warrior's culture, namely the ability to face death squarely and honestly, coming together to pay full and handsome tribute to their dead on a national day of mourning. All the major institutional figures in the land, led by State President Carlo Azeglio Ciampi, joined the people of Rome in a dignified ceremony, held in the magnificent Basilica of St Paul Without the Walls.

Italian tricolours flew from many of the windows along streets leading to the Basilica whilst billboards displayed the faces of all 19 dead with the simple words, 'Rome Hugs You to Itself'. Inside the crowded Basilica, Monica Filippa, the young widow of 33-year-old Carabiniere Andrea Filippa, kneeled for a long moment over her husband's coffin, stretching out her hand as if for one last touch. Slowly and quietly, she bent forward, finally resting her head on the coffin as she burst into tears.

The reaction to the Nasiriya dead was not surprising, given the widespread opposition to the US-led military invasion of Iraq. In February 2003, a huge crowd, perhaps as many as three million people, had peacefully marched through Rome to protest against the forthcoming invasion. Parties from the centre-left opposition, a variety of Catholic lay groups, hard-line party Rifondazione Comunista, trade unionists, Rome Mayor Walter Veltroni, ex-State President Oscar Luigi Scalfaro, anti-globalisation activists, Palestinians, Kurds and non-EU immigrant groups joined with showbiz personalities, such as American film director Spike Lee and Italian Oscar-winning comic Roberto Benigni, as well as thousands of ordinary Italians, for a demonstration that took over the centre of the Eternal City. The peace flags and an eclectic variety of street music reflected an Italy to feel good about, for a change.

Romans again took me by surprise more recently, on the evening of 2 April 2005, the night that Pope John Paul II died. At ten o'clock that night, not long after news of the Pope's death had broken, 60,000 people stood so quietly in St Peter's Square that even from a distance you could clearly hear the water gently flowing in the square's two handsome fountains. For seven or eight minutes, after the formal announcement of the Pope's death had been greeted with a round of applause, a quasi-silence and an eerie calm descended upon the square.

Then there are the students who marched against the local Mafia, the 'Ndrangheta, in the Calabrian town of Locri in November 2005, in protest against the killing two weeks earlier of a local politician, Francesco Fortugno, doctor, husband and father of two. He had been gunned down in broad daylight in the centre of town on a Sunday afternoon, minutes after voting in Italy's first-ever centre-left primary election. As he stood chatting to two colleagues, a masked man had approached him and fired at point-blank range, hitting him five times and killing him almost immediately. The man, with the help of a waiting accomplice, then effected a speedy and unhindered getaway. Police investigators found no bullets to pull out of the wall or surrounding objects; only five had been fired and all five had hit their target. This was an 'Ndrangheta hit job.

On the day of Fortugno's funeral, young members of his

party, La Margherita, had boldly flown a banner bearing the slogan 'And Now Kill Us All', by way of protest over the 'Ndrangheta's hold on the region. Now Italy's most powerful criminal organisation, stronger and more dangerous than Cosa Nostra in Sicily and with an estimated annual turnover of €36 billion, or 3.4 per cent of Italian GDP, the 'Ndrangheta had flexed muscle in order to intimidate those like Francesco Fortugno who were determined to fight their stranglehold on the local economy, local government and public contracts. In and around Locri itself, a town of 13,000, there were 26 Mafia murders in 2005.

I have witnessed many less dramatic, less public moments when Italians have taken me by surprise. There were the two young Protezione Civile guys who pulled me out of a ditch on a rainy Sunday after I skidded off the country road, as I hurried in to do TV commentary work. There were Domenica and Anna Maria, gynaecologist and obstetrician, who came round to our flat and sat up with us all night as Dindy went through labour before giving birth to Róisín. Then there was the irascible Bruno, last of the Etruscans, builder by trade but raconteur by inclination, who oversaw the building of our house even though he was dying from cancer.

Then, too, there are all those other ordinary moments – early-morning bike rides by the lake in my home of Trevignano, long hot summer days on the beach, chilly February days in the magic of Venice, evenings of food and wine and chat that are part of the Italian experience, and all things that make you feel good about Italy.

It is for those moments, for the Paolas, Rosarias and Domenicas of this Italian world, for those young Calabrians who want rid of the Mafia, for those individuals and families who, despite everything, manage to believe in the concept of service to the Italian State, that I want the Italian football team to win.

Not, mind you, that you think those thoughts at the time. There and then, I was just disappointed that Italy had lost. While most neutral commentators probably felt that France were the outstanding side at Euro 2000, even those not well disposed towards Italian soccer (and, as usual, there were a lot of them about) acknowledged that, on the night, Italy had more than matched the reigning world champions.

The architect of this near-success story was coach Dino Zoff, himself a living legend who had captained Italy's 1982 World Cup winning side. The Italian squad, although it contained world-class talent in players like Alessandro Nesta, Paolo Maldini, Fabio Cannavaro, Francesco Toldo and Francesco Totti, was probably a little short of the overall strength of the French squad. Yet Zoff maximised resources, rode his luck and very nearly went all the way.

Zoff's handling of his squad was exemplary, not only in relation to his inspired team selection (one example was the surprise choice of goalscorer Marco Delvecchio in the final) but also, and perhaps more importantly, in creating the calm, controversy-free atmosphere that had reigned at the Italian training headquarters in Geel, near Antwerp. How many coaches could have handled the potential time bomb prompted by the debate about whether to use Francesco Totti or Alessandro Del Piero without eventually seeing it go off in his face? (Zoff opted for Totti, incidentally, leaving Del Piero on the bench for most games. He brought Del Piero on as a substitute in the final, only for the striker to miss two relatively easy chances that would have swung the result in Italy's favour.)

State President Ciampi, who was present in Rotterdam for the final, accurately caught the nation's mood by visiting the Italian players in their dressing room after the game to tell them that they should return to Italy with their heads held high and 'full of pride'. Furthermore, the next day he nominated all 22 squad members 'Cavalieri Della Repubblica', an honour previously bestowed on the 1982 World Cup winning team by the then president Sandro Pertini.

There was, however, one significant exception to this mood of nationwide approval, namely centre-right opposition leader and AC Milan owner Silvio Berlusconi. At the very moment that the Italian football community was lavishing huge praise on Zoff and Italy, Berlusconi chose to launch an astonishing attack on the national coach. At a news conference on the day after the final, Berlusconi was asked for his opinion on Italy's close-run defeat.

'We should and could have won,' he replied. 'There were certain things happening on the pitch that you could not ignore. You cannot leave the source of their game, Zidane, free to run the show and prompt all their actions, especially in a final. Even an amateur coach would have realised what was happening and would have won the final by stopping Zidane ... It was simply unworthy.'

Some coaches might have ignored Berlusconi. Not Zoff. Perhaps emotionally stretched after the Sunday final, he found Berlusconi's comments deeply offensive. Summoning a hastily convened news conference on Tuesday morning, he told reporters that he was resigning, adding that he had been 'very upset' by the criticism and that he had been so angry he had been unable to sleep. 'I don't understand why he [Berlusconi] has to denigrate somebody else's work,' he said. 'I have been publicly denigrated and treated with huge disrespect and this really annoys me ... It is not Berlusconi's technical analysis but rather his personalised evaluations that have upset me.'

Zoff was perhaps wrong to resign but he was right to dismiss Berlusconi's 'technical analysis' regarding Zinedine Zidane. So successful was the Italian handling of Zidane that the great Frenchman had had by far his worst game of the tournament, being consistently closed down by an Italian midfield whose combative attitude to him largely contributed to a first half of tense, dramatic stalemate.

Four years later, I met Zoff on the fringe of a news conference in Rome and asked him if he did not, in hindsight, regret his decision to resign. No, he said, I could see the way things were going, the criticism that was coming my way, and felt that it was better to jump rather than be pushed.

The Rotterdam story may be a reminder that, in Italy, the good guys do not always win; indeed, they more often get hounded straight out of town. Zoff had done a brilliant job and had been rewarded with a kick in the teeth.

This was only sport, not (Bill Shankly, forgive me) a matter of life and death. By comparison with the treatment that modern Italy offered its Mafia-investigating magistrates, Zoff had got off lightly. After all, the bravery and courage shown by Falcone and Borsellino in fighting organised crime was rewarded with a campaign of isolation, jealousy and suspicion from sections of the media, the judiciary and the political classes, which left them exposed and unprotected. By the end of their days as investigators, both men felt so threatened, so closely watched by hostile forces, that the only place in Palermo's Palazzo di Giustizia they felt safe to talk was the lift.

The Rotterdam story has always struck me as emblematic, and for two reasons. Firstly, it illustrates the extent to which football in Italy is a frontline issue. It is hard to imagine England coach Sven-Göran Eriksson or German coach Juergen Klinsmann handing in their resignations just because opposition leaders David Cameron or Gerhard Schroeder had criticised them. Secondly, like just about every other significant political, financial, industrial or news story in Italy over the last decade, this one bears the formidable imprint of Silvio Berlusconi.

It would be comforting to suggest that Italian football represents an oasis of limpid transparency, rigorous administrative efficiency and total moral probity in an otherwise corrupt Italian environment. It would be nice to be able to say that, in the context of the chaotic, corrupt and scandal-ridden labyrinth of modern Italy, football provides a touchstone of excellence. Nice, but not true.

Italian football, like football in any other part of the world, merely reflects the society around it. Hence, football in Italy is currently undergoing a crisis, ranging from financial meltdown to match-fixing and drugs scandals, that reflects the much wider economic, political, cultural and social crisis afflicting the country. In that sense, Italian football offers a unique looking glass through which to observe modern Italy.

This is not to say that either Italy or Italian football are in terminal decline. Both will live to fight another day, yet both are certainly stuck in a moment and not sure how to get out of it.

When I first came to work as a football writer in Italy in December 1985, I contacted former *Guardian* correspondent George Armstrong, who had been an occasional contributor to the Dublin-based *Sunday Tribune*, for which I had been the sports editor. I told George that I wanted a break from Ireland and was moving to Italy, intending, at least at first, to cover mainly football.

'Oh good,' said George. 'Football is just about the only thing that starts on time in this country, at three o'clock every Sunday afternoon.'

Twenty years later, the president of FIGC (Federazione Italiana del Gioco Calcio – the Italian football federation) Franco Carraro told me the same thing, albeit in greater detail: 'Italian football organises 710,000 games per annum between professional and amateur games. These games all begin punctually and, in 99.9 per cent of cases, all end punctually. Football, despite all its problems, is still the best organised, most punctual activity there is in Italy.'

Carraro has a point. Italian football has much to be proud of. Just take the matter of perceptions of Italy. Most non-Italians would tend to perceive Italian political life as some form of corrupt opera buffa that has passed from revolving door government to the era of Silvio Berlusconi, united all along by the single constant of judicial or Mafia-related scandal. Italy, a G8 country with an economy as large and powerful as that of Great Britain, often appears to carry limited political clout and even less political credibility.

Yet, no serious football professional – fan, player, coach, manager or club director – has ever treated Italian football with anything other than deep respect. While Italy's politicians have often served their country badly, regularly rendering it ridiculous in the eyes of the world, Italian football and Italian footballers have been among the best on the planet in the last 25 years, winning one World Cup and six European Cups/ Champions League trophies. While modern Italy has become notorious for its poor standards in matters of public administration (over-bureaucratisation, low rates of State pay, inadequate educational, health and transport infrastructure), Italian football has represented a mark of total excellence over the last quarter of a century.

It is also true that in a country where academics, politicians and industrialists alike regularly lament the lack of innovative industrial research, Italian football has set a standard of excellence admired and copied in other parts of the world. Where once only England sent out its coaches to teach the world football, men such as Fabio Capello (Spanish title with Real Madrid) and Giovanni Trapattoni (German title with Bayern Munich; Portuguese title with Benfica) have shown that there is a highly professional method to Italian winning ways.

Walking along the seafront in Naples on a mild February day in 1994, on the eve of a friendly international between Italy and France, I bumped into former Arsenal, Juventus, Sampdoria and Inter Milan player, Irishman Liam Brady. Having known Brady and had occasional contact with him since 1980, we stopped for a chat in a nearby café. I had not spoken to him at any length since he had left Italian football, midway through the 1986–7 season, when he had moved from relegation-battling Ascoli to West Ham. I was curious to know how he found things back in English and Scottish football. (He had also managed Glasgow Celtic for two seasons.)

One of his first answers was very revealing. Italian footballers, he said, were instinctively professional. Without being ordered about, they knew how to live a professional life, how to train, to eat and not drink. It came naturally to an Italian, he said, to know what foods were rich in protein and which in carbohydrates and when to eat them. As for their English counterparts, well ... he could only shrug his shoulders.

More than a decade on from that conversation, standards in the much-hyped Premiership have clearly moved on. Yet, the increasing number of foreign coaches in English football would suggest that the benchmark has been set somewhere to the east of Dover. Unquestionably, Italian football was amongst the first to set that benchmark.

It is also worth recalling that, from 1980, Italian football introduced an open-door policy towards foreign players – enticing great players like Michel Platini, Diego Maradona, Zico et al to Italy – that was at odds with the protectionist Italian economy of the day. If you were an Udinese supporter in the early 1980s, it was OK to shout for Brazilian Zico, but almost impossible to go out and buy yourself a Japanese car rather than a Fiat.

In those pre-single market days, Serie A football represented an international element of cultural and commercial exchange in an Italy that was otherwise hermetically sealed off (economically, linguistically and politically) from the rest of the world. If you think this too strong, just look at Ford's abortive attempts to buy out the State-owned car producer Alfa Romeo in 1986. With the Ford deal practically concluded, the Italian government of the day, led by the subsequently disgraced Socialist Prime Minister Bettino Craxi, moved the goal posts and handed Alfa Romeo to Fiat instead.

The following pages hope to cast light on some of the elements that made and still make Italian football both glamorous and fascinating: the outstanding players; the industrial barons; the wall-to-wall media coverage; the scandals; the triumphs; and, more recently, the failures.

Obviously, this book is in no sense an academic or sociological survey of Italian football, rather a personal reflection on 20 years of football-watching in Italy during which I have been present for many memorable moments, such as Napoli and Maradona's first title triumph at the San Paolo in 1987, or AC Milan's historic 3–2 defeat of Napoli at the San Paolo one year later en route to Berlusconi's first title triumph. There have also been less edifying moments, such as the pitch invasion by three AS Roma *ultras* (die-hard fans) who, in a show of menacing force, 'persuaded' Roma captain Francesco Totti and other players to suspend the March 2004 derby between Roma and Lazio.

For better or for worse, Italian football throughout that time has by turns been exciting, technically excellent, winning and scandal-ridden, but never boring. Part of the reason may be that football is not so much Italy's national sport as a virus woven into the DNA of the average Italian.

Once, during the course of an interview with Italy's 1982 World Cup hero Paolo Rossi, I asked Rossi if he could sum up just what football meant to Italy and Italians. 'In Italy, 90 per cent of people are crazy about football,' he said. 'The other 10 per cent say they are not interested ... and then you see that they too like to sneak a look at the sports papers, just to check the results.'

ONE
HAMMER IN THE BRIEFCASE

Things were not going well. Inter Milan's German international Karl-Heinz Rummenigge was standing in my way and the dour look on his face suggested that perhaps it was not such a smart idea, after all, to attempt a one-man invasion of the team bus. In truth my timing was hardly ideal. Inter had just lost, for the first time in club history, to little Pisa in a game played at the Arena Garibaldi, within walking distance of the celebrated Leaning Tower.

The mood on the team bus was as grey and sombre as the Tuscan sky on that January 1986 evening. Yet I simply had to get on the bus, sombre mood or not. Irishman Liam Brady was my man and I had to get to him. With an apologetic smile, I pushed past the perplexed Rummenigge only to find a scowling Marco Tardelli next up. That might have been the not-so-pretty end of my solo expeditionary force had I not been able to catch the eye of Brady, who was sitting some way down the bus. With a tired nod, Brady indicated to Tardelli and another player, Andrea Mandorlini, to let me pass.

'You shouldn't be here, Paddy, and I don't want to talk to you,' came the greeting from my illustrious compatriot. As conversation starters it was hardly encouraging and I was soon back off the bus, without a quote, phone number or indeed hope for future, fertile collaboration with one of Serie A's most gifted stars.

I'd arrived in Italy in December 1985, less than one month earlier, in search of a new direction as a journalist, and Brady had seemed like a logical place to start. After all, went my naive reasoning, Brady would be glad to help out the only Irish sports writer then permanently based in Italy. Given his often polemical and frustrating relationship with the Irish media, 99.9 per cent of whom never bothered to travel to Italy to watch him play in those pre-Internet, pre-satellite TV, pre-Champions League days, I thought that Brady would appreciate having someone on hand who could tell the real story of his immensely successful Italian career. Furthermore, I had met and interviewed Brady at various times over the previous six years, even following him around for a week during his Arsenal days in London, and had always found him courteous and helpful, if understandably cautious with his words when faced with the reporter's notebook.

In those days, Brady was a Serie A icon. All you had to say was that you were Irish and Italians would often reply 'Ah, like Liam Brady'. When Italian football re-opened its frontiers to foreign stars in 1980 (they had been closed since Italy's ignominious exit from the 1966 World Cup finals at the hands of modest North Korea) Brady was the first foreigner purchased by Italy's most famous club, Juventus.

In seven seasons between 1973 and 1980 at Arsenal, he had established himself as one of the brightest talents in European football. Arsenal fans still warm to the memory of Brady – in particular for his role in setting up a memorable late winner, scored by Alan Sunderland, in the 1979 FA Cup final win over Manchester United. Many Arsenal fans, however, probably do not realise that they never saw the best of Brady. That was reserved for Italian fans.

In two title-winning seasons with Juventus, and subsequently in two years with newly promoted Sampdoria, Brady played probably the best football of his tremendous career. His close control, vision, passing and silken left foot were always destined to shine brightly in the Serie A of the 1980s, a cerebral, tactical league that was light years away from the hurly-burly of the (then) English First Division.

Brady left his mark on Italian football not just through the quality of his football but also for one particular incident, which, to this day, is still admiringly recalled. It came on the last day of the 1981–2 season, at a time when Brady already knew that Juventus had decided to offload him in favour of French ace Michel Platini. (The regulations of the day permitted only two foreign players per Serie A club and the club already had the brilliant Pole Zbigniew 'Zibi' Boniek on their books.) Juventus were away to Calabrian side Catanzaro and needed a win to see off nearest rivals Fiorentina. When Juventus were awarded a second-half penalty, it was Brady who knocked it away with nonchalant elegance to wrap up the title. For many Italian commentators and fans, Brady had shown remarkable professionalism, not to say class, in winning the game for the club which had just betrayed him.

Recalling that 'betrayal' years later in his autobiography, *Una Vita A Testa Alta*, the then Juventus president Giampiero Boniperti wrote:

> Brady, Boniek, Platini – we had one too many. If only we had been able to hold onto all three of them, with Brady playing behind those two, we would have become one of the greatest teams of all time. I remember I rang Brady and an hour later he was at my door. 'Brady, we've signed Platini, I'm really sorry,' I told him … He was in tears and I had a lump in my throat, too.

Brady played great football, spoke good Italian, and was widely admired and respected. By that January day in 1986 on the Inter

Milan bus, he seemed thoroughly integrated into Italy and Italian football. In that sense, he had done better than many of his Anglo-Saxon comrades, men like Jimmy Greaves, and later Ian Rush and Paul Gascoigne.

In 1961, Greaves had made a high-profile transfer to AC Milan but fell out with the club's autocratic coach Nereo Rocco, and even though he scored nine goals in his first twelve league games, he was back in England before Christmas of that year where he was snapped up by a grateful Bill Nicholson of Tottenham Hotspur for the famous purchase price of £99,999 (to avoid him being weighed down with the 'first £100,000 player' tag).

Rush, like Greaves an astonishing talent in front of goal, failed to shine either on or off the pitch with a poor Juventus team in the 1987–8 season. In Italy, he remains best known for his requests for strange food, such as baked beans, tea and biscuits and Welsh ale. Furthermore, in a quote he doubtless regrets, he once described his Italian experience as 'like living in a foreign country'.

Having said that, Rush did better than yet another famous Brit, the redoubtable Paul Gascoigne, whose dramatic days at Lazio in the early 1990s were marked by a succession of injuries, squabbles with paparazzi, an inability to speak Italian and the occasional belch into a TV reporter's microphone.

In fairness, I have to point out that in my time in Italy, I have come across a number of British players, such as Gordan Cowans (Bari), Graeme Souness (Sampdoria), Ray Wilkins (AC Milan) and David Platt (Juventus), who all managed to fit in pretty well. Yet, none of them lasted as long as Brady or made anything like the same impression. His accomplishments put him on a par with the legendary Welshman John Charles of Juventus. Always elegant, on and off the field, Brady consistently cut a *bella figura* in Italy. Years later, sitting in a bar with him in Naples during one of his periodic return visits to Italy, I was not much surprised to note that the waiters all remembered him well.

In short, Brady was just about the best person a newly arrived greenhorn could meet. Or he would have been. His emphatic rejection on the bus put paid to that. It took me some while afterwards to establish a decent working relationship with him and then, alas, just as I was getting to know him and understand something about Italian football, he was shipped back to England and West Ham. (Typically, Brady chose to play down the circumstances of his departure from his last Italian club, Ascoli, with whose vulcanic owner, Constantino Rozzi, he had a less than satisfactory relationship, especially with regard to wages due.)

As I beat a crestfallen retreat off the bus, I was left to reflect that things were not going as planned. This, after all, was glamorous Italy, cradle of civilisation, the Hollywood of football, the home of the reigning world champions, where men, women and children understood, as nowhere else, the complex subtleties of the beautiful game.

Yet, somehow, things were far from glamorous. The Pisa press room reminded me of the canvas tent at the Mid-Antrim point-to-point where the gentlemen riders changed into their colours. It was shoddy, ill-equipped and old-fashioned. Worst of all, it was dominated by a loudmouthed blustering man called Romeo Anconetani, the Pisa president, who had appeared in the press room to give us his 'thoughts' on the match. Given the result, you might have expected him to be happy. Yet, he chose his hour of victory to settle scores in a long-winded, high-decibel rant that suggested he was pompous, arrogant, semi-literate and semi-lunatic. With hindsight, of course, one realises that he was among the more reasonable of Italian club presidents.

The president's performance was entertaining, in its way, but my major concern was the no-show of Inter players in the press room. How was I to know that the Inter officials had called a *silenzio stampa* (press blackout)? Thus it was that, armed with the sort of courage that comes from true ignorance, I had opted for the raid on the Inter team bus. Twenty years on, the idea seems vaguely whimsical. Nowadays, such action would probably earn you six months in Guantanamo prison.

Stomping down the road, away from the bus and into the cold, dark Tuscan night, I began to think that things were not as they should be. This was a far cry from the siren call of Mediterranean sun, glamour and football glitz that had brought me here in the first place.

The idea of going to Italy had sprung into being one year earlier during a Christmas break in Barcelona. I was with my then girlfriend, now wife, Dindy. We had travelled up the coast on a bus one day, stopping at San Feliu de Guixols where we sat out at a beach restaurant, eating a pleasant lunch. This, we agreed, was a much better life than that offered by the pre-Emerald Tiger, 1980s Ireland, where we then lived. That was the Ireland of majority pro-abortion and anti-divorce referenda votes, dominated by a sanctimonious, hypocritical, complacent and repressive Catholic Church. It was a stifling place and the urge to get out was hard to resist.

For most would-be emigrants, the biggest question concerns future livelihood. What exactly will you do for a living? For us, this was not an issue. As an established Dublin-based journalist, I was foolhardy enough to imagine that I could get by as a freelancer, whilst Dindy had already spent more than three years teaching in Spain. No, for us, the biggest problem was where we would go.

Dindy was a confirmed Hispanophile, whilst I was a Francophile, both of us having studied the respective languages at university. Dindy had lived and worked in Barcelona for three years while I had spent two years in France, first in Paris and then in Arles where I had a first, magical taste of the Mediterranean. So which would it be, France or Spain?

One Sunday morning, we sat down in a coffee shop at the top of Grafton Street in Dublin, determined to resolve this thorny issue. In the end, using a logic taken from the Dag Hammarskjöld guide to diplomacy, we opted for the 'compromise' solution of Italy. After all, it was a truly Latin country and sort of halfway between Spain and France (our European geography has much improved since). Above all, we concluded gleefully, it will certainly be a lot warmer than windy, wet Ireland.

The next consideration was where, exactly, in Italy. For someone with an eye on football, Milan would have seemed a logical base. After all, two of the country's three most powerful clubs (then and now), AC Milan and Inter Milan, were based there whilst the third, Juventus, was just an hour down the *autostrada* in Turin.

Again, the atlas was consulted. Even we could work out that Milan sat in the foothills of the Alps and was clearly about as Mediterranean as Belfast. No, no, it would have to be Rome. The Eternal City looked to be a much more exotic, intriguing and warm destination.

In those days of foolhardy naivety, the fact that I had never been to Italy, even as a tourist, and did not speak a word of Italian seemed no obstacle. Being a good linguist, I reasoned with stupefying arrogance, I would soon 'pick up' the language. Indeed I did, but certainly not 'soon' and not without being frustrated and initially much handicapped by the slow-learning faculties of 33-year-old brain cells.

In truth, though, there was more reason to our madness than there might have seemed. At the *Sunday Tribune* in Dublin, I had been very aware of just how difficult it was to get good, first-hand reporting about Brady in particular and Serie A in general from Italy.

As a journalist who had started out covering everything from the Troubles in Northern Ireland to the Irish rugby team for monthly magazine *Magill*, I felt confident that Italy would prove a rich enough source of Vatican, Mafia, lifestyle and other stories to keep my struggling freelance head above water.

That was the theory, at any rate. The practice was to prove rather different. Italy and Rome, initially, were impenetrable. Almost nothing worked along lines that the Anglo-Saxon mind could recognise. You were in a European country, that was for sure, but one where the influence of an Arab, Greek, ancient Roman and even Mussolini past, to name all but the obvious, conditioned the local mindset.

To emigrate to any big city, where you are without friends and relatives and where useful contacts are few and far between, can be hard enough. To swap the title of sports editor for that of impoverished freelance was harder still. To arrive in a city where you do not speak the language and where your only guaranteed income is a handsome IR£55 per week (thanks to dear old Tom O'Shea, sports editor of the now defunct *Evening Press*) was also tough. In such circumstances, to have chosen Rome was an act of mindboggling folly, not to say masochism.

Rome is, of course, a city of breathtaking beauty, a place so stylish, handsome and self-possessed that, 20 years on, it still sets my heart pacing just to walk around the *centro storico*. It is also, however, the *caput mundi*, an ancient centre of civilisation that has seen foreigners, from Hannibal to Attila, come and go for thousands of years. The arrival of an impoverished Irish hack was never likely to register too much on the Roman Richter scale.

The culture shock was tremendous. Faced with the *forestiero* (foreigner or outsider), Romans tend to take a martial arts approach to the normal courtesies that elsewhere represent social interchange. In the pursuit of everything from a flat to a phone to match tickets, I was regularly dismissed with unbelievable rudeness. People hung up on the phone; enquiries were met with either silence or a curt 'no'.

Those, of course, were the pre-Internet days when such was the Italian commercial nous that travel agents refused to give information over the phone. Could you give me a price for a London–Rome return flight, please? Oh no, sir, you will have to come into the office for that information. And Italians now wonder why the country is in economic crisis.

One morning shortly after our arrival, at the famous flea market of Porta Portese, we gained a useful insight into the Roman experience. As we struggled with our confusing lire (just imagine, there are idiots who actually want to re-introduce that accursed currency with its trillions and zillions of zeros), a neighbouring stall-holder shouted across to his colleague, imagining that we could not understand: 'Rip her off, Giovanni, she's not Italian.'

Flea market retailers, in any part of the world, are not usually looked on as beacons of moral rectitude. Yet, two further and rather more serious experiences in those early days indicated dramatically that the Italian playing field was not quite level.

Firstly, there was the question of money, or rather the lack of it. Fortunately, we were not dependent on my modest income since Dindy had found a job as a teacher at the British Institute of Rome before we set out from Ireland. However, given that we had sent ourselves to Italy, there was no multi-national company, embassy or newspaper office to cover any of the costs of moving and setting up in another country.

For that purpose, we had travelled to Italy armed with a little nest egg in the shape of an Irish income tax rebate cheque, relative to my *Sunday Tribune* job. The sum of money in question was just under IR£3,000, a veritable fortune to us and our economic guarantee for the settling-in period.

It only remained to go to the bank, which I duly did almost as soon as I arrived – and that was where the problems began. First of all, I was directed to the huge head office of Credito Italiano out in the 'Mussolini Ideal Town' suburb of EUR

(Esposizione Universale di Roma), where they could deal with foreign currency. A certain Mr Petriello (not his real name) relieved me of the cheque but, puzzlingly, told me to come back the following day to collect the money. Given my limited Italian and even more limited understanding of the Italian banking system, I reluctantly accepted, all the time suspecting however that something was not right.

The next day, of course, the cheque had somehow not been cleared. A week later, nothing had changed. To cut a long story short, a month passed and several frustrating trips out to EUR were made, but Mr Petriello refused to cough up. It was difficult, he said, getting an Irish cheque cleared. (In truth, in those days, people like Mr Petriello kept trying to tell me that Ireland was not a member of the then European Community.)

Convinced at this point that I was on the receiving end of a good old runaround, my mental state switched to deeply para-noid mode. Everything, it seemed, was difficult. The *mura di gomma* (rubber wall) effect was at work. One morning I announced to Dindy that I was going to make another visit to Mr Petriello and that this time I would be carrying a hammer in my briefcase (I intended to purchase the offending weapon at a hard-ware shop). Why a hammer and what exactly I hoped to achieve, I am not quite sure. The choice of weapon says much about my fast-deteriorating mental faculties.

Before this dastardly plan could be enacted, however, Dindy intervened. She had told all her colleagues at the British Institute about the cheque saga. By chance, one of them just happened to have a Credito Italiano employee in one of her classes, who also worked at the head office in EUR. On our behalf, he got in contact with Mr Petriello and came back two days later to tell us that Mr Petriello had said he would pay half the cheque. At this point, all my hammer-wielding paranoia was justified.

We sent back a message along the lines of 'No Way,

Sunshine'. Then, two weeks later, we finally got a lucky break when Dindy was sent to teach the senior management at an investment institution linked to Credito Italiano. She lost no time in outlining our problem to her new pupils. Her story of the cheque prompted an initial embarrassing silence, followed quickly by a hasty exchange of opinions. One of the managers gave Dindy his phone number and told her to ring him the next day. When Dindy rang him from the bar close to our flat, he told her that things had been 'sorted out' and that I could now go out to EUR and collect the money.

Next day, I did indeed travel to EUR to pick up the money from a smiling Mr Petriello. He could not have been more courteous or pleasant. As he handed over the money, I remember looking at his elegant, tanned and manicured hands. Now, if I had got a good blow in at those fingers with my hammer, I mused pacifically, that might have taken the smile off his face. Six weeks had passed since the day I had lodged the cheque.

Twenty years later, my faith in the Italian banking system remains circumspect. Twenty years later, too, the Governor of the Bank of Italy, Antonio Fazio, was forced to resign in the wake of scandal prompted by his handling of a bank takeover in which he had, allegedly, unfairly favoured Banca Popolare Italiana over Dutch competitor ABN AMRO in a battle for control of another Italian bank, Banca Antoniana Popolare Veneta Spa (Antonveneta). At press time, Mr Fazio is still under investigation but has not been formally charged. Although he denies any wrongdoing, saying that he had 'always acted in full respect of the law', the whole incident did remind me of my, admittedly much less serious, experience 20 years earlier: 'Rip 'em off, Antonio, they're not Italian.'

Our initial impact with Rome was also much coloured by a dismally wet autumn. I had travelled out with Dindy in October 1985 to settle her into her new job at the British Institute, staying three weeks before returning to Dublin to work out my notice with the *Sunday Tribune* through to December. The plan was for me to use the three weeks to find us a home. Inevitably, it did not work out that way. Apartment-hunting was both baffling and disorienting. The landlord classes of Rome, when faced with a newly arrived foreigner, smelt blood.

In three weeks of stuttering phone calls (from rickety old phone boxes) and painstaking scrutiny of *Il Messaggero*, I saw 23 apartments, which ranged from the dusty to the dilapidated to the miserable. Most of them looked as if, at a pinch, they might do for a low-rent funeral parlour. There was only one constant: they were all overpriced.

One prospective landlady required six months' rent in advance, plus a hefty deposit on her furniture, plus references and pay slips from both our employers. Given the difficulty of finding a place, we were almost ready to meet these demands. We did, however, want to know from her, before handing over the loot, when the apartment would be available.

Over a two week period, I kept asking when the apartment would finally be ready. It will be ready when it is ready, she informed me. Her tone suggested that, as a foreigner, I ought to be grateful to her that she was about to do me the honour of ripping me off handsomely and that furthermore I should be grateful to her for keeping me waiting, without as much as an apology, whilst she and her navel contemplated one another. After all, what was my problem? I was only out on the street, looking for somewhere to live. Big deal. She had more pressing matters to worry about ... *Va'fan'bagno, Signora.*

For much of those first three weeks, it rained. As I left Rome it was raining and when I got back in December it was still raining. Our duvet, brought with us from Ireland and packed into a travel bag, developed a dose of mildew from the damp of the little *pensione* off Corso d'Italia where we were staying. So this, then, was the sunny, glamorous Mediterranean. This was another blip on the learning curve. Surely we knew that Rome gets as much annual rainfall as London, the only difference being that in Rome's case, the rainfall tends to be concentrated into the November–March period?

After my miserable failure on the apartment front, I was feeling less than sanguine about matters as I sat on the airport bus on my way back to Ireland. The bus had got stuck in your average Roman, rainy-day traffic jam, so much so that I was in danger of missing the flight. As I looked out the bus window at the sheets of falling rain, I began to feel guilty about leaving Dindy behind. Things were further complicated by the fact that she had broken her left wrist, which at the time was encased in plaster.

Six weeks previously, she had travelled out to Rome for an interview with the British Institute. Her interview was so successful that she not only got the job but also received an invitation to dinner that night with the British Institute proprietor, Patrick Clare, a man not frightened of a glass of good red wine, or indeed any colour of wine. Whether it was the wine, or a freshly mopped marble staircase in the *pensione*, or the height of the steps on that staircase, is hard to say, but Dindy came a cropper the next morning, breaking her wrist in the process. Six weeks and two operations later, it was still heavily strapped, stuck up in the air in a most uncomfortable-looking manner.

Now I was leaving her there, with a broken wrist, no apartment and seemingly dismal prospects. 'This place is a dump. Let's just abandon the whole idea and go back to Ireland,' I volunteered.

Wisely, and not for the first time, she chose to ignore my mutterings.

In the end, we solved the apartment problem thanks to the help of an Irish friend, Liz McKenna, who was then the local rep for Irish travel firm JWT. She was about to give up the lease on a small apartment in Via Col della Porretta, near Piazza

Sempione and the Via Nomentana, a tranquil and relatively green residential zone not far from the centre.

At first, I was reluctant to take Liz's apartment because it did not have a phone (a pretty essential item for a freelance journalist in the days before mobile phones). After my three-week search, however, we got wise, realising that this was as good as if not better than it got, phone or no phone.

We were very comfortable in the apartment. It was on the ground floor, was maybe 110 square metres in size with parquet floors, just one bedroom, a small kitchen, a small bathroom and a pleasant *salotto*. At the time, we did not realise it but it had the inestimable virtue, for a Mediterranean house, of being cosy and warm in the winter and relatively cool in the hot summer. Best of all, for me, was the *terrazzo* (balcony) that ran along the whole side of the flat. When the warm weather came, we used it all the time, enjoying the huge novelty of eating and sitting out all evening long. I was so pleased with the *terrazzo* that I called it 'Monte Carlo', since I felt it represented some sort of exotic pleasure. (A couple of years later, when I first visited the modern, money-driven squalor that is the real Monte Carlo, I felt rather sorry that I had named my *terrazzo* after it.)

Piazza Sempione, too, in those days seemed very exotic. For a start, it hosted a daily, bustling, eminently well-furnished open-air market where it was possible to buy all manner of fruit, vegetables and meat. The only problem was dealing with the stall-holders and the shopkeepers. No one was especially friendly or helpful, and I soon learned that if I did not literally push my way to the front of the queue, I could spend an hour before getting my bread or *gorgonzola-mascarpone mista*. Even today, I am still occasionally taken aback by the brazen way in which Romans jump the queue and then turn on you viciously if you have the temerity to protest. Piazza Sempione did, too, boast a splendid *enoteca* (a bar, sometimes a restaurant, where you can buy wine by the bottle, demi-john or case). There was no ritual I liked better than trotting down there with my empty demi-johns and listening to the owner's philosophising as we filled up on his excellent supply of *vino sciolto* (literally 'loose wine', meaning unlabelled wine bought by the litre).

It was, though, a very different world to anything we had expected. For a start, all the lights were out by nine-thirty in the evening. Walking around the area after that hour was like being in a ghost town. Nothing was open and no one was about. It was so eerie that I used to go down to the square and wait for Dindy's ten o'clock bus from her evening work at the British Institute. This was no Dolce Vita.

The experience of being a newly arrived foreigner in Rome was certainly a humbling one. I remember one morning, maybe three or four months after we arrived, sitting on the bus as it travelled down Via Nomentana. On my lap, I had a briefcase that had been given to me as a going-away present by a colleague, Gerry Callan, a superb writer on boxing who had worked with me at the *Sunday Tribune* and who had been grateful for the space I had given him. By this stage, I could understand what was being said around me. As I sat there, gazing out the window, one lady standing beside me on the crowded bus said to her friend: 'Look at the poor divil with the briefcase. He must be a foreigner. Who does he think he is fooling? He's probably just got a sandwich in it. Maybe, where he comes from, he thinks it makes him look important and that it will help him find work ...'

I was almost tempted to protest and maybe say something rude to the good lady. Of course, I said nothing. Rather, I just sat there reflecting on their comments and thinking to myself that, in the space of a few months, geography and our self-inflicted emigration had transformed me from a busy, young, middle-class professional into a struggling freelance who could be taken for a boat person. On the greasy pole, I had slid down several notches.

A few months earlier, I had been ensconced in an office in Baggot Street, Dublin, the sports editor of a national Sunday newspaper. My phone rang all day long with calls from outraged readers, frustrated correspondents, PR consultants inviting me to reception after reception, people wanting to pitch stories, others looking for tickets. These days I did not even *have* a phone. (Getting one installed took about a year, even though it only required the reactivation of an existing line.)

In those days, I used to work out of the Associazione della Stampa Estera (Foreign Press club) in Rome, which provided (and still provides) a splendid work environment. The problem there was that I was out of phone contact when I went home in the evening or if I opted to work at home in the morning. For a struggling freelance, this was a recipe for disaster. In many senses, I had dropped off the edge of my known world. It would take some time before I could find the right knob to pull in order to release the parachute and ease the Rome landing.

The ladies on the bus were, of course, dead right about the briefcase. After all, it was neither 100 per cent leather nor *firmato* (designer labelled). Then, too, my hair was unkempt, and I was wearing a woolly jumper and leather jacket. If I had only had the gumption (and cash) to invest in a neat series of Valentino suits early on, life would have been much easier. One of the stifling realities of Italy then and now is that appearances count. I had come from a northern European workplace where journalists dressed not so much casually as nearly always badly. Not many of my colleagues in Dublin wore suits to work.

To dress sloppily or badly in Italy is the same as walking around with a sign on your head saying 'I'm an idiot'. Often, when I am standing in arrivals at Rome's Fiumicino International airport watching people coming off a flight from Dublin or, indeed, London, I think to myself that the average newly arrived passenger looks like an East European refugee. The festive-worn clothes, all bright for the holiday, are usually too bright, or too dull, or too mismatched, or not matched at all – in short, a mess. Mind you, within hours, these same people will be walking about the Eternal City in their shorts, stopping at a streetside café to order a beer followed by a cappuccino. Italy is, of course, a tolerant country. Any other society would instantly repatriate people for such outlandish behaviour.

In those far-off days, though, the learning curve was steep. You had to dress well or be considered low rent. A year or so after I arrived in Rome, I got a gig as a Vatican stringer for the news agency UPI. The Rome bureau chief, Peggy Polk, needed someone to go across to the Vatican every day and pick up the infamous *Bollettino* or Vatican news bulletin, which was and still is released every day, sometime between midday and two o'clock.

This was hardly an arduous assignment, but it was one from which you could learn a lot about the mysterious workings of the Vatican. Doyen of the Vatican *sala stampa* (press room) in those days was the late Max Bergerre, a Frenchman who had been a wartime diplomat in Rome. When Max saw my name up as the UPI guy for a 'pool' of journalists that was to cover an audience granted by the late Pope John Paul II to the late King Hussein of Jordan, he got worried. Eventually he came over to me.

'Paddy, you're in the pool tomorrow, aren't you?'

'Sure, Max.'

'Well, ahm, you do know that this is a papal audience, with the Pope and the King of Jordan, and that it takes place in the Library in the Apostolic Palace and, ahm, we need to be very smart and respectable. You do understand, don't you?'

'Don't worry, Max, I'll have my best bib and tucker on tomorrow.'

Next day, I turned up at the Vatican press room in a dark suit. Poor old Max just about did a cartwheel of delight when he saw me. For months, he had seen me slop into the *sala stampa* in jeans and jumpers and, obviously, he thought I was going to turn up for the Pope and King Hussein in the same sort of garb. After all, he himself was someone who turned up in the press room almost every day in a three-piece suit.

'*Oh, ça, c'est très elegant,*' he beamed at me.

Covering the Vatican for UPI also meant that I regularly got to be close up to 'Himself', the Pope, that is. On one occasion, this almost prompted a minor family incident. My mother-in-law, Marie Clare, a strong believer and daily communicant, happened to be staying with us one Easter. Knowing her religious inclinations, I said to her on Good Friday morning that I was off to the Vatican beat and that, if she liked, she could come, too.

Good Friday is obviously a very special day in the Church calendar and the Pope marks it by, among other things, donning black robes (it is the only day in the year that he does this) and coming down into the Basilica of St Peter's to hear confessions from ten of the thousands of pilgrims, faithful and tourists mingling around the church. (The Vatican always says that the ten are picked at random but, in reality, they have to be 'screened' first.)

Unlike Marie Clare, I knew that this was the programme. So, I marched her into St Peter's, placed her close to the confessional booths that I knew John Paul II would soon be using and told her to hold on to her place in the front row on the rails in order to see the action. I then left her there to resume my duties. Half an hour later, the Pope entered the Basilica by the side lift, followed by myself and three other journalists who were part of that day's Vatican pool. My mother-in-law could hardly believe her eyes. There was her Northern Irish Protestant (worse, Presbyterian) son-in-law doing a man-to-man marking job on John Paul II, following his every move, notebook in hand.

That night, when we returned to our flat in Via Col della Porretta, Marie Clare quietly took Dindy aside and asked anxiously: 'Do they know about him in the Vatican?' In other words, were the Holy See authorities aware that a Northern Prod was on their hallowed beat?

Years later when, through the offices of the Pope's then private secretary, now Archbishop of Cracow, Stanislaw Dziwisz, I organised a private audience with John Paul II for Marie Clare, she was truly grateful. By that stage, however, she had long since come to accept her son-in-law's Vatican work.

The initial learning curve, of course, included items both banal and Byzantine. To whom did you use the formal '*lei*' for you, rather than the informal '*tu*'? You had to be careful about city centre bars because they charged double if you sat down at the café table. (I still regularly see enraged tourists arguing with indifferent Roman waiters about this one.)

As newly arrived immigrants, of course, we made plenty of mistakes. On our very first weekend in Rome, we went for a meal in the splendid theatrical surrounds of Piazza Navona, once the Stadium of Diocletian. It was October, the sun was shining and we wanted to celebrate our brave new Italian venture by eating out in one of Rome's most sought after locations. When the bill arrived, we discovered we did not have enough money. No problem, we thought, we will pay with the credit card. Big problem. It was not that credit cards were not accepted, it was more that no one had ever seen or, God forgive us, ever used such a thing. Money is money, said the waiter, plastic is plastic, that is something else. There was nothing for it but for Dindy to call a taxi and dash round to the *pensione* to dig into the piggy bank below the mattress, while I waited and consoled myself with another glass of sparkling white.

In those early days, too, it was impressed upon us that we needed to acquire a *codice fiscale*, a sort of social security number.

This was another instructive experience. We headed off to a huge public office not far from the Vatican where hundreds of people, apparently on the same mission, were gathered. A fellow sitting at a table handed us a form to fill out. Then it was just a question of a morning-long wait before eventually a public service employee emerged, shouting names at the top of her voice. Everyone crowded around like earthquake victims looking for a food parcel as they desperately tried to recognise the Romanised version of their name. If you thought your name had been shouted out, you raised your hand and the *codice fiscale* was sent surfing down through the crowd to you. It sounds chaotic, but it worked. Dindy and I still use the *codice fiscale* issued to us that day.

One learns the hard way. I remember we spent a quiet, but rather lonely New Year's Eve together in the apartment that first winter. After midnight, when the bells started ringing and fireworks went off, I foolishly suggested we go out for a walk around the neighbourhood to join in the festive celebrations. There was almost no one out on the streets. We soon discovered why.

From apartment balconies, people shouted down at us. At first, I thought they were wishing us a Happy New Year. As fireworks then crashed down onto the street beside us, it became clear that the 'greetings' from the balconies above were rather more hostile. At first, we thought it was just a mistake. Surely they were not aiming at us? Bang, zzzippp, wwhaap, as more fireworks crashed around us. Indeed, they were aiming at us. We soon beat a hasty retreat back to the apartment and safety. Now, when I read the casualty toll on New Year's Eve (every year, people are killed or injured by fireworks), I can understand just why.

Then, too, there was the day when the loo blocked (a not unusual Mediterranean experience). That happened, as these things often do, when my parents were staying with us. It happened, too, on a national holiday, 1 May. In our desperation, we rang an 'emergency service'. Later that day, two rather shifty fellows from the emergency *idraulica* (plumbing) service arrived. They took one look and immediately told Dindy the problem could be resolved for the sum of 500,000 lire (about £200), the equivalent of one month's rent. Dindy told them to go away, deciding that we would struggle on until we could get the local plumber to come round next day. The two men said OK, but would she sign a form just to prove that they had answered our call. She duly signed.

In due course, we received a bill for 1,500,000 lire from our 'emergency' plumbers, for 'the use of a laser-jet suction pump' etc. Furthermore, if we failed to pay immediately, we would be charged a monthly interest rate of 14 per cent on the outstanding sum.

Clearly, we were not going to pay. So, first, we wrote a letter to the paper (I knew people at the Rome daily *La Repubblica*), recounting the whole tale. Then, another of Dindy's British Institute classes, this time down at the Ministry of Justice, came to the rescue. One of her pupils, a magistrate's assistant, took the details of the case, the name of the firm and made some phone calls. Mysteriously, we never heard any more from the 'laser-jet' plumbers.

For me, those early days were full of a sense of surprise, usually of the negative variety. I had expected a warm, easy-going, open and modern Italian society that fitted in with some daft notions I had concocted for myself, largely from a diet of Pasolini and other film makers. I had not bargained for a closed, tough, cynical and aggressive society that chooses to almost deface its great cultural wealth with some of the most ugly post-industrial urbanisations known to man. Italy is, of course, still the famous *bel paese*, but take a ride some time on the little train that heads south from Naples through the city's hinterland to Pompeii to see another much less attractive Italy.

There was surprise, too, about the unexpectedly conformist

and conservative nature of the society. Rome itself was a city with no youth culture, no floating population out on the town and the streets, no sense that there was a space for singles or young couples. True, there was the splendid fun of Trastevere, the one area in the city that throbbed with nightlife, but this was the exception rather than the rule.

For young northern Europeans, it was especially difficult to understand just why and how so many young Italians were still living at home well into their late twenties and early thirties. Where was their sense of spirit and adventure? Curiously, 20 years later in November 2005, *The Economist* observed the same phenomenon: 'The fact that 40 per cent of Italians aged thirty to forty are reportedly living with their parents is not just a happy sign of family harmony or attachment to Mamma's cooking. Many young Italians stay at home because they cannot find work or because they do not earn enough to afford a place of their own.'

Those same cultural differences were forcibly underlined to us by Mary, a young Irish woman married to an Italian, who told us about her experiences as a newly-wed. Her husband, Stefano, now in his early thirties, had worked from his teens as a tour bus driver. For more than a decade, he had continued to live at home, giving practically his entire salary to his parents, who in turn lodged the money in a savings account for him. The idea was that the money in the savings account would one day be used to buy an apartment for Stefano and his future wife.

In time, Stefano's parents did just that, buying and overseeing the renovation and furnishing of Stefano's 'bridal suite'. What Mary did not realise was that, even after the pair were married, Stefano's father kept a key to the apartment and would come round every morning about half past nine, let himself into the house and have a look around to reassure himself about the general upkeep. On occasion, he would complain to Stefano about Mary, pointing out her housekeeping deficiencies. Worse still, when it came close to their pay day towards the end of the month, his father would turn up with a list of repairs, improvements or renovations that needed to be done on the apartment. In the end, in despair, Mary decided that the only solution would be to move out of Rome, as far away from her in-laws as possible. When last heard of, they were living happily on the Adriatic coast.

In those early years, too, Dindy used to teach a class for a nationwide insurance company. Her pupils were mainly women who held senior secretarial or lower management positions. They were all typically well turned out, glamorous, hard-working and smart women of the sort who went to bed every night at nine in order to be up at five to wash their kitchen floors prior to an hour-long commute to work. (In those days, people assured us that a kitchen floor should ideally be washed three times a day, after each meal.)

Along with the women employees, their department head also attended the class. He was male, self-important and not too bright. All the women did much better than him in class. Eventually, a delegation of the women came to Dindy after a class and begged her not to ask their boss 'hard' questions or, if he did give a wrong answer, to pretend that it was the right one. If you do not do this, he will just suspend the class, the women said. Dindy continued to teach her class just as she would teach any other class. The shortcomings of the department head became ever more apparent. English lessons were soon suspended.

At the time, I found the story hard to understand. Not now. Do not for a second think that this particular manager was some sort of exception. He had probably been given the job on the basis of a *forte raccomandazione* (i.e. relatives or friends had pulled strings for him) rather than on merit. One of the great mysteries of modern Italy is its almost total lack of meritocracy, especially in the public service. All over the country, senior executives – be they bank managers, hospital administrators, surgeons or professors – owe their positions more to *raccomandazione* than to their ability.

On a more banal front, those early days also involved learning how to live in a condominium. Our balcony was splendid, but next door, separated from us only by a low wall and fence, was Ralph, a large German Shepherd. On the occasions his elderly owners went out, Ralph would bark and bark and bark. Neighbours were always complaining about him. In the end, the condominium cleaner suggested that we should get up a petition, asking people to urge Ralph's parents to do something about him. We had tried talking to the elderly couple but they failed to understand our point of view. So, in the end, we got up the petition and were the first to sign it. And the last. No one else signed. Next day, when I went out to our car (a beat-up Fiat 127), I found that someone had bent the carwipers into a neat S-shape and written '*Va'fan'culo*' (go fuck yourself) on the windscreen.

For me, what I loved most about those early days were the summers, travelling around Italy, eating and drinking the best food on earth. In our little Fiat 127, we would head up the Aurelia road, heading for the beach of Pescia Romana on the Tuscan coast, about 150 kilometres north of Rome. It was a ridiculously long journey but the wide empty beaches made it worthwhile.

I loved the heat. I remember one day we parked near to a beach in the Gulf of Trieste, and came back to find that a biro I had left on the car dashboard had become so hot that it had melted itself into a neat arc. Now, that was hot.

In January 1986, the long hot summers and the many joys of travelling up and down Italy were all in front of me. I was still trying to find my feet – not to mention press tickets. Part of the emigration masterplan had envisaged me seeing as much Serie A football as possible. (After all, you did not need to speak fluent Italian to watch a football match.) Given that I was living in Rome, this meant watching AS Roma at the Olimpico, as Lazio, the city's other major club, was at the time languishing in Serie B. The problem was that press tickets were issued on a seasonal basis and had already been issued the previous summer, long before my arrival. Surely, I reasoned, as an ex-sports editor, there will still be some press tickets available on a match-by-match basis?

Yes and no, was the answer. Yes, if Roma was playing Avellino, Bari or Como. No, if the team was at home to Juventus, AC Milan or Inter Milan. In other words, if Roma was playing a minnow, then I could get in. Yet, when it came to a game with a side like Juventus, there was no room at the inn, even when, as on several occasions, the accreditation request was made on my behalf by the *Guardian* in London.

Frustrated by this state of affairs, I went to the Roma head-quarters to meet the man who handled match tickets. In those days, Roma, like many other clubs, did not even have a full-time press officer. Mr Rossi (not his real name) soon made it clear that he had plenty more important things to do than resolve the prob-lems of a long-haired freelance in a leather jacket, without a tie or much Italian. He did at least lighten my darkness, explaining that I was about six months too late for a season press ticket but telling me how to resolve the problem for next season. In the end, in those first few months, I got press tickets for all the Roma home games against the minnows, and bought stand tickets (when I could find them) for clashes with the big sides.

That particular Roma side was well worth taking the trouble to watch. Coached by current England manager Sven-Göran Eriksson, and including some outstanding players such as the present AC Milan manager Carlo Ancelotti, Polish midfielder Zbigniew Boniek, Brazilian schemer Cerezo and striker Roberto Pruzzo, the team played easily the best football of any side in Italy that season. It was only an unexpected home loss to Lecce that stopped them in their tracks and handed the title to Michel Platini's Juventus.

To the layman, the difference between a press ticket and a stand ticket might not seem much of an issue. To the journalist, it matters very much since it may afford access to players. It seems almost unbelievable now, but in the late 1980s you could still walk into the dressing room after a Serie A match and sit down to talk to a player. I recall vividly walking into the Juventus dressing room during the 1986–7 season to be confronted with the languid figure of Michel Platini smoking a cigarette as he answered questions from a posse of journalists. Platini's intelligence, his ironic disdain for the inanity of the average hack question, his wonderful football skills and his sheer elegance made him one of my all-time favourite footballers. Face to face with him, I was at a loss for anything to say. I really only wanted to tell him how much I had enjoyed the football I had seen him play. Serious journalists, of course, do not do things like that. So I just stood and admired, listening to the other hacks prattle away.

The learning curve of those early days, of course, was not all negative. How could it be? Right from our very first days in that little *pensione* off Corso d'Italia, I had discovered proof of something that had attracted me to Italy in the first place: the sense that this was a country where *il calcio* was much, much more than just a game.

In those early days, I watched a lot of games in a little bar just down the road from the *pensione*. Here I discovered to my delight that even watching a match in the local bar entailed a certain protocol. There was a certain hierarchy to be observed when it came to the seating arrangements for a European Cup (as it then was before it became the Champions League) game. You could not just walk in and sit down. This was football, a serious business, and seats had to be booked.

The proprietor, however, had noticed me every morning in the bar as I painstakingly struggled through the pages of *Gazzetta Dello Sport*, complete with my pocket dictionary. One morning, as I paid for my cappuccino and cornetto, he asked me if I would like him to reserve a seat for that night's match. I was delighted, feeling I had passed some unseen test and been accepted into an inner circle. Better still, the bar owner had spotted my steadfast application and intended to reward it. When I turned up that night, I was placed ceremoniously in the front row, given the title of *esperto* (expert) and a welcome glass of red wine. This is much better, I thought. From then on for the first few weeks in Rome, I was in the front row for all the big games.

Watching matches in the local bar, however, had its drawbacks. In particular, I remember one night, during a Juventus versus Verona European Cup tie, when a fierce row broke out between the *juventini* (a minority) and the *anti-juventini* (just about everybody else in the bar, except my rigorously neutral self). The proprietor became heatedly involved in the row, too. Frustrated by the direction the discussion was taking (and perhaps the direction the match was taking, given that Juventus went on to eliminate Verona), the *anti-juventino* proprietor switched off the TV in a fit of total pique. As learning experiences go, this was a good one. From that day on, no one ever had to explain just how much one half of Italy loathes Juventus.

Initially, though, our life in Italy was deeply frustrating: I was earning very little; I had to work without my own phone number; press tickets were hard to come by for big matches; and it took weeks of tough bargaining to get an Irish government cheque cashed. Worst of all, it rained all the time.

Those first months were so difficult that I vividly recall my sense of joy when I travelled down to Avellino in early February 1986 for a World Cup warm-up friendly between Enzo Bearzot's Italy and Franz Beckenbauer's West Germany. For the uninitiated, Avellino is about level with Naples, inland in the Campania region.

It was a miserable day, with the rain yet again pouring down, but I was delighted to be there, on a big match occasion. When we walked into the press room at Avellino's Partenio stadium, local functionaries gave the foreign journalists, mainly German obviously, a little commemorative medal to mark the day. If I had been handed a solid gold bar, I could not have been more pleased. I still have that commemorative coin and carry it around with me in my computer case as a sort of good-luck charm.

As is often the way of friendlies, the game itself was no great shakes, West Germany winning 2–1 thanks to goals from Herget and Matthäus. Italy's goal was scored by Aldo Serena, then with Juventus. If anything could have been read into the game, it was that Italy, the defending world champions, were going to have difficulty holding onto their title in Mexico later that year. Likewise, those were still the days when you could tell that, rain, snow or sunshine, a German team would almost definitely make it to the final. It was not hard to make those predictions, nor was it surprising either when Italy went out of the 1986 World Cup, beaten 2–0 by Michel Platini's France in the second round, while West Germany went on to the final, to be beaten by Diego Maradona and Argentina.

The trip to Avellino was enlightening, for more than just football reasons. I had had to change train at Benevento and then travel across country. As we sped through the countryside, it was impossible not to see the wreck of house after house, destroyed by the Irpinia earthquake of six years earlier. There were still houses half-standing, or more accurately, half-houses still standing. Often a wall had been taken away to reveal a wallpapered kitchen complete with sink and other fittings, looking for all the world like a disused stage set. I wondered about the level of corruption, inefficiency and lack of political will that had failed to knock down these houses and build new ones. Over 25 years after the earthquake, notwithstanding an estimated €24 billion worth of earthquake relief funds over the years, there are still thousands of Irpinia victims living in temporary accommodation.

This is a very Italian story. The earthquake on the night of 23 November 1980 had been devastating, resulting in the deaths of 2,735 people and the total destruction of 36 villages on the border between the Campania and Basilicata regions. In all, maybe just over a hundred villages or towns in the area were seriously damaged. Yet, by the time various earthquake relief bills had passed through parliament, the area affected by the earthquake had been 'expanded' to include no fewer than 687 *communi* (local authorities) in a zone that stretched from Napoli on the west coast to Puglia on the east coast, and as far north as Lazio, the region around Rome. What had happened? Every local authority, politician, builder and architect had tried to climb onto the relief bandwagon and take advantage of the State-sponsored building of new houses. Even one of the most prominent of those local politicians, the subsequent Italian Prime Minister Ciriaco De Mita, admitted to parliament some years later that there had been 'the regrettable phenomenon of the progressive enlargement of the original geographic area in which the original tragedy took place'.[1]

Travelling across the country by train that day, I did not know any of this, but even a child could see two very obvious things. Firstly, the relief work here had been shamefully slow; and secondly, by Western European standards, it was (and still is) a relatively poor region. For me, it was a first look at the Italian south – *Il Mezzogiorno*, as Italians call it – and one that told its own tale. (*Mezzogiorno* literally means midday, but the term was first used during the nineteenth century, copying the French use of *Midi* for southern France.)

After the game that day, I got a lift home to Rome from Giuseppe Smorto, then the sports editor of *La Repubblica*. Giuseppe was a source of invaluable help in those early days, giving me all sorts of useful advice. That journey home also introduced me to fellow passenger Gianni Mura, then and now a senior football writer for *La Repubblica*. I have read thousands of columns by Gianni in the years since, and have rarely been disappointed. Not only does he unfailingly go to the heart of the footballing matter, always seeing the game in the broader context of the society in which it is played, but he invariably does so in an original and witty prose style. He is also something of a gourmet. When you arrive in the press room on the opening day of a World Cup finals or a European Championship tournament, Gianni is your man, as he will have already carried out a thorough reconnaissance of all the local restaurants.

Those early days, too, were marked by one truly horrendous event. At around nine o'clock in the morning of Friday, 27 December 1985, four men believed to be operatives of the Palestinian Abu Nadal 'Black September' brigade burst into the crowded departure lounge of Rome's Fiumicino International airport. The men moved towards the TWA and El Al check-in desks and began firing randomly, as well as chucking hand grenades around. In those days, there used to be a bar right in the corner of the departures hall, close to the TWA and El Al desks. One of the attackers turned his kalashnikov on the bar and began firing into the crowded café, filled with passengers, their families and friends.

From behind the El Al desk, three Mossad agents were the first to react, almost immediately returning the attackers' fire. At the end of a gruesome shoot out that lasted maybe two minutes, 15 people were dead (another died later) whilst 77 had been injured. In the area close to the café and the check-in desks, bodies, suitcases and overturned rubbish bins lay on top of one another. Amongst the dead was twelve-year-old Natasha Simpson, daughter of Daniela and Vic Simpson, who both worked (and still work) for the US news agency Associated Press. Vic himself and nine-year-old son Michael had been injured in the shooting. Daniela had been spared only because she had stepped outside the terminal building to take the family dog for a walk.

I did not know either Daniela or Vic at the time, but I felt bad for them. Years later, I know both of them, regularly coming across them on the Vatican beat. Years later, too, I still feel bad for them, all the more so because I like and respect both of them.

Following the attack, the airport was closed for three hours and a temporary barrier of screens was erected across that section of the hall where the killings had taken place. Yet, when the airport opened up again, people crowded in, seemingly un-deterred, many of them worried, indeed some angry, that they might have missed their flight. Doubtless they were aware of what had happened, but life, in this case a holiday trip, goes on.

I went out to Fiumicino on the day after the shooting. It was business as usual, almost as if nothing had happened. The café was open, even if there was a shallow hole in the floor caused by a hand grenade as well as obvious bullet holes in and around the check-in desks. The airport cleaners had worked through the night, sterilising and cleaning away the grisly mess of the day before. All seemed normal with hundreds of people moving through the departure hall, rushing for flights, tugging at their bags, hurrying children along, doing all the things that people do before they get on a plane. The speed with which 'normality' had returned made me feel better, despite the horrors of the day before. The barman at the fateful café told me: 'When we opened this morning people at first seemed embarrassed, but very quickly they came up and ordered their coffees just like any other day ...'

By way of a footnote, I should add that Abu Nadal, believed to have been found dead in a Baghdad apartment with gunshot wounds in August 2002, was convicted and sentenced in absentia by a Rome court for having organised the Fiumicino airport attack.

Working for *Magill* magazine in Ireland, I had occasionally covered the Troubles in my native Northern Ireland. That work, though, had been essentially about talking to and interviewing people. This seemed very different. I had never actually covered what today would be called a serious terrorist attack. I had left Ireland, too, partly to get away from the Troubles, from the apartheid-divided Northern Ireland in which I grew up – and a curse on both your houses, Protestant and Catholic, loyalist and republican. Walking around Fiumicino that day, I began to think the not exactly original thought that Protestant-Catholic tensions were in the halfpenny place by comparison with this Jewish-Islamic, Middle Eastern thing.

As a resident Irishman in Italy, I am occasionally interviewed about Ireland or asked to give talks to students or literary societies. Italians have a sparklingly positive view of Ireland. Younger Italians love the place, in particular the sense of freedom, liveliness and vibrant youth culture that positively throbs through Dublin. Today, Ireland (it was not always like this, folks) strikes a dramatic contrast with closed, non-meritocratic, constipated Italy where only auld fellows in their late sixties get to run anything, and then run it badly along happily nepotistic, corrupt and inefficient lines.

When I talk to Italians at gatherings like this, I often begin by pointing out that I am a Northern Irish Protestant by birth (Kilrea in County Derry) and that my wife, Dindy, is a Southern Irish Catholic by birth (Dublin). We are the future of Ireland, I say, adding that this, of course, is why we do not live in Ireland. Having said that, Dindy and myself lived, and could do so again, as a 'mixed' couple in Dublin, without anyone taking the blindest bit of notice. The same, mind you, might not be quite so true of Northern Ireland.

The point was, however, that notwithstanding the apartment crisis, the press ticket shortage, the cheque-cashing dilemma, the lack of a phone, and the rain, anything back then was better than Ireland – just about. Walking around Rome in those early days, be it coming upon a dimly lit little piazza late at night or just watching people strut their stuff in Piazza Navona on a Sunday morning, everything seemed glamorously, splendidly, stylishly different. Romans, male but even more female, like to flaunt it. If you have got good hair, then let it cascade all over the place. If you are well endowed in the bosom department, then let the neckline drop to somewhere around your belly button. If your legs look good, then the shorter the skirt, the better. Above all, wear as much gold or silver glitter as you have got – on your fingers, around your neck, in your hair or in your ears. It all looked exotically different then. To the boy from Kilrea, it still does.

Such was (and still is) the sense of ongoing, unprompted Roman street theatre that Dindy and myself used to have a little joke in those early days about film maker Federico Fellini. He was no genius, we would say to one another; all he did was turn his cameras on the everyday eccentricities of Italians and Italian living.

By the time we set out for Pisa on 5 January 1986 for the interview-that-was-not-to-be with Liam Brady, Dindy and I were already beginning to understand that Italian clouds have Italian silver linings. That day was a mini-disaster, so far as meaningful contact with Brady was concerned, but there was the splendid consolation of finding a terrific post-match restaurant. One of the great joys of living in Italy is that, just about no matter where you are, you are sure to find a good restaurant. That this one was 'good' was emphatically confirmed when later that evening, Pisa striker Paolo Baldieri, local hero and goal-scorer earlier that afternoon, turned up with friends to eat.

So good, indeed, was the meal – and the Chianti – that we lost sight of time and managed to miss our return train to Rome. That, in turn, prompted some feverish train station accountancy, as we calculated if we would have enough money to buy new tickets for the trip home to Rome. By dint of emptying all pockets, wallets and pencil cases, we scraped together enough and got home around four in the morning, tired and thirsty and having stood for half the journey. Not for the first time, our little outing had been a useful learning experience. It might have been worse. Karl-Heinz Rummenigge could have had me arrested for storming the Inter team bus. What is more, we had seen the Leaning Tower. What more could you want?

TWO
MUSSOLINI INVENTS SERIE A

On the afternoon of Wednesday, 22 May 1963, I was in a hurry to get home from Kilrea primary school. The BBC was due to broadcast the European Cup final between AC Milan and Benfica, being played that afternoon at the mythical Wembley stadium. In those days, you did not get to see much live football on TV, let alone a chance to see two great European clubs.

I cannot claim to have known very much about either team, as I was busy following (still follow, in a distant way) the fortunes of Burnley, then featuring Northern Irish compatriots such as full-back Alex Elder and inside-forward Jimmy McIlroy. I recall little about the game, although I do remember the Beeb's legendary commentator Kenneth Wolstenholme getting very excited about Portugal and Benfica ace Eusebio, especially after the latter scored an opening eighteenth-minute goal.

There was a lot of TV talk, too, about Milan's golden boy, the then 19-year-old Gianni Rivera. I vaguely remember the opportunism of Brazilian Jose Altafini, scorer of the second-half goals which enabled Milan to win 2–1 and become the first Italian team to win the European Cup. I have absolutely no memory of the Milan captain who held aloft the winner's trophy that day, a certain Cesare Maldini. Little did I realise then that I would become very familiar with all of the above.

Maldini went on to become as successful a coach as he had been a player, serving as number two to Enzo Bearzot when Italy won the World Cup in 1982, before going on to win three European Championships with the Italian Under-21 team. Those successes earned him a crack at the senior side, which he led to a memorable World Cup qualifier win over England at Wembley in February 1997 on the way to the 1998 finals in France. For all that, Cesare Maldini is perhaps best loved by football fans worldwide for having fathered one of the modern game's truly sublime players, Paolo Maldini.

Altafini, for his part, went on to become a popular, entertaining and often enlightening TV commentator (most recently with Sky Italia). His enthusiastic, distinctive Brazilian style has made him something of a household name in Italy.

It is the fate of the third of the three Milan players mentioned above, namely Gianni Rivera, that interests me most. Maldini senior and Altafini took the two most obvious retirement roads open to the modern footballer – coaching or media work. Rivera, however, went into politics. Without any seeming difficulty, he moved from being the David Beckham or Francesco Totti of his day to parliament, serving as a junior minister for Defence in four different centre-left governments between 1996 and 2001. An Italian MP from 1987 to 2001, Rivera currently serves as a Euro MP and as the Sports Planning councillor on Rome City Council.

Curiously, though, if you check out Rivera's official website (www.giannirivera.it), you will find that, in spite of a solid, 18-year career in politics, more than half his official 'bio-pic' is devoted to his football career. No one, it seems, dares to argue that a young life totally dedicated to training for and playing football is hardly the ideal preparation for the responsibilities of public office. On the contrary, given the dubious background and scholastic formation of many Italian politicians, lots of Italians would see Gianni Rivera as much better prepared for public life than many of his political peer group. Football in Italy has a level of credibility and seriousness that makes it much more than just the nation's favourite game.

Such considerations were far from my mind, though, in 1986. On arrival in Italy, I had a very sketchy knowledge of recent Italian football history, one that started with that Wembley day of Rivera, Maldini senior et al, and moved on to Italy's 1982 World Cup triumph, via various scandals such as the infamous 1980 match-fixing affair which almost ruled ace striker Paolo Rossi out of the 1982 World Cup finals.

The first thing to learn was some basic terminology. For a start, what is the word for football in Italian? You might expect it to be a derivative of the original English word, as it is in many other languages – *le football* (French), *fussball* (German), *futebol* (Portuguese) or *fútbol* (Spanish) – but in Italian, the word for football is *calcio*, which means 'a kick' and also 'calcium'.

According to sixteenth-century Italian philosopher Antonio Scaino, writing in his treatise entitled 'The Game of the Ball' in 1555, the term '*calcio*' relates to the fact that the game was started by kicking the ball. Given Scaino's descriptions of the football of the day, it seems that for much of the rest of the time, the ball was handled.

Scaino describes a game played in a large, walled space with up to 40 players on each team, the object being to get the ball behind enemy lines, rather like in modern American Football. Players are asked to present themselves on the playing field without armour so as to be able to 'hit the ball':

It is necessary that each team has a captain who will principally oversee the battle, will pick suitable players, some who may be good runners, others stout fellows well able to resist the contrary impact, others good at close encounters with the ball and others again most useful when applying themselves to the skirmish. These latter

shall be placed in the vanguard with behind them the
stout fellows, and behind them those good at handling
the ball and behind them again the runners.

Scaino goes on to point out that this *calcio*, whilst not as refined as
the other games of the day, does 'give great pleasure to spectators'.
Nor is it surprising to discover that these early games were often
banned because of the high number of casualties they caused.

In more recent times, of course, modern Italian football owes
its development to England, and particularly to English merchants
based in the northern industrial triangle of Genoa, Milan and
Turin. The first recorded team is Edoardo Bosio's International
Football Club, which was founded in Turin in 1887. Six years
later, in June 1893, a certain G.D. Fawcus and friends marched
into the office of the British Consul in Genoa, a Mr G. Payton.
After the ritual cup of tea, Fawcus addressed the Consul: 'We
would like you to understand our requirements for the summer
season. We are all of us subjects of Her Majesty, who live and work
in Genoa, and to us it seems only fair that we might, as we would
do at home, indulge ourselves in some sporting activities, above
all in the game of football.' Later, in September of that year, the
Genoa Cricket and Athletic Club was founded. As the title would
suggest, football was not initially the club's primary concern, but
the name was changed in 1896 to Genoa Cricket and Football
Club. To this day, the club retains the English version of the city
name rather than the Italian 'Genova'.

It is no coincidence that modern Italian football began in
the industrial triangle where wealthy entrepreneurs and large
urban populations provided two of the game's basic ingredients.
In many senses, Italian football remains profoundly marked by
its origins, southern football being very much the poor relation
of the wealthy, industrialised north. Juventus in Turin, and
AC Milan and Inter Milan have dominated post-war Italian

football, and are still the country's three most powerful clubs. Between them, these three have won 51 of the 77 league championships contested since 1929. (Bologna, Cagliari, Fiorentina, Lazio, Napoli, AS Roma, Sampdoria, Torino and Verona are the other winners.)

In 1898 the Italian football federation, FIGC, was founded with the first ever league title contest being played in that same year. Three Turin teams – International Torino, FC Torinese and Ginnastica Torino – and Genoa competed in that first championship, which lasted just one day and was won by Genoa. Within seven years, two famous names – Milan in 1901 and Juventus in 1905 – had picked up their first of many titles.

On Sunday, 15 May 1910, the national team made its first appearance, beating France 6–2 in a game played at the Arena Stadium in Milan. That day the team wore white shirts largely because, as the Football Commission reports of the time state, white shirts were the cheapest available and could also be substituted with 'an ordinary white shirt or a rowing singlet'. It was only on the occasion of Italy's third international match, eight months later on 6 January 1911 (a 1–0 defeat by Hungary again at the Arena Stadium in Milan), that the team wore blue shirts for the first time, in homage to the house of Savoy, Italy's royal family, led at the time by King Vittorio Emanuele III. The Italian word for blue is *azzurro*, which is why the Italian national team has been known as the *azzurri* ever since. (In the meantime, of course, the Savoys have been sent packing, following a 1946 referendum in which a majority of Italians voted for the dissolution of the monarchy. Vittorio Emanuele III's grandson, also called Vittorio Emanuele, now lives in Switzerland.)

It was during the 20-year Fascist dictatorship of Il Duce, Benito Mussolini, however, that Italian football really made the world sit up and take notice. Mussolini was convinced that his totalitarian regime had to stake out a moral dominion over every sphere of the individual citizen's life, including sport and recreation. Furthermore, like many politicians after him, he quickly realised that sport could provide priceless, positive PR and photo opportunities for him and his regime. In the foreword to a book by Olympic athlete Ugo Frigerio in 1933, Mussolini had written: 'Sporting achievements enhance the nation's prestige and they also prepare men for combat in the open field and in that way they testify both to the physical well being and moral vigour of the people.'

In 1926, Mussolini purged the entire national set-up, re-organising football along lines 'more consonant with the new life of the nation'. He even tried to convince people that the game was not an importation from the dreaded *inglesi* but rather the logical development of the old Florentine *calcio*.

Mussolini's 1926 reforms not only re-organised the administration of football (basing it in Rome) but, more importantly, also ensured him direct control of all appointments to the sport's governing bodies. It was therefore a Fascist-controlled FIGC which instigated the first truly national league championship in the 1929–30 season. (Until then, there had been northern and southern leagues.) In many senses, then, it could be argued that it was Mussolini who invented Serie A.

FIGC is still the governing body of Italian football, from Serie A to amateur level. It holds overall authority, while the day-to-day running of the top level of the game is handled by the Lega Nazionale Professionisti (the football league, known as the Lega), based in Milan (founded as the Lega Calcio at Rapallo, near Genoa, in 1946). For example, Italy's World Cup coach Marcello Lippi is employed by the FIGC, while the Lega runs Serie A and Serie B, overseeing disciplinary proceedings, registering player and coach contracts, and registering (but not negotiating) TV rights contracts. Beyond Serie B, there are a further eight levels of organised and licensed football under the

FIGC's control, from Serie C1, Serie C2 and Serie D to a bewildering number of local leagues called Excellenza, Promozione, Prima Categoria, Seconda Categoria and Terza Categoria.

In late January 2006, the historic link between Mussolini and modern Italian football was forcibly impressed upon me when attending a three-day congress on the subject of 'Italian Football: Values, Perspectives and Reform'. The opening ceremony for the congress was held at the headquarters of CONI, literally the Italian Olympic committee but in practice the governing body of Italian sport since it oversees the activities of all the various federations, including the FIGC.

CONI's headquarters are at the Foro Italico, once called the Foro Mussolini, the sports complex on the banks of the Tiber at the foot of Monte Mario, not far from the centre of Rome. The complex, which was built between 1928 and 1938, contains the Olympic Stadium, the handsome Stadio dei Marmi small running track, an Olympic swimming pool, tennis courts and CONI itself. Walking past the CONI headquarters on your way up to the Olympic Stadium, you walk straight into a huge obelisk bearing the words 'Mussolini Dux'.

Mussolini makes himself even more felt inside the CONI complex. When FIGC president Franco Carraro opened the congress in the Salone d'Onore, he did so in front of an enormous mural of Il Duce surrounded by admiring blackshirted Fascist officials, whilst the massed ranks of the army and the *popolo* all look up to him, clearly urging him to show the way.

The level of Fascist involvement in football during the 20 years of Mussolini's rule is illustrated by the success of Bologna, winners of five titles between 1929 and 1941. For much of this time, the FIGC was led by Leandro Arpinati, a Bologna-based Fascist, who encouraged Bologna's city council to help the club and who also oversaw the building of Bologna's Dall Ara stadium, still considered an important expression of Fascist architecture.

Not even Arpinati, however, could save his winning coach, the Hungarian Jew Arpad Weisz, who was sacked in 1938 in the wake of the introduction of Mussolini's infamous racial laws, inspired by those already introduced by Hitler in Germany and which effectively banned Jews from public office of any kind, excluded them from the medical, legal and teaching professions, and even prohibited them from owning a radio. Weisz died during the Second World War.

When the fledgling World Cup appeared, Mussolini did not need prompting. With Italy staging the 1934 finals on home ground, he wanted success. With pragmatic cynicism, legislation banning foreign players was reversed and suddenly the Italian national team was able to field a number of Argentine stars of Italian origin, three of them – Orsi, Monti and Guaita – playing a key role in Italy's 1934 World Cup triumph. (Monti had actually played for Argentina in the 1930 World Cup finals.)

Curiously, that same Italo-Argentine tradition is carried on today by the Juventus midfielder Mauro Camoranesi, who made his debut for Italy in a 0–0 friendly with Portugal in February 2003 and who has since gone on to establish himself as a key figure in the current Italian national team. In so doing, Camoranesi became the sixteenth Italo-Argentine to play for Italy, and the thirty-fifth 'foreigner' of Italian origin to line up for the *azzurri*. (Brazilians and Uruguayans, as well as one Swiss, one Paraguayan, one American and one Scotsman, have played for Italy.)

But the key figure in the Italian team of the Fascist 1930s was coach Vittorio Pozzo. A confirmed Anglophile who picked up important ideas as a student in England when watching Manchester United's centre-half Charlie Roberts, Pozzo not only led Italy to two successive World Cup wins in 1934 and 1938 but also won the football tournament at the 1936 Berlin Olympics. Authoritarian and paternalistic, Pozzo probably did more than anyone to establish some of the traditional characteristics of the modern Italian game – robust, if not to say cynical in defence, clinical in attack and skilfully precise across the board. Accused of having collaborated too enthusiastically with the Mussolini regime, Pozzo died in relative obscurity in 1968 after having coached the national team for 19 years, from 1929 to 1948. Football writers, however, should remember Pozzo because, both before and after his stint with Italy, he worked as a sports journalist. Not many of us can claim to have moved from the sports desk to the training ground, let alone with such success.

Pozzo's finest hour probably came at the 1938 World Cup in France. Whilst the Italians had been accused of making the most of home advantage in 1934, the same could not be said of 1938. The Fascist stigma, however, stuck to both Pozzo and that team. For example, if you ever get a chance to watch the grainy black-and-white film of the Paris final, you can see Italy's captain Giuseppe Meazza (after whom the stadium at San Siro in Milan is named) making a rather half-hearted Fascist salute as he steps up to lift the Jules Rimet trophy.

In 1997, almost 60 years later, I met and interviewed the goalkeeper of that team, the so-called *Gatto Magico* (Magic Cat), Aldo Olivieri. Although then 77 years old, he was sharp and lucid. When I asked him about the team's relationship with Mussolini and Fascism, he confirmed immediately that the team and Vittorio Pozzo were under huge pressure from the regime to win. As for the side's 'commitment' to Fascist politics, Olivieri claimed that he and his team-mates were interested first and foremost in football and that they had little choice but to support the national (Fascist) interest of the day.

This was also a period when Italian football began to attract the attention of big business. The respective presidents of Milan and Juventus at the time were Piero Pirelli (of the Milan-based tyre company) and Edoardo Agnelli (of the Agnelli family, founders of automobile giant Fiat – Fabbrica Italiana Automobile

Torino). In this same period, the original San Siro football stadium was built (the first game there was, of course, a Milan derby, played in September 1926 and won 6–3 by Inter), while advertising hoardings at the stadia and player product endorsements made their first appearances. By 1937, there were 52,000 licensed players in Italy.

In his book *Football and Fascism, The National Game Under Mussolini*, Simon Martin argues that when Italian players travelled outside Italy during the 1930s, whether with their club or the national team, they were closely identified with the Mussolini regime. In Marseilles during the 1938 World Cup finals, for example, there were unconfirmed reports of riots, with police being called in to restrain anti-Fascist protests.

It is arguable that the link between Fascism and football was only finally severed in 1949 when Italian football was struck by arguably its greatest post-war tragedy, the Superga plane crash outside Turin on 4 May 1949 involving the outstanding club side of the day, Torino. Winners of five consecutive titles from 1945 to 1949, Torino were so powerful that Pozzo once picked ten of the club's players in an Italian XI. A total of 31 people, including the entire squad of 18 players as well as club officials, journalists and air crew, were killed when their plane crashed into the Superga hillside in conditions of greatly reduced visibility. The disaster prompted national mourning, and the players were honoured by an emotional funeral, which was attended by thousands and marked by the spectacle of the funeral cortege being led by the empty 'Conte Rosso', the team bus. Superga was to Italian football what nine years later the Manchester United disaster in Munich would be to English football.

Italian football took a long time to recover from the Superga disaster. The AC Milan success in the 1963 European Cup, which I watched as an eleven-year-old in Kilrea, was the first significant Italian international success since the 1938 World Cup victory in

Paris. That success, however, marks the definitive post-war renaissance of Italian football, a renaissance that obviously owed much to the Italian economic miracle of the 1960s and 1970s.

Between 1963 and 1970, AC Milan and Inter Milan won four European Cups and one Cup Winners' Cup, whilst, in the same period the national team won the 1968 European Championship and lost the 1970 World Cup final to Pele's Brazil. (It was in that same period, however, that the national team was also a spectacular casualty at the 1966 World Cup in England, when they were eliminated by North Korea.)

Before the successes of the 1960s, though, there had been at least one key development in Italian football. In the 1951–2 season, Inter had won the league title (*scudetto*, or shield) using a tightly organised defensive scheme that had been deployed to great effect by Uruguay when winning the World Cup in 1950. The scheme was called *verrou* from the French for 'doorlock' or 'padlock' because it had apparently first been used by the Swiss national team in 1938. For Italian writers, *verrou* quickly became *catenaccio* (bolt or padlock), and thus was born a term that has, ever since, been much used and abused.

If the 1950s introduced us to the term *catenaccio*, they also introduced the Italian public to the phenomenon of mass foreign imports. In the summer of 1957, for instance, the entire Argentina attack arrived in Italy. Called the 'Angels with Dirty Faces', the trio in question were Omar Sivori, who joined Juventus, Antonio Valentin Angelillo, who was signed by Inter, and Humberto Maschio, who went to Bologna. They were just some of a whole wave of Latin Americans, Swedes and other foreigners who, then and now, played a key role in Italian club football.

If the 1960s had been dominated by the Milan clubs, AC and Inter, the late 1970s and early 1980s were dominated by Juventus, coached by Giovanni Trapattoni, which not only won six titles in a ten-year period between 1976 and 1986, but also provided the backbone of Enzo Bearzot's World Cup team both in 1978 (in which Italy were eliminated by the beaten finalists, the Netherlands) and in 1982 (which, of course, Italy won). In a sense, that too is where I entered the Italian fray. When I arrived in Italy in the 1985–6 season, the football community was preparing for the 1986 World Cup with a wishful, backwards-looking glance at 1982. Even Bearzot did not seem to believe that he and his *azzurri* could repeat themselves. (They went out to France in the second round.)

In January 1986, most of this Italian football history was unknown to me, yet it was all relevant. Mussolini's political interference in football set the stage for a strong link between politics and football that has continued in the guise of Silvio Berlusconi. Great Argentine players, such as Sivori, had enlivened the Italian football scene, and arguably one of the greatest of them all (Maradona) had arrived just two years earlier. Where the clubs of the north (Inter, Juventus and AC Milan) had dominated, so would they continue to dominate, not just in Italy but also in Europe.

Above all, Italian football, like Italy itself, seemed buoyant and self-confident. It was about to take off on a helter-skelter ride of unprecedented success that would be followed by more recent, partial decline. Enthralled, bemused and often amused, I was there to watch the ride, hurling from the ditch all the way.

THREE
MARADONA

Naples is getting ready to party. It is Sunday, 10 May 1987 and the city's football team, Napoli, stands poised on the brink of the greatest day in its history. As my train pulls into the city on a balmy, sunny morning, two American tourists in my carriage look out of the window at the sea of light-blue banners, flags, scarves and bunting that seem to adorn just about every building in sight. 'Oh my, something big must be happening today,' says the lady to her husband.

I smile to myself and think that not since Allied troops arrived here in September 1943, to find a city reduced to rubble and its inhabitants desperately short of food and water after a four-day insurrection against the Nazi occupation, has Naples had such good reason to celebrate. It is the penultimate match of the season and Napoli, today at home to Fiorentina, are leading the title contest, three points clear of their closest rivals, Inter Milan. A win will earn them two (rather than today's three) points. (The system was changed in the 1994–5 season.) So Napoli can wrap up the title this afternoon. Indeed, many of the normally superstitious Neapolitans appear to be tempting fate because several of the flags and banners hanging off tenement terraces and small kitchen balconies bear the inscription '*Napoli, Campioni d'Italia*'.

Naples is a city that sometimes makes headlines for the wrong reasons: traffic chaos, acute housing problems, high unemployment and, above all, a serious organised crime problem in the shape of the local Mafia, the Camorra. This afternoon, then, is special, something Naples has craved for 60 years – the Italian league title, Napoli's first ever *scudetto*.

One man has made all this possible. Argentine Diego Armando Maradona has single-footedly powered Napoli to the top of the Italian league. His stupendous genius, his ability to get team-mates to play with and for him, and his footballing intelligence have, in three seasons, proved the biggest elements in a process that has seen Napoli transformed from relegation battlers to title contenders.

The Napoli fans quite literally worship Diego. The traditional patron saint of Naples is San Gennaro, a fourth-century Christian martyr whose coagulated blood, allegedly collected by a devout follower, is still contained in a silver reliquary in Naples Cathedral. Twice a year, that blood still 'miraculously' liquefies for the benefit of the faithful. By 1987, San Gennaro is facing serious competition from the poor boy from Villa Fiorito, a shanty town suburb of Buenos Aires. During the past week, a prayer has begun appearing in Neapolitan shop windows:

Our Maradona
Who Takes the Field
We Have Hallowed Thy Name
Thy Kingdom is Napoli
Lead Us Not Into Disappointment
But Deliver Unto Us the Title
Amen.

Other Napoli fans have left nothing to chance. One story, widely reported in the Naples press, concerns Giuseppe, a fishmonger's assistant. He, apparently, is one of the few to be little moved by the impending title contest. When his boss orders him to wear a Napoli football shirt, with Diego's No.10 on the back, rather than his usual shop apron, for the week prior to the Fiorentina game, he refuses. His boss gets furious, arguing that his employee's lack of respect for Maradona and Napoli will bring bad luck to the team. The discussion becomes so animated that the boss sacks his assistant. Three days later, a humbler Giuseppe returns to ask for his job back. OK, says his boss, you can have it back on two conditions: firstly, you will wear the No.10 shirt; and secondly, you will sing 'Ho Visto Maradona' for me. (This was a song then much in vogue, comparing Maradona to the legendary Brazilian Pele.)

In the end, the fishmonger and all the other Neapolitans need not have worried. Twenty-nine minutes into the first half, striker Andrea Carnevale works a clever one-two with Bruno Giordano on the edge of the Fiorentina area before scoring the game's opening goal. Even an equaliser eleven minutes later from a talented 20-year-old called Roberto Baggio (incidentally scoring his very first goal in Serie A with a trademark precise free kick) fails to dampen the celebrations. In the meantime, the electronic scoreboard at the San Paolo tells the wildly enthusiastic, 82,000-strong crowd that Napoli's closest rivals, Inter, are losing 1–0 away to relegation battlers Atalanta.

If the two scorelines remain like this, then Napoli can even afford to lose to Fiorentina and still lift the title this afternoon. But Fiorentina, happy with their away point, declare an armistice during an endless, tedious second half punctuated only by the growing sense of impending eruption – not from nearby Mount Vesuvius, but from the delirious Napoli fans.

At last, the final whistle blows. The score is 1–1 and Napoli are champions. Even though the moat around the San Paolo ensures that there is no pitch invasion, a posse of reporters, cameramen and assorted officials still crowd the players as they set off on a series of laps of honour.

Inevitably, Maradona is the most sought-after player. Yet, he shuns the reporters and the cameras, making straight for the fans, not just at both ends of the grounds but also at different points along both sides of the pitch. As he comes round in front of the makeshift press box, situated on a lower tier of the stand and close to the pitch, I watch in amazement as he stops to salute the fans. He is totally lit up, the barrel chest defiantly thrust forward, the stocky physique looking as tough as centuries-old teak. He gestures to the Napoli fans, first clenching his fist, and then opening wide his arms and blowing kisses. At one moment, he is the poor boy from the gutter, saying, 'This One Is For You'. At another, he is the King of Naples, demanding and receiving not just tribute, but total adulation. Football is not often like this.

Afterwards, the huge press corps at the San Paolo waits anxiously for the one soundbite, the one set of quotes that really matters. As is his wont, Diego keeps us waiting. Two hours after the final whistle, and after some pretty hectic dressing-room celebrations, he finally emerges.

'For me this championship title means a lot more than winning the World Cup,' he says. 'I won a Junior World Cup in Tokyo and I won the World Cup in Mexico last year but on both occasions I was alone, I had no friends with me. Here, however, all my family, the city of Naples, are with me, because I consider myself a son of Naples.'

There never was and probably never will be a footballer quite like Diego Armando Maradona. Whenever and wherever people talk football, they will talk about Maradona. His name will inevitably evoke the same general reaction. Those who saw him play will tell you that he was one of the greatest footballers of all time, if not *the* greatest. Sadly, they will add, he was also a cheat whose eventual drug addiction besmirched the world game.

When one first came across Maradona, it was immediately obvious that this was a very different type of player, handled by very different people. Maradona was walled in by a clan of minders – brothers, sisters, mother, father, personal trainers, physios, managers, agents, PR advisers, friendly hacks and body-guards. Common sense told you that, in spite of the clan's highly protective attitude to their man, not all of them could have been in it for the good of Diego. He was perhaps the first modern football icon-player, the first systematically to exploit, develop and market his success even as he played. Long before he had arrived in Naples in the summer of 1984, he and his first manager, Jorge Cyterszpiler, a friend from his teenage days, had formed Maradona Productions.

In what is arguably the best of many books written about Maradona, *Hand of God* by Jimmy Burns, Cyterszpiler candidly recalls that in handling Maradona, his aim had been 'to form the first company ever devoted to promoting the image of a foot-baller'. Cynics would argue that, from the outset, Cyterszpiler (and many others involved with Maradona) was looking for the chance to make big money.

Such was the extraordinary Maradona talent that everybody wanted a slice of the action. From the military junta of generals to President Carlos Menem in his native Argentina, from world bodies such as UNICEF and FIFA and a host of multi-national sponsors, not to mention the world's media, Napoli football club, the city of Naples and, last but not least, organised crime, everybody wanted in.

I recall a conversation with the Napoli press officer, Carlo Juliano, one December afternoon in 1986 when he pointed out that the Napoli club telex machine in the previous hour had received two one-off work offers for Maradona, one from Egypt and the other from Japan. Both required him to play exhibition matches. One offer was worth around £85,000 and the other £200,000. Given that estimates at the time claimed that Maradona Productions was earning him approximately £1.7

million per annum, a huge amount of money at the time, via his salary with Napoli and contracts with sponsors such as Puma, Toyota, Fuji Xerox and Aojama Enterprise, he could afford to turn down these two. Another individual from a different background and at a different time might have handled things differently. In the age of Beckham-mania, the concept of the star footballer as a one-man industry is nothing new. Twenty years ago, however, multi-nationals and television interests were only just kickstarting a rapid development of the international 'footbiz' industry we now take for granted.

Not everybody appreciated the aggressive marketing of Maradona. Many in Italy, as well as in Barcelona where he spent two largely unsuccessful years before transferring to Napoli, saw him and his clan as greedy upstarts. Obviously, Maradona's complex personality did not help. Obviously, too, as time went by and revelations about his private life emerged, Diego offered his detractors plenty of material with which to attack him.

For me, all of that was to come later. As an outsider myself, struggling to make a living in the closed, casually xenophobic world of 1980s Italy, I felt an instinctive sympathy for him. Throughout all his vicissitudes – and there have been plenty of them, each one more ghastly than the other – he has retained my sympathy. He was such a wonderful player that I wanted, still want, to forgive him everything.

When I arrived in Italy, there was a large body of footballing opinion, particularly British and Spanish, which felt that Maradona was an overrated player – full of clever tricks, but not solid or consistent enough to justify the exalted reputation that had accompanied him almost since his first appearance as a ball-juggling ten-year-old on Argentine TV.

I begged to differ. I had first seen him when he played for Argentina in a friendly against Ireland at Lansdowne Road in June 1979. We had heard about this potential phenomenon, of how he had made his Argentine first division debut for Argentinos Juniors at the age of 15 (ten days before his sixteenth birthday) and of how he had been excluded from Argentina's 1978 World Cup winning squad at the very last moment. We had heard, too, that he had thrown a tantrum when Argentine coach Cesar Menotti told him he would not be in the squad for the finals.

Maradona came on in the second half of that game against Ireland and he made an immediate impression. His balance, his pace, his self-assurance, his footballing intelligence and, above all, his touch with that magic left foot, were all clearly something out of the ordinary. A few days after that match, he underlined the point when scoring a spectacular individual goal in a 3–1 win against Scotland at Hampden Park.

When I contemplated the idea of moving to Italy, the thought of watching Maradona play for Napoli had certainly been a major factor, both in terms of business and pleasure. I was, therefore, on his side from day one.

That he was different from other footballers, off the pitch as well as on it, soon became hard to ignore. I recall an early visit to the San Paolo, on the last Sunday of 1986, prior to the Christmas break. Napoli had just beaten Como 2–1 to confirm their position on top of the Serie A table. After the match, along with the other journalists, I waited for Maradona to emerge for a final pre-holiday press conference. As usual, he kept us waiting. Finally, a walking scrummage made its way down the corridors from the dressing room. Somewhere in it was Maradona. All around me, Naples-based colleagues, those whose work involved daily coverage of Napoli football club, became agitated. They pushed and shoved their way to the front, not to ask Diego a question or to push a microphone into his face, but rather to shake his hand, hug him warmly and even kiss him.

If it had not already seemed obvious, it became crystal-clear then that the vast majority of the Neapolitan press (at that particular moment) was willing to give Maradona an easy ride. Keep us on top of Italian football, Diego, and we will turn a blind eye to your exotic nightlife, irregular living, intermittent training and questionable friendships. On that afternoon, it seemed as if the majority of the media was more interested in humouring Maradona than in asking him awkward questions. Later, towards the end of his Italian experience, they would not be so remiss.

As early as 1986, a report by Napoli's Nucleo Mobile (Flying Squad) had drawn attention to Maradona's friendship with the Giuliano family, one of the most powerful organised crime families in the city.[2] According to the police, the Giuliano family approached Maradona via a seemingly innocuous phone call. Diego, the voice said, Don Loigino and Don Carmine Giuliano would like to meet you.

Police investigators discovered no fewer than 71 photos showing Maradona in the company of the Giulianos, most often at the clan HQ in Forcella but also at local restaurants such as the Rosolino, where Diego attended a Giuliano wedding reception for a cousin of Don Loigino in March 1989. In many of the photos, Diego appears at ease and relaxed, in the company of friends.

Later, when questioned about his relationship with the Giuliano family by magistrate Federico Cafiero de Rano, Maradona admitted that he had met the Giuliano family but had had no idea who they were. He claimed that a Napoli fan had invited him to the Giuliano home and that, as he often did, he had accepted the invitation. He also claimed that over the years in Italy, he had had his photo taken alongside thousands of fans, which was clearly true.

Even if Diego did not know who the Giulianos were – which is, frankly, hard to believe – they certainly knew who he was and just what an interesting business proposition he might represent. From the moment that word leaked about negotiations between

Barcelona and Napoli in 1984, it is only logical to assume that the Camorra sat up and took note. After all, clandestine betting rings and sales of Napoli-related merchandise were just two of many 'business' activities controlled by the Camorra that were likely to blossom with the arrival of the world's greatest player.

Argentine colleagues, present on that May 1987 day when Napoli lifted the title, also came back from Naples with an interesting tale to tell. After the post-match press conference, a dozen or so Argentine journalists were invited by Maradona to a private party. They were told to wait at a special point outside the stadium where they would be picked up and driven to the party.

They were taken to a house in Nola, one of the many small, ugly suburbs in the greater Naples area. The house was huge and modern, a mansion built like a bunker, furnished with closed-circuit TV cameras and mini watchtowers peopled by men with walkie-talkies. Once they had been given the all clear at the gate, they were shown into the bunker-villa where one hell of a party was already in full swing, with plenty of champagne being served in silver-lined goblets. In one room a giant TV screen showed replays of Maradona's greatest goals.

Many of the guests seemed wealthy, and keen to flaunt their wealth by wearing designer label clothes and gold jewellery. Curiously, when the reporters asked about their host, their questions were met with blank looks. Early that morning, they all returned to Naples convinced that their host could only have been a local Camorra godfather.

In Maradona's early years, however, Italian and Naples media were either unaware or simply uninterested in speculation about links between Maradona and the Camorra. On the July 1984 day when Maradona was formally presented to the Napoli public at the San Paolo, a French journalist, Alain Chaillou, had the temerity to ask both Maradona and club owner Corrado Ferlaino about 'rumours' that the Camorra had contributed to his £4 million (approximately) purchase fee. By way of an answer, Chaillou was told by Ferlaino that his question was an 'offence' against the 'honest city' of Naples and he was unceremoniously shown the door.

By December 1986, the day of Napoli's 2–1 win over Como, the sports media were much more concentrated on his football. 1986, of course, had been the year of Maradona's controversial but extraordinarily dominant role in Argentina's World Cup win in Mexico. In just one match against England the two sides of Maradona had been thrown into sharp relief: the genius who scored one of the greatest goals of all time; and the cheat whose 'Hand of God' opening goal should clearly have been disallowed. One reporter at that Christmas press conference in Naples probably thought he was asking an easy first question when he called on Maradona to sum up the year just past.

'At this stage, I would say that 1986 was not the best year of my life,' he said. 'It brought me many good things but it also gave me some very nasty shocks.'

It was easy enough to identify one of the 'nasty shocks'. It had come on 20 September when a 22-year-old unemployed accountant, Cristiana Sinagra, a good-looking blonde, had claimed on a state TV news bulletin one Saturday night that Diego was the father of a baby boy born to her earlier that same day. She furthermore claimed that the child was the fruit of a four-month 'affair' with Maradona that had gone on from December 1985 through to April 1986.

From the outset, there was something about the way Cristiana Sinagra faced the cameras that suggested she could be telling the truth. Faced with the threat of a paternity suit, Maradona did not at first deny he was the father of the child. Instead, a carefully worded statement was issued on his behalf in which he complained of the undignified manner in which the whole matter had been made public and of the damage done to the image of both Napoli football club and of Maradona.

In the meantime, the Sinagra family had come face to face with Maradona's popularity. When Cristiana and her baby boy, named Diego Armando Junior, left hospital, they had to do so in secret at two o'clock in the morning in order to escape the wrath of Napoli fans, concerned that their idol's form might suffer as a result of the threatened paternity suit. When Maradona led out Napoli for a home game against Udinese on the Sunday after the Sinagra TV revelation the previous evening, he was greeted with a banner reading 'Maradona, King of Naples'. Then, as now, the Napoli fans were on his side.

Cristiana Sinagra, however, did not go away. In the end, after a nine-year legal battle during which Maradona consistently denied he was the boy's father, a 1995 ruling from Italy's Cassazione, or final Court of Appeal, decreed that Diego Junior was indeed Diego Maradona's son and, as such, legally entitled to use the surname Maradona.

Ten years on from then, in the autumn of 2005, the issue still clearly rankled with Maradona. Talking in his new role of TV presenter on his own show on Argentine television, *La Noche del 10*, he said of Diego Junior that 'to accept is not to acknowledge', adding, 'I have two daughters who are the love of my life and I am paying with money for past mistakes. A judge can force me to pay but not to say my love. My love is called Dalma and Giannina [his daughters].'

In the following days, he hammered home the point, telling Argentine channel TN that he had daughters and that 'the other was merely a mistake', continuing: 'I can accept a judge's ruling but in no way will I accept that Diego Junior is my son, like it or not ...'

Like his mother, Diego Junior refused to go away. In 2003, he confronted Diego Snr, whilst the latter was playing a round of golf at Fiuggi, during one of his occasional visits to Italy. Diego Junior slipped onto the golf course for a first ever face-to-face meeting with his father. The older Maradona told the boy that he would get in contact with him in future. No such contact was made, and the next thing Diego Junior heard was his father's public repudiation of him in September 2005, which prompted him to comment that his father was 'mad'. In December 2005, Diego Junior went on to sue his father for 'lack of financial support, moral damages and defamation'. (Incidentally, Diego Junior has himself tried to make it as a professional footballer, but without much success. By the end of 2005, he was training with the Serie D side Angri.)

Diego Senior may not be mad, but he is certainly different. One of the first and most disturbing things that I noticed about him was his Caesar complex, his insistence on talking about himself in the third person. During that 1986 end-of-year press conference after the Como game, he talked about how uniden-tified 'bad people' were out to get 'Maradona', adding: 'Maradona has suffered a profound shock ... Maradona wishes no one ill, yet somebody is trying to hurt Maradona.' Watching the whole Maradona 'show' and listening to him spout on in the third person (something he continued to do throughout his time in Italy) was very disconcerting. He looked and sounded like a pampered prima donna, oscillating between petulance and paranoia.

The revelation of the Sinagra love-child, too, had been equally disconcerting. It was the first tangible confirmation of the 'unorthodox' life led by Maradona in Naples, although Spanish colleagues had drawn my attention to stories, carried in gossip columns and glossy magazines during Maradona's time in Barcelona, reporting on his allegedly 'unprofessional' lifestyle off the pitch. It was suggested that outrageous parties, if not to say orgies, were regular happenings in his luxury villa in

Pedrales, outside Barcelona – especially if his long-time, live-in girlfriend Claudia Villafanes happened to be out of town. Lavish food, lots of drink and maybe some other stimulants would be consumed during parties which were attended by various ladies of the night and where people often ended up in the villa's swimming pool. In *Hand of God*, Jimmy Burns relates the experience of Ramon Miravitillas, editor of the popular magazine *Interviú*, who told him:

> My relationship with Maradona during the time he was in Barcelona consisted of me having to listen to, and seemingly discredit, a stream of approaches from young women with old, tired and sad eyes who, in exchange for some money, were happy to tell me how much and by whom they'd been fucked during the intimate parties organized by the clan.

In my ignorance and innocence, I tended to dismiss such gossip from Catalonia, arguing with myself that the whole thing had been exaggerated by a Catalan press that simply could not wait to see the back of the little upstart Argentine. Perhaps he had thrown parties with call girls and others in attendance, but then so too had other footballers. Surely, it had only happened occasionally? Surely, for the rest of his time, Diego was leading a reasonably clean-living, good-eating, hard-training, long-sleeping footballer's life? Maybe he had a drink at some of his parties, but surely that was where it ended?

I even recall hearing a radio interview in Italy in the autumn of 1986 when Maradona solemnly gave his support to a national campaign against drug addiction. 'If my words about drug addiction and its evils were to save one of you,' he told listeners, 'then that will be worth more to me than a hundred league goals for Napoli.'

Ten years later, with his football career prematurely curtailed by his chronic drug addiction, Maradona admitted that he had used cocaine for the first time in Barcelona in 1982, at the age of 22. Back then, at the San Paolo on that December 1986 afternoon, I could never have imagined that the career of the world's greatest footballer would end up going down the toilet in a cloud of cocaine.

At the same time, it was becoming clear that Maradona was indeed leading an irregular lifestyle in which he was probably indulged not just by his inner clan but also by Napoli football club. (Argentine colleagues have often suggested that the Maradona lifestyle certainly did not improve when he broke with his original manager, Jorge Cyterszpiler, in 1985, replacing him with Guillermo Coppola, a man not disinclined to enjoy the good things of life.)

Nowadays, when former players and football critics in Italy recall Maradona, many of them speculate on how things might all have turned out differently if he had moved to, say, Juventus rather than Napoli. (Juventus did in fact seriously consider buying Maradona from Argentinos Juniors in 1979, three years before his move to Barcelona.) Had he gone to Juventus, the autocratic club run by the Agnelli family, critics suggest, he would have been better protected against the outside world, against his sycophantic clan and his own worst self.

Perhaps, and there again, perhaps not. Certainly, his experience at Barcelona seemed to suggest that Maradona was not the ideal client for a major club with a huge sense of its own tradition and standing in its community, not to mention a tendency to believe that, at the end of the day, all their players, even star ones, were simply employees. What is certain is that Juventus would not have cut Diego the amount of slack granted him at Napoli. What is less certain is whether, by the time he arrived in European football in 1982, Diego would ever have prospered at any club that tried to tie him down too tightly, control his private life and limit his nightlife.

He had already become too much cock of his own walk, too spoiled by his hangers-on. Off the record, Argentine and Italian colleagues would report on how Diego's every whim was met. If Maradona wanted something – be it a new shirt, a new car, caviar or a bottle of champagne – then he got it. It was his money, after all.

When he arrived in Naples, he had asked Napoli to provide him with a house similar to the spacious villa in Pedrales, outside Barcelona, that he had just left. Finding somewhere with a swimming pool, tennis court and five-a-side football pitch, however, was almost impossible in Naples. In the end, he settled for a comfortable, quiet but ordinary enough two-floor flat on Via Scipione Capece in the upmarket area of Posillipo. The only original features of his apartment were a huge garage for his cars and a downstairs gym for his personal training, overseen by Ferdinando Signori.

The apartment did, though, have one other important advantage in that it was relatively quiet, given that Posillipo is far from the madding Neapolitan crowd.

By that December in 1986, Diego could and indeed often did dictate his own terms to all and sundry. In those pre-satellite TV days in Italy, when clubs were much more dependent on gate receipts than on TV rights money, he was Napoli's financial lifeline. Season ticket sales in Maradona's first season soared to over 60,000 while the box office takings that year saw the club earn slightly more than double the record $7.5 million they had paid Barcelona for him. In Maradona's first two seasons, Napoli earned more from gate receipts than in the previous 24 seasons combined. By the end of Maradona's time at Napoli, it was alleged the club had earned around £35 million via gate receipts, sponsorships and related contracts.

* * *

Yet, Maradona's relationship with Naples and Napoli was about more than money and mutual convenience. On that title-winning Sunday in May 1987, when he called himself a 'son of Naples', his words were not empty rhetoric, trotted out for the occasion. In many ways, Maradona and Naples were ideally suited for one another. For many Italians, particularly those from the richer, industrial north, Naples is a byword for just about everything that is wrong with contemporary Italy. It seems engagingly exotic, yes, but also alarmingly chaotic, disorganised, corrupt and, in the end, distinctly low-rent.

Once, during a Northern League party congress in Milan in January 1997, a delegate cheerfully informed me that when he hears a Neapolitan song on the radio, he thinks he is listening to Arab music. The same man, a well-heeled small businessman, also wanted to explain to me the dynamic of a serious train accident the previous week, in which Italy's fast train, the *Pendolino*, had crashed in Piacenza, resulting in eight deaths. 'It is very simple, you see,' he said. 'The driver was from Naples. What do you expect? You can't put a Neapolitan in charge of a train, they don't have the cultural preparation for a job like that.'

Naples, then, is a bustling, colourful urchin by comparison with historic, aristocratic Florence, Milan, Rome, Turin and Venice. Where the good burghers of Turin and Milan, like those of Barcelona, would have seen Maradona and his entourage as garish upstarts, Naples embraced him as 'one of us', the poor kid who had started out on the wrong side of the tracks and made it none the less.

When he first arrived in Naples on 5 July 1984, more than 60,000 fans turned out for his official presentation at the San Paolo. He was, in the all too ephemeral sense of sporting success, the new Messiah. He would deliver, he would put one over on those toffee-nosed northerners, he would ensure that Napoli football club could compete with AC Milan, Inter Milan, Juventus et al.

Remarkably, and this was arguably his greatest achievement as a footballer, Maradona did just that. He delivered. He brought a fleeting moment of success to Naples, leading them not just to that 1987 title but to a second one in 1990, with a UEFA Cup victory to boot in 1989. Neither before nor since had the football club experienced anything like it.

After Maradona departed Italy in drug-addicted ignominy in April 1991, Naples began a gradual slide first into Serie B, then into insolvency and finally into a born-again existence in the fourth division.

In social terms, the football success was like a meteor. At the time of the 1987 title win, there was much talk about how this could be a turning point in Naples' history. Now, it seems as though things, if anything, have got worse. Such was the climate of social unrest in Naples in 2004 that 116 people were killed in vicious gang warfare, while whole zones of the city, such as Scampia, remained practically off-limits to the police, and a 50 per cent unemployment level amongst young people in certain areas continued to prove itself a useful recruitment weapon for the Camorra.

Amongst those killed in gang warfare in March 2005 was 57-year-old Nunzio Giuliano, brother of Don Loigino and Don Carmine Giuliano, the Camorra bosses with whom Maradona had so often been photographed. A one-time godfather with a prominent role in the family 'business', Nunzio Giuliano had distanced himself from the Camorra in the late 1980s, following the death of his son Vittorio from a drug overdose in December 1987. In the grim world of the Mafia, however, that decision had not spared him the wrath of Camorra bosses, probably furious with him and his family for the dishonour brought to the 'extended family' by the decision of three of his brothers, Don Loigino, Guglielmo and Salvatore to turn State's witness and collaborate with investigators. On the evening of 20 March, as he rode home on a Honda SH motorbike, another bike came along-side him. In the busy traffic of Naples, he may not even have noticed as the pillion passenger pulled out a gun and hit him with a round of fire that killed him instantly.

Naples in 2005 was also the city where businesswoman Silvana Fucito earned herself a European Hero citation from American weekly *Time*. She had had the courage to refuse to pay the *pizzo* or protection money demanded by the Camorra. In response, the Camorra burnt down her paint factory one September night in 2002, in the process also burning down 20 adjacent apartments. For her pains, Ms Fucito found that, rather than venting their anger on the Camorra, the local residents blamed her. Her reaction was to form the San Giovanni Anti-Racket Association, accusing 15 people (eleven of whom were subsequently arrested, tried and sent to prison) of Mafia-style extortion. Naples remains Naples.

In such a context, a figure like Maradona made an enormous impact, even years later, as was seen on the night of Thursday, 9 June 2005 when the prodigal son returned. It was Maradona's first visit back to Naples for 14 years, since that April 1991 night when he had slipped out of the country just days before FIGC's disciplinary commission gave him a 15-month suspension for testing positive for cocaine in a routine post-match drugs test.

The occasion was a testimonial match for his former Napoli colleague, defender Ciro Ferrara. (A constant aspect of the Maradona phenomenon is the affection, high esteem and loyalty granted him by former team-mates.) Ferrara is himself a much-loved son of Naples but he found himself upstaged on his high-profile day. In theory, the testimonial was Napoli versus Juventus and the cast included not only famous Napoli names of the past, such as Salvatore Bagni, Alemão, Bruno Giordano, Careca, Fernando De Napoli, Daniel Fonseca and Gianfranco Zola, but also famous Juventus names, past and present, including Alessandro Del Piero, Gigi Buffon, Zlatan Ibrahimovic, Zinedine Zidane, Gianluca Vialli, Fabrizio Ravanelli and Pavel Nedved. For the San Paolo faithful, though, there was only one player they wanted to see. Up went the chant: 'Diego, Diego.' Eventually, out he came, complete with a strange retinue of bodyguards, all dressed in black with their heads shaven.

Maradona then put on a display of his once legendary ball control, just as he had 21 years earlier on his first appearance in front of Napoli fans. As the crowd roared its approval, he broke through the posse of minders, photographers and TV cameramen to rush over to the terraces, just as he had done on the day of that first title, blowing kisses, clenching his fists and lapping up the adulation.

The curious thing about all of this is that a large percentage of those at the San Paolo that June 2005 night was too young ever to have seen Maradona play. Such is the power of the myth, however, such is the collective Neapolitan folk memory of what, for a short time, Maradona had meant for Naples and Napoli, that no amount of sordid stories of drug addiction, prima donna behaviour or squalid licentiousness will ever destroy the Maradona image in Naples.

In other parts of Italy, though, that image has long since been badly dented. For many Italians, in the north and elsewhere, the Sinagra case proved their worst suspicions. As, over the next four years, Maradona appeared to lead a blatantly unprofessional life, fingers wagged. Failure to turn up for training, failure to turn up to the pre-match training camp (*ritiro*), point-blank refusals to play in key games, criticism of the team coach and regularly returning late from his holidays in Argentina all became more rule than exception.

Even Maradona's golden earring, hardly a cause for concern in these days of piercing, convinced some of his then critics that he was more of a gypsy than a serious professional footballer. The begrudgers had a field day in November 1989 when he staged a lavish million-dollar wedding in Buenos Aires to his girlfriend, Claudia Villafanes. A jumbo jet was hired for the 1,200 guests, 2.5km of pale-green carpet was laid, Josef Goebbels' 1933 Rolls Royce was wheeled into service and, as usual, Diego got into a scuffle with an over-anxious photographer.

Many of the reservations that non-Neapolitans felt about Maradona came to a head at the 1990 World Cup in Italy. I remember sitting in the press room at the Meazza stadium in San Siro shortly before the kick-off of the competition's opening game – holders Argentina versus Cameroon – discussing the Maradona phenomenon with the late Peter Ball of *The Times*, a good friend and a very astute observer of the world game. Peter surprised me by expressing the opinion that, for all that Maradona was a footballing genius, he was still one of the least-loved, least-admired and least-respected 'great players' ever to grace the world stage. I was taken aback. Even allowing for all the enmity prompted by the infamous 'Hand of God' goal against England, I still imagined that true football lovers warmed to him.

Minutes later, as the match began, there was plenty of material to prove Peter's thesis. Throughout the game, Maradona was booed by a largely Milanese crowd. Partly the booing was linked to purely domestic considerations, given that Maradona's Napoli had, just a few weeks earlier, snatched the league title from under the noses of AC Milan in controversial circumstances. That win (Napoli finished just one point clear of AC Milan) had been overshadowed by a coin-throwing incident during Napoli's away tie with Atalanta. The match ended 1–1 but Napoli were subsequently awarded victory and two points at a FIGC hearing. The club had argued that their Brazilian midfielder Alemão, the player hit by the coin, had been unable to carry on. The Milan fans, and many others, felt that Alemão had been encouraged to 'play-act' by, among others, his team captain, Diego Maradona.

Argentina were beaten by Cameroon that day. Speaking after the match, Maradona pointed out that the northern Italian fans had cheered on black Cameroon against his Argentina, and quipped: 'At least I've saved the Milanesi from the accusation of being racist.'

Playing on painkillers for a badly swollen left ankle, Maradona did not have a fantastic World Cup. One of the recurrent strains on him was the extent to which both Argentina and Napoli were willing to resort to painkillers or other medication for his recurrent ankle, knee and back problems. Both teams needed him badly and were always desperate that he play. Furthermore, by 1990 his drug problems and his non-professional lifestyle meant that he was no longer the player of 1986. Yet, such was his class that, even at Italia '90, he surfaced from his lethargy for fleeting moments that were enough to see him set up the goals that beat both Brazil in the second round and host country Italy in the semi-finals.

As fate would have it, that semi-final was played in Naples. Diego had infuriated many Italians by remarking prior to the match that it was ironic that the rest of Italy was now calling on Neapolitans to be good Italians and get behind the team. For the rest of the year, said Diego, most Italians do not give a damn about Naples. It was close to the bone, but accurate.

Those words and Argentina's 1–0 win that night in Naples put Diego and Argentina firmly on the hate list for the final, played at the Olimpico in Rome. As the Argentine national anthem played, the mainly Italian fans jeered and whistled. As the TV cameras moved along the line of Argentine players, it focused on a furious Maradona, who was clearly muttering 'Hijos de putana' (sons of bitches). It was classic Diego – theatrical, passionate and scurrilous. Given all the wonderful football he had played in Italy, and given what he had done for Napoli, I felt he deserved more from his adopted country. The Italian worm, however, had turned against him.

In many senses, though, the negative treatment at Italia '90 did not come as a surprise. Writing a profile of Maradona for the *Guardian* on the eve of that tournament, I put it this way: 'Not everyone shares this enthusiasm [of Neapolitans] for Maradona. In his Italian time, he has been accused of frequenting too many night clubs, of having a drink problem, of snorting cocaine, and of being too much of a womaniser.'

There, it was out. We all knew it, and some of us even wrote it. Diego had a drug problem. In a famous 1998 interview, Czech coach Zdenek Zeman, the 'whistleblower' in the infamous Juventus dope trial (see Chapter 9), said that people on the inside track were already talking about Maradona's drug problems when Napoli bought him in 1984. Zeman and other insiders may have known about it but the rest of us could only sense the extent of the problem, even if by 1990 it was clear that Maradona was coming to the end of his Italian and, eventually, his footballing road.

He had not done much to help himself. There was a minor but perhaps significant incident in January 1990 that indicated the extent to which he was potentially out of control. A football writer for the Naples daily *Il Mattino*, 62-year-old Giuseppe Pacileo, had the temerity to give Diego a 3.5 out of 10 *pagella* (mark) for his performance in Napoli's 2–2 home draw with Udinese on Sunday, 14 January. A mark of 3.5 was equivalent to saying that he had been worse than useless, more of a help to Udinese than to Napoli.

Enraged by this affront to his dignity, Diego stormed around to the studios of local TV Canale 34 the next evening, where Pacileo was a regular guest on the Monday night football programme *No.1*. To the consternation of the studio team, Maradona, on air, ripped up a copy of Pacileo's article and then shoved it into the hapless journalist's mouth.

The final act in Maradona's Italian drama started in, of all places,

Red Square in Moscow. Frozen Muscovites hurrying through the square on a bitterly cold Tuesday night in November 1990 might have been surprised to notice a great deal of activity around the Lenin Mausoleum. The world's most famous footballer was being given a special, late-night guided tour. Diego, friend of Cuban leader Fidel Castro, admirer of Che Guevara, the poor working-class boy, was paying homage to the founder of Communism.

The problem was, however, that Diego was not in Moscow on a sight-seeing trip but rather to play a European Cup tie against Spartak Moscow. That late-night visit to Lenin's tomb had come about because Maradona had arrived in Moscow by private jet only hours earlier, and 24 hours after the rest of the Napoli team.

On the Monday of that week, Maradona had refused to travel with the club. When worried team-mates had gone to his flat in Posillipo, they were told by one of his minders, Fernando Signorini, that Diego was sleeping. Indeed, he was. Sleeping off the effects of a night of sex and cocaine out on the town.

When Diego eventually recovered his senses, he seems to have regretted his refusal to travel. Perhaps his sycophantic inner clan were beginning to realise that this time even Maradona had gone too far. In the end, he hired himself a jet, travelled to Moscow and was left to sit on the bench by coach Alberto Bigon for the first half by way of punishment.

He came on for the second half and, typically, almost set up a goal that would have put Napoli into the next round of the competition. This time, however, Maradona was not able to play his way out of trouble. The match ended up going to penalties and Napoli were eliminated, thus waving goodbye to upwards of £17 million worth of box-office and contract-related revenue.

Napoli boss Corrado Ferlaino and his team director, Luciano Moggi (today one of the key figures behind the ongoing Juventus success story), seem to have decided that enough was enough. Within a month, Ferlaino had taken Diarma (the company that had replaced Maradona Productions) to court, arguing that Maradona's behaviour had affected his earning power. At the time, Napoli contributed to Diarma in exchange for a share of the company's earnings. Given his recent performances, argued Napoli, the club should be allowed to reduce its contribution because they expected a £3 million fall in revenue over the next three years of a contract that ran to 1993. Ferlaino added, lest anyone had failed to get the point: 'Following Maradona's tantrums, Napoli believes its image to have been devalued and that the profits will not be as previously forecast.'

Maradona responded by giving an interview to Spain's Canal-Plus TV in which he indicated that he might well leave Napoli before the end of the season. This was one of his more accurate predictions (although his departure did not come about in the manner he might have anticipated). 'The end is nigh,' he said. 'I want calm, I've put up with enough already ... No contract is going to curtail my freedom.' He added that he would never play again for Argentina, saying: 'I'll be the number one fan of the side's next number ten.'

Four years later, of course, at the 1994 World Cup in the USA, 'the next number ten' for Argentina was Maradona, caught up in one of the biggest dope scandals of modern sport.

In the wake of that European Cup elimination in Moscow, things went from bad to worse. In February 1991, he was cited for his alleged involvement in a 'sex and drugs' investigation by the Naples state prosecutor's office. Maradona's voice had been picked up eight times in 10,000 hours of tapped phone calls, which were part of an undercover investigation into the Camorra.

Newspapers which had either ignored or been unaware of his alleged involvement with the godfathers of crime were now giving front-page prominence to all the sordid details of the investigation. Leaks from the police report claimed that in the early hours of 7 January 1991, Carmela Cinquegrana, a '*grande maîtresse*' of the Spanish quarter allegedly linked to the Camorra boss Mario Lo Russo, received a phone call from someone claiming to speak on behalf of Maradona and asking for 'two women'. Carmela insisted that Maradona ring her back, which he did rather groggily later that morning – at 3.38am to be precise – to confirm the 'booking'. The police report continued: 'The famous footballer Diego Maradona on a number of occasions asked Signora Cinquegrana for "gear" in no small quantities. By this we understand cocaine.'

As a result of the investigation, five people, including Carmela Cinquegrana and Mario Lo Russo, were arrested on charges of involvement in a dope trafficking network between South America, Italy and France. Maradona was cleared of any involvement in drug trafficking but charged with possession of cocaine.

Lots of beans were now spilt. As details of the investigation emerged, so too did details of the seamy side of Maradona's life. It transpired that it was through his brother-in-law, Gabriel Esposito, that he had got to know nightclub owner Italo Iovine, nephew of a Camorra clan boss from Caserta. Through Iovine, Maradona was introduced to Carmela Cinquegrana.

Another figure to emerge from the investigation was Felice Pizza, known as Geppino. A former underground railway worker, Geppino soon became Maradona's night-life secretary, procuring women and cocaine for him. The Hotel Paradiso in Posilippo, close to Maradona's apartment, was apparently a regular venue for these in-season friendlies, while the asking price could be £300 per girl per night.

The publicity surrounding the investigation prompted all sorts of people to come forward with testimony against Maradona. There was 'Susy', a Brazilian dancer who worked at the 21 Club, a rather sordid nightclub in Naples. She told her story to both magistrates and reporters alike, saying: 'He gave me

£300 for one night. He said that I was beautiful, the most beautiful. He kissed my lips; he wasn't particularly doting but he knew what to do. I recall that he particularly liked to suck my big toe.' Another unnamed woman, who denied being a call girl but said she was an 'admirer' of Maradona, told *La Repubblica*: 'He might have been a remarkable athlete on the field but in bed, he was no big deal.'

Some of those who came forward had rather more serious stories to tell. There was Pietro Pugliese, a former security guard, Camorra hit-man (he subsequently admitted to five gangland killings) and 'friend' of Maradona who turned up one morning at the Naples Palazzo di Giustizia asking to speak to the magistrate handling the Maradona case. He told a complicated story about a package of 'newspapers' that a woman friend of his had carried from Argentina to Italy, on behalf of Maradona's manager, Guillermo Coppola. For organising all of this, Pugliese alleged that he had been paid approximately £5,000. Obviously, he suggested, the package contained not newspapers but cocaine.

Both Coppola and Maradona admitted the arrival of the package but denied that it had contained cocaine, while Coppola claimed that he had paid Pugliese money by way of a contribution to his plan to build a football school on the outskirts of Naples.

The investigation prompted more questions than answers but, in the immediate short term, it was bad publicity for Maradona. However, it was only the *antipasta* for what was to follow just one month later.

It was late in March when newspaper stories speculated that Maradona had tested positive for cocaine, following a routine dope test after a Serie A game against Bari on 17 March. At first, neither the club nor the FIGC was willing to confirm the story. Eventually, it proved impossible to contain.

Maradona was now cornered. The conspiracy of Neapolitan silence about his misdemeanours had been well and truly blown.

He was now involved in three different inquiries: the 'sex and cocaine' Mafia investigation; the paternity suit brought by Cristiana Sinagra; and the litigation with Napoli regarding Diarma, his marketing company. Worst of all, though, was the positive dope test.

With hindsight, it is hard to believe that these events just coincided. Why had Maradona never tested positive before? We now know that, by his own admission, his cocaine habit had started back in Barcelona in 1982–3. Is it possible that all the other dope tests undergone by Maradona prior to that March 1991 game against Bari had not been carried out with total rigour? Did sympathetic officials turn a blind eye? Was he now caught out because he was no longer wanted either in Naples or in Italian football?

What we do know for certain is that when, seven years later in 1998, judicial investigators looked into CONI's dope-testing laboratory at Acqua Acetosa in Rome where footballers' samples were tested, they discovered that tests were carried out in a haphazard manner, if at all. Laboratory technicians told investigators that on those occasions when tests had proved positive, they were simply 'forgotten about'. Had this happened to previous Maradona positive tests? Was he now being caught out because it was politically convenient? (See also Chapter 9.)

In the end, he did a runner. On the night of 1 April 1991, he slipped out of Italy like a thief in the night, passing through Rome's Fiumicino international airport at around midnight. Few people were there to see him off and, when the news of his departure broke the next day, not many expected to see him back again. Allegedly, his wife Claudia was amongst those who encouraged him to leave, believing that Naples was simply no longer a good place for him to be.

Alas, it seemed that Argentina was no better a place for him. Three weeks after Maradona slipped out of Italy, in the early evening of 26 April 1991, members of the Buenos Aires anti-drug squad raided an anonymous flat in the working-class Cabillito area of the city. When they entered the apartment, the police found the world's most famous footballer stretched out naked and fast asleep in a dingy bedroom. The police also found cocaine in the flat, which led to the arrest of Maradona on suspicion of cocaine consumption and possession. As the groggy footballer struggled to wake up and pull on his clothes, he turned to one of the policemen and asked him if there was no way of undoing the arrest. 'There's no turning back,' replied the cop. 'There are two hundred people outside.'

Many people in that crowd did their best to prevent the arrest of Maradona, surrounding the police as they emerged from the apartment and cutting off the path to their car. In the end, the police had to retreat and wait in the flat for four hours before they could take Maradona off to the clink.

It seemed that some fans in Argentina were willing to forgive him almost anything. Shortly after his return from Italy but prior to his arrest, a poll in the newspaper *Clarin* claimed that 69.5 per cent of Argentines still considered him their idol while 63 per cent felt he should not be punished for his failed post-match dope test.

Many people were clearly finding it hard to come to terms with the depths to which Maradona had fallen. As I watched him slip out of Italian football and out of my bailiwick, I felt above all saddened. Sure, he had created plenty of his own problems, but Italy, Naples and the entire football industry had not much helped. The media pressures, the national footballing razzmatazz, the pressure to play when half-injured, the exaggerated expectations, not to mention the Camorra, had all played their part in Diego's downfall.

Fifteen years on, like most others who saw him play, I prefer to recall him as a player whose total skill and innate footballing

Liam Brady and family enjoy the views by Lake Como in 1985, during his spell with Inter.

Brady was one of the first overseas players to reach Italy after restrictions on foreign signings were lifted in 1980, playing for Juventus, Sampdoria, Inter Milan (pictured) and Ascoli before returning to Britain and West Ham in 1987.

Italy is a great country in which to bring up a small child – Relaxing with Róisín in our garden in 1995.

One of the great Juventus teams, led by the inspirational
Michel Platini. They went on to win the Intercontinental
Cup just as I was touching down in Italy in 1985.

Juve's 'wonder team' of the late nineties:
Zinedine Zidane is surrounded by team-
mates Ciro Ferrara (left of picture), Attilio
Lombardo (second right) and Paolo
Montero (right), having scored in
their 4–1 demolition of Ajax in the
Champions League in 1997.

Before the ban on foreign imports and even
longer before Maradona arrived, another
Argentine star was gracing Serie A – Enrico
Omar Sivori of Juventus, training in 1961.

One of the earliest British successes was John Charles, dubbed Il Buono Gigante ('The Gentle Giant') by Italian fans after he joined Juventus from Leeds in 1957 for a record £65,000.

Jimmy Greaves scored a creditable nine goals in just 12 games for AC Milan in 1961, but failed to settle in Italy, returning to England and the grateful Bill Nicholson of Spurs by Christmas.

Ian Rush also found it hard to adjust to life in Italy, returning to former club Liverpool after only one season – and just seven goals – at Juventus in 1987-88.

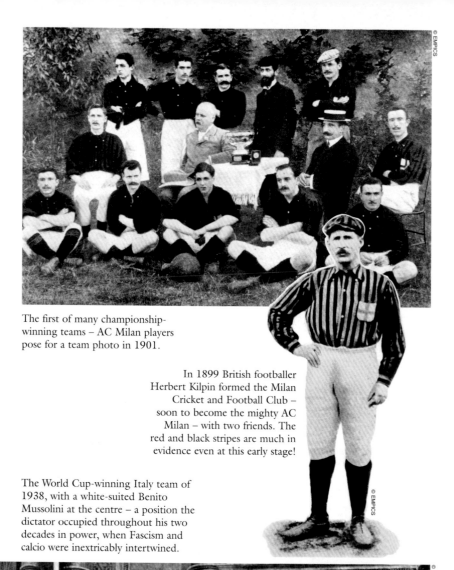

The first of many championship-winning teams – AC Milan players pose for a team photo in 1901.

In 1899 British footballer Herbert Kilpin formed the Milan Cricket and Football Club – soon to become the mighty AC Milan – with two friends. The red and black stripes are much in evidence even at this early stage!

The World Cup-winning Italy team of 1938, with a white-suited Benito Mussolini at the centre – a position the dictator occupied throughout his two decades in power, when Fascism and calcio were inextricably intertwined.

To say that Diego Armando Maradona single-handedly led lowly Napoli to the pinnacle of Italian football is no exaggeration – celebrating the UEFA Cup win in 1989.

Maradona's emotional return to Naples in 2005 for Ciro Ferrara's farewell match. Despite leaving under a cloud in 1991 amid drugs charges, the Napoli fans' love for the Argentine remains undimmed.

Maradona's invitation on to the judging panel of Miss Italy 2005, broadcast on state television, underlines his continuing place in the Italian popular consciousness.

In case there was any doubt who had helped them get there, Milan's players hoist media billionaire and club owner Silvio Berlusconi aloft with the European Cup in 1990.

Berlusconi had moved to the forefront of national politics by the time his club won another Serie A title in 1999.

By 2002, Berlusconi had become a recognised international stateman, here being entertained by German chancellor and Borussia Dortmund fan, Gerhard Schroeder, at a Champions League match.

© EMPICS

The Dutch connection: Without
doubt Berlusconi's millions
brought added glamour to Milan
in the late eighties with signings
Marco Van Basten (above)
and Ruud Gullit (left).

The sometimes irascible Bruno was our builder, but he was also a great many other things besides – and is sadly missed by everyone in our village.

With Dindy, meeting Pope John Paul II at his summer residence at Castel Gandolfo. As Vatican stringer for UPI, I regularly followed 'Himself' on the Vatican beat.

intelligence sent shivers down the spine. His cocaine habit was the expression, not of a need to enhance his performance – never was there a player who less needed chemical help to play football – but more of his own inner confusion.

In the years since, I have often been struck by the high opinion in which Maradona is held by the one community that matters to him, namely his fellow players. Typical was this comment from Paolo Maldini, the AC Milan captain and genuine 'model professional' who, during a series of interviews in January 2005 to mark his 20 years in Serie A football, declared his admiration: 'Diego Maradona was not only the greatest player but also the most honest. He was a model of good behaviour on the pitch – he was respectful of everyone, from the great players down to the ordinary team members. He was always getting kicked around and he never complained – not like some of today's strikers …' That is also the Maradona I prefer to recall.

For the impoverished freelance, too, Maradona was a godsend. He was always making waves of some sort. Within six months of settling in Italy, and partly thanks to Maradona, I had established a regular round-up of clients including the *Guardian*, the *Irish Times*, the *Scotsman*, news agency UPI and radio stations such as the BBC, RTE and Deutsche-Welle. None of them paid very much (£30 for a radio interview and £100 to £150 for a newspaper feature was as good as it got) but it was work.

Pope John Paul II was also a good source of work for me in those early years. In October 1986, he staged one of those innovative, idiosyncratic events that were so typical of his pontificate by holding a World Day of Prayer for Peace in the small, handsome Umbrian town of Assisi, birthplace of St Francis. In attendance were 150 religious leaders, including the Dalai Lama, the Archbishop of Canterbury, Buddhist monks, Lutheran ministers, Japanese Shintoists, Jewish Rabbis, Muslim Imams, Sikhs, African animists, Jains from India, Zoroastrians and a delegation of Native American Indians. It was, by any standards, a remarkable event and one that attracted the attention of the world's media. For my purposes it also attracted the attention of Paul Gillespie, then foreign editor of the *Irish Times*. He agreed to take a piece from Assisi, which subsequently ended up on the front page. Thus began a collaboration with the *Irish Times* that is ongoing to this day.

In the summer of 1988, my relationship with the *Irish Times* became even more solid thanks to Malachy Logan, the sports editor (then and now). One day Malachy rang me to ask if I would be interested in regular collaboration with the paper. He took the then bold step of promoting a European football column, which I still write today. This work was vitally important because it established a formal link with Ireland's most prestigious and authoritative daily, the only one that would conceivably be interested in regular Rome coverage, and I became a contributor to the foreign and news desks, too. Eventually, in 1993, I was offered a retainer for foreign, news and features coverage. How many other papers, I often wonder, would happily accept that its Vatican correspondent also writes regular football columns?

As for Maradona, there is one memory that has never left me. It came from the very first Napoli versus Juventus game I saw, during my first winter in Italy. It was a game that brought together the established northern super-power and the scruffy southern upstarts, a game that saw the languid, elegant skills of Frenchman Michel Platini opposed to the explosive dynamism of Maradona.

Halfway through the second half of a tight match in which both Platini and Maradona had strutted their stuff, Napoli were awarded a free kick on the edge of the area. Maradona, of course, stepped up to take it. The free kick had been awarded on the left side of the area, not exactly the ideal position for a left-footer like Maradona.

Rather than position himself to the right of the ball, to hit it with his left instep, Maradona stood to the left of it, as if he were about to hit it with his right foot. Standing like that, it looked to the Juventus defenders as though he were not yet ready to take the kick. Out of the blue, and without a run-up, Maradona hit it billiard-style with a vicious, sliced outside-of-the-left-foot strike. It curled into the net for a truly majestic winner. Napoli held on for a 1–0 win.

That goal has remained with me ever since, and for two reasons. Firstly, after the match, Platini had the graciousness to applaud the goal as the 'invention of a great player'. Secondly, and more tellingly, I recall walking around the centre of Rome the next day being amused by the number of times I saw fans re-enact the Maradona free kick, be it at the bar or in the street (and no doubt in their offices, too), re-creating the vicious, sliced effect that had fooled the Juventus defence and beaten goal-keeper Stefano Tacconi.

In a land where football matters, Maradona struck a mighty major chord. Football is not often like this.

FOUR
BERLUSCONI: FOOTBALL AND POLITICS

In Palazzo Chigi, government house in Rome, lunch is coming to an end. In the impressive surrounds of the palazzo, begun in 1562 by architect Giacomo della Porta for the Florentine noble family of Aldobrandini (one of whom, Ippolito, reigned as Pope Clement VII from 1592 to 1605), Prime Minister Silvio Berlusconi is entertaining a small gathering of resident foreign correspondents, prior to Christmas 2005.

The lunch has been very, very good. We started with a *caprese* (mozzarella, tomatoes and basil), followed by *pennette tricolore* (three types of pasta to reflect the colours of the Italian flag). After that we had a *tagliata di filette Chianina*, for the meat dish, followed by a selection of cheeses and ice cream. To wash it all down, there were bottles of Capichera Vermentino 2004, Elio Grasso Barbera d'Alba 2002 and I Vignaioli di Santo Stefano, Monte d'Asti 2004.

The Prime Minister had kept the journalists waiting. When he arrived in the *salotto* where we were being entertained with a glass of *prosecco*, he burst in like a whirlwind, immediately apologising for being late and going round the gathering one by one, shaking hands with everybody. He was his ebullient and energetic self, cracking jokes as he focused on each person. Mr Berlusconi is one of those high-energy, driven people who believes that, with his not inconsiderable charm, he can win over anyone.

Throughout the lunch, the Prime Minister ate and drank

sparingly, since he was busy answering questions from the correspondents. Each of us was allowed one question. As luck would
have it, I found myself to be last in line, so I slipped in a couple
of extra questions, one of them on a subject dear to Berlusconi's
heart, his very own football club, AC Milan. Putting a question
that has fascinated me for years, I asked Berlusconi just how big
a role AC Milan had played in his political success. Curiously, he
downplayed the club's impact. 'Certainly, no one has ever won as
much as I have,' he said, 'not only with AC Milan but also with
other sports teams ... but the reality is that I owe my political
success to the historical context of 1994 ...'

As Berlusconi sees it, his overnight-sensation success at the
ballot box in 1994 came about because he stepped into a vacuum
created by those political forces which had ruled Italy without
interruption since 1946 and which, in 1994, were laid low by the
infamous 'Tangentopoli' scandal.

When dealing with modern Italy, it is almost impossible to
ignore Silvio Berlusconi, the country's richest man and (at press
time) twice its Prime Minister. This applies as much to football as
to politics or business. Indeed, Berlusconi has been one of the
major players in Italian football over the last 20 years. Given that
Berlusconi's relationship with football has increasingly developed
political undertones, it is impossible to reflect on Berlusconi the
football impresario without, however briefly, putting him into
that very 'historical context' to which he himself refers.

When the victorious Allies looked out across Italy at the end
of the Second World War, they had a problem, one that had been
identified by Winston Churchill in his famous Fulton, Missouri
speech in 1946 when he declared: 'From Stettin in the Baltic to
Trieste in the Adriatic, an Iron Curtain has descended across the
continent.' Trieste, of course, lies in the north-east of modern
Italy. In other words, in 1946, Italy was a frontline state, border-
ing on the Communist Eastern bloc. That consideration was to

dominate Italian political life right up to 1989 and the fall of the Berlin Wall. Given the strength of the Italian Communist party (the PCI – Partito Comunista Italiano) and its important role (via partisan fighters) in defeating Nazi-Fascist and Mussolini-Fascist forces in the Second World War, there was the very real danger that the PCI might win the first post-war elections in 1948, then perhaps setting up a government in Rome not dissimilar to the puppet governments of the Warsaw Pact countries.

If that seems far-fetched, just remember that one year later, in 1949, the PCI leader and dominant figure of the time, Palmiro Togliatti, wrote this about Soviet dictator Joseph Stalin: 'The role that Stalin has played in the development of human thought is such that he has earned himself a place which until now very few have occupied in the history of humanity.' In March 1953, the PCI daily, *L'Unità*, responded to the news of Stalin's death with a front-page banner headline that read: THE MAN WHO HAS DONE MOST FOR THE LIBERATION OF THE HUMAN RACE IS DEAD.

Put simply, the main thrust of Italian politics from 1946 to 1989 was focused on one issue and one alone: keep those dirty red Commies out of government. To this end, all manner of unlikely bedfellows joined the cause. Leading the way were the Catholic Church, the Christian Democrat party and subsequently the Socialist party, aided and abetted in a variety of clandestine ways by a motley crew of secret service agents, including CIA, MI6, Mossad and Italian operatives.

For example, speaking to the Italian parliament in August 1990, seven times Italian Prime Minister Giulio Andreotti publicly admitted for the first time the existence in Italy of Gladio, an organisation intended to activate a network of clandestine fighter groups in the case of foreign (i.e. Soviet) invasion. Gladio, which was heavily dependent upon the training and direction provided by the CIA, was formally ratified by a (possibly illegal)

1956 agreement between SIFAR (Servizio Informazioni Forza Armate – the Italian military secret service) and the CIA. Furthermore, Gladio's structures remained secretly in place right through to 1990, and in that time may well have been used for surveillance of and possible action against internal enemies (of the left) rather than against an invading Soviet force.

From 1948 to 1989, therefore, Italian politics were frozen solid in Cold War logic. Throughout that period, there was close to one party rule, with every government in those years either led or controlled by the powerful Christian Democrat party. Two factors changed all of that. Firstly, there was the 1989 fall of the Berlin Wall, which, *de facto*, robbed the Christian Democrats and their allies of their winning electoral card since there were no longer any 'reds under the bed'. Secondly, from 1992 to 1994, Italy became gripped in a massive corruption scandal, 'Tangentopoli' or Bribesville, which featured all the ruling parties of the last 40 years, who were found to have systematically looked for kick-backs for personal and party funds in return for the allocation of public works contracts.

As prominent figure after figure in the former ruling parties either came under investigation or was imprisoned, caught out by the brilliant investigative work of a Milan-based set of investigating magistrates known as the 'Clean Hands' pool, it was obvious that the General Election of 1994 risked becoming a walkover for the PDS (Partito Democratico della Sinistra – the Party of the Democratic Left), the new-look, new-name, post-Berlin Wall version of the old Communist party, the PCI.

Into the space left by the discredited Christian Democrats and allies, however, stepped media tycoon Berlusconi, prompted perhaps by a visceral loathing for Communism but almost certainly by concern for the future of his vast, politically well-connected media empire under a new leftist regime. Masterminding a brilliant, whirlwind campaign at the head of his own brand-new party,

Forza Italia, Berlusconi pulled off a remarkable political triumph to win the April 1994 General Election.

Even though he downplayed its importance at the Christmas 2005 media lunch, one of the ingredients in that political success was certainly Berlusconi's winning image as owner of AC Milan, and his administration of the club reveals as much about Berlusconi himself as it does about Italy and Italian football.

On the evening of 5 July 1986, a promising, slightly bewildered 21-year-old Dutch striker called Marco Van Basten drove through the gates of San Martino, the magnificent eighteenth-century villa at Arcore, north of Milan, owned by Berlusconi. Van Basten was on his way to a secret rendezvous, summoned by Berlusconi who, just four months earlier, had bought one of Italy's most famous clubs, AC Milan.

The young Van Basten was not to know it, but his secret meeting was to lay the foundations not only for huge sporting success for AC Milan but also, at least partly, for future political triumphs for Mr Berlusconi. Van Basten would prove to be a key element in an impressive array of playing and managerial talent brought together at AC Milan by Berlusconi, talent that very quickly saw the club establish itself as amongst the best in the world.

Destined to be nicknamed the 'Swan of Utrecht', because of his elegant, angular looks, Van Basten was to become one of the great strikers of the modern game. Winner of the World and European Player of the Year awards while with AC Milan, he climaxed his first season in Italian football in 1988 with a superb European Championship tournament in Germany. Playing for the Netherlands against the USSR in the Munich final, he wrapped up the Dutch victory in true Roy of the Rovers fashion by scoring one of the greatest goals of all time, volleying home, from a prohibitively tight angle, a 60-yard crossfield pass.

Van Basten also experienced huge success in the Milan shirt. Within two years of that July rendezvous at Arcore, AC Milan were winning their first league title of the Berlusconi era, and one year after that they were at the Nou Camp in Barcelona winning the European Cup. The new-look AC Milan not only blazed a trail of spectacular footballing success but it also set new standards, at least for Italian clubs, in terms of commercial organisation, professional management and salary levels.

Travelling down that road with Van Basten and the Milan team was its powerful owner, a hands-on tycoon who brought to the club not only financial resources but also energy, enthusiasm, new ideas and a not inconsiderable knowledge of football. Berlusconi has never been a man to hide his light under a bushel and, at times, it seemed that he was not only Milan's inspirational guiding light but also its very *anima* (soul). Where there was Milan success, there was the broadly smiling face of *padrone* Berlusconi, either standing proudly over the latest piece of heavyweight silverware won by the team or being thrown in the air by his jubilant players.

Lest anyone failed to get the point, Berlusconi underlined the crucial nature of his own role and contribution to AC Milan, particularly in the regular interviews he granted to Italy's sports dailies such as *Gazzetta Dello Sport* and *Corriere Dello Sport*, papers which, then and now, represent Italy's (much less vulgar) equivalent of Anglo-Saxon, mass-circulation tabloids. Colleagues recall how, in those days, Berlusconi would himself take questions about AC Milan on the phone. In September 1991 he was quoted in *Gazzetta Dello Sport* as saying:

I've been a football coach myself, you know, and not of the firm's kick-around team but of regular teams that played in FIGC's youth and junior team championships, teams that won every competition they took part in. I never interfere in the work of our coaches [at AC Milan] but if you are the president of a club, above all, if you are someone with the sort of experience that I have had as an entrepreneur in the handling of people and of normal business activity, then you simply have to try and stimulate people, make suggestions and express your opinions in your relations with your managers, even your football manager.

I don't want to play down the contributions made by anyone else but my presence as AC Milan president over the last four years has been at the very least very important if not absolutely crucial. The club president has a 360-degree role – he intervenes when he has to, he holds his patience if that is necessary and he motivates people during difficult periods. This is a highly important role and it is my belief that no club can obtain important successes if it is not led by someone who possesses a whole series of skill that form part of the entrepreneur's talent.

Nowadays, Berlusconi is one of the best-known and most-talked about Italians in the world. Whether he is addressing the European Parliament, making Nazi jibes at German Euro MP Martin Schulz (July 2003) or in court defending himself against charges of bribery (June 2003), he has rarely been out of the limelight.

For much of the last decade, too, his judicial problems have cast a less than flattering light on his native land. He has been charged with (but not convicted of) corruption, bribery of judges and tax inspectors, false accounting, tax evasion and illegal party financing in nine different judicial investigations. His first government in 1994 was brought down when he was served with a judicial warrant while chairing an international convention on organised crime in Naples.

For his part, Berlusconi has always argued that he has been the victim of a political witch-hunt, orchestrated by left-wing magistrates. As proof of this claim, he regularly points to the fact that, despite all the varied charges, he has never actually been convicted. This is indeed true, but his various acquittals bear closer inspection. He owes his clean judicial record, with regard to some of these charges, not to a final acquittal but to the fact that the 'statute of limitations' had come into operation. In other words, although sometimes initially found guilty, he was then subsequently acquitted during the appeal process because time had run out.

More recently, of course, he has stood loyally by the side of President George W. Bush, giving both Italian moral and military support to the US-led invasion of Iraq, notwithstanding the fact that Italian public opinion was overwhelmingly opposed to the US invasion.

Ranked by *Forbes* magazine as the twenty-fifth richest man in the world, he is the head of a €10 billion business empire that comprises advertising, banking, film, insurance and publishing interests as well as, and above all else, a huge private media empire that controls Italy's three biggest commercial TV channels – Rete 4, Canale 5 and Italia 1 – which between them claim approximately 45 per cent of the national audience share.

For much of the last decade, it has been difficult to live in Italy and avoid Berlusconi. His empire invades every corner of Italian life. If you read the Milan-based daily *Il Giornale* or the weekly news magazine *Panorama*, take out a pension with insurance company Mediolanum, buy books published by Mondadori, sit in a multi-cinema owned by Medusa, showing films distributed by Medusa, look for a late-night pizza in the *Pagine Italia* (*Yellow Pages*), or go for a night out to Milan's Manzoni Theatre, then you have stepped into the wonderful world of Mr Berlusconi. His Fininvest holding company has either a 100 per cent or a majority shareholding in each of these concerns.

* * *

Born into a comfortable middle-class Milanese family on 29 September 1936, the son of the manager of the Banca Rasini and educated by priests of the Salesian order at the austere Sant'Ambrogio boarding school, Berlusconi graduated from Milan university where he studied law. Media portraits love to record how the young Berlusconi supported himself through his early years by taking jobs as a singer and compere on Mediterranean cruise ships and in various Milanese nightclubs, often accompanied at the piano by school friend Fedele Confalonieri, today the president of Mediaset, the company which controls Berlusconi's three television channels.

Berlusconi first made waves in Italy in the early 1960s when he founded Edilnord S.p.a., a building company supported by his father's bank, the Rasini, and by a Swiss company, Finanzierungesellschaft fur Residenzen Ag, registered in Lugano, a company of undisclosed ownership that was subsequently looked into by Palermo-based anti-Mafia investigators. Berlusconi and Edilnord struck rich with the conception and construction of Milano 2 (built 1970–9), a luxury compound for 10,000 inhabitants in the green suburban north of the city, containing a hotel, a conference centre, a running track, swimming pools, underground car parks, cycle paths, pedestrian walkways and cable television (the latter to avoid the ugly mess of TV aerials that, even today, besmirch the skylines of Italian cities).

Surrounded with trees, lawns and artificial lakes, the Milano 2 garden city offered quality living for the budding masters of a Milanese universe where the advertising, telecommunications, finance and fashion industries were all booming. Significantly, too, in an Italy where kidnapping and Red Brigade violence were to become daily occurrences, Milano 2 offered a high level of security thanks to an extensive nightwatchman presence. Furthermore, in an Italy where many regions simply fail to enforce building regulations and by-laws, Mr Berlusconi's innovative creation offered an oasis of 1950s mid-American order and tranquillity in sharp contrast to the chaos of the modern Italian city.

When originally installed, the Milano 2 cable TV system offered six channels, of which three were occupied by the State broadcaster RAI and two set aside for foreign channels. That left one channel empty. At the instigation of Milano 2 residents, the free channel was used as a local news service called Telemilano, which began broadcasting in 1974.

At first, Berlusconi was only marginally interested in the Telemilano project. By July 1976, however, when a ruling from Italy's constitutional court decreed that privately owned channels could transmit legally in their own regions, Berlusconi had understood the potential for private broadcasting.

In the following years, he bought up transmitters and repeaters in the Lombardy region around Milan and began region-wide broadcasts. By 1980, Telemilano had been renamed Canale 5, today the flagship of the Mediaset empire, and was broadcasting an American-style package of films, TV series, quizzes, variety shows and, last but not least, football.

Two events over the next years had a key impact on the rise and rise of the Berlusconi television empire. In late 1980, he acquired the rights to the Mundialito or Copa d'Oro tournament in Uruguay, a celebration of the fiftieth anniversary of the first World Cup that featured all the previous World Cup winners – Argentina, Brazil, Italy, West Germany, home side Uruguay and the Netherlands (not World Cup winners themselves but replacements for England, who opted out).

The success of the broadcasts of this tournament, played in December 1980 and January 1981, not only served to remind Berlusconi of the huge impact of televised football on the Italian public, it also helped forge a national identity for Canale, which was, at the time, legally bound to broadcast only in the Lombardy region. Berlusconi got around that restriction by using a complex system of synchronised tapes of pre-recorded programmes on local stations up and down Italy, thus creating the illusion of a nationwide broadcaster.

The second key event of those early years came in 1984 when magistrates in Rome, Turin and Pescara ordered the blackout of Berlusconi's channels (by now, he had three). The magistrates argued that Mr Berlusconi's creative system of simultaneous broadcasts was illegal. Within four days, Socialist Prime Minister Bettino Craxi had introduced a ministerial decree that, *de facto*, legalised the Berlusconi operation and allowed his channels back on the air. Later, the decree, which under the Italian constitution has only a 60-day lifetime, was pushed through parliament by Mr Craxi himself. From that moment on, despite various half-hearted attempts by the Italian parliament to regulate Italy's broadcasting free-for-all, Berlusconi had all the room for manoeuvre, development and growth he needed.

Mr Craxi, who died in self-imposed exile in Tunisia in 1999 after having been convicted of corruption charges, had been a long-time friend of Mr Berlusconi. When Berlusconi married his second wife, the actress Veronica Lario, in a civil marriage in Milan town hall on 15 December 1987, there were just four witnesses present – Bettino Craxi and his wife, Anna, and Berlusconi's old friends Fedele Confalonieri and Gianni Letta, later his government cabinet secretary.

Loyalty to trusted collaborators and friends is a constant factor in the Berlusconi phenomenon. People like Letta and Confalonieri have been at his side almost all his adult life. Even at AC Milan, Berlusconi has stuck with the same trusted advisers with managing director Adriano Galliani and directors Ariedo Braida and Silvano Ramaccioni all in place at the club from the day he bought it in 1986.

The concept of the powerful *padrone* owning a football team was and is nothing new in Italy. Italy's makers and shakers simply feel they are nobody until they have a football team under their corporate wing.

The industrial baron style of ownership had been pioneered by the semi-aristocratic Agnelli family from Turin, founders and majority shareholders in automobile giant Fiat and *de facto* owners of Italy's most famous and most successful club, Juventus. By the mid-1980s, the 'Old Lady', as Juventus is often called, had long been considered part of the Agnelli family silver, with 'l'Avvocato' (the lawyer) Gianni Agnelli combining the role of Fiat president with that of number one Juventus fan. He, too, regularly intervened directly in club affairs, and personally negotiated the purchase of Michel Platini in 1982.

In Milan, different generations of the Moratti family of oil millionaires have owned Inter Milan. Today's Inter is payrolled by Massimo Moratti, son of Angelo, who was in charge of the club during a golden period in the 1960s when it won three Serie A titles and two European Cups.

Historically, families such as the Morattis and Agnellis tended to make their influence felt discreetly, rarely identifying themselves specifically and personally with the team's success. No one had ever seen l'Avvocato Agnelli jumping into line for a photo-call alongside a new trophy. Nor had anyone ever dared to throw him in the air after Juventus had lifted yet another title. At the very most, Agnelli might have been snapped by the photographers during a training session at the crumbling old Stadio Comunale (since re-built for the 2006 Winter Olympics). He would be seen chatting quietly with the team coach or with one of the many Juventus stars, players such as Sivori, Charles, Boniperti, Bettega, Platini, Boniek et al.

Berlusconi was different. From the beginning, he hitched his formidable rising star to the Milan bandwagon. At his first pre-season presentation of the new team, in July 1986, he had the players flown into Milan's old Arena Stadium in a helicopter to the accompaniment of Wagner's 'The Ride of the Valkyries'. 10,000 fans, too, were on hand to see the show. Later that summer, speaking to the players in the privacy of his San Martino villa, he told them that he was 'not accustomed to finishing second'. Berlusconi could see only too clearly the potential gains to be had from creating a winning 'synergy' (one of his favourite words at the time) of football success, consumer advertising and national television audiences.

From the beginning, his AC Milan was a very different club. For a start, it was listed under the 'cinema and show business' arm of his holding company, 'Fininvest'. In those early days, other Fininvest companies were closely involved. By 1988, the team shirt was sponsored by insurance company Mediolanum (which also covered player insurance) while travel requirements were handled by Five Viaggi, both Fininvest companies. The club's sports gear was provided by Robba di Kappa, a successful, independent firm but a good client of Publitalia, the powerful Fininvest advertising company and money-making machine.

The Berlusconi-owned Milan also got quickly into the merchandising act, opening a Milan Point shop close to the city's celebrated *duomo* (cathedral) where fans could buy not only Milan gear but also match tickets. The Lombardy bank Cariplo, omnipresent in the Milanese hinterland, was enrolled to help with ticket sales. So well did the early Milan go that season ticket sales at one point went over the 70,000 mark. On top of that, a magazine called *Forza Milan* went into print, with a circulation of over 100,000 copies. It sounds old hat now, but it was vibrantly new for Italy at the time.

Berlusconi also set new standards when it came to levels of pay. By 1989, tax declarations showed that striker Van Basten and captain Franco Baresi were on an annual wage of around £850,000 each, attacking midfielder Roberto Donadoni was on £600,000, and players such as Carlo Ancelotti (later to become club coach), Paolo Maldini and Mauro Tassotti were on £500,000. Furthermore, these high wage levels were stimulated by a 'productivity' bonus system (then unknown in Italy) whereby the more the club won, the more wages its star players earned.

These salaries were way ahead of the rest of Europe. For example, five years later, in the mid-1990s, Manchester United's charismatic Frenchman Eric Cantona, one of the highest paid players in the English Premiership, was estimated to be on a salary of just over £500,000 per annum.

Even the club's legendary training centre of Milanello, near Varese, 80 kilometres north of Milan, was revamped. If you go there now, it is hard not to be impressed by the sense of organisation, order and sheer professionalism. When you arrive outside the big iron gates, you have to announce your presence on the intercom. Usually, you have been given an appointment for a specific time and until that time comes, the gates remain closed and the journalists wait outside. Inevitably, and always on the dot, the gates open and you and your TV crew can move in, driving past the plush lawns, the manicured pitches and along the tree-lined avenues that give a hint of the nearby Alpine foothills. Before you go any further, however, you have to pick up your identity tag. Only then are you free to circulate and wait for the players. Here again, Milan tends to be very professional. If the club says a player will be available for an interview then he will turn up. Likewise, if they tell you that the said player will not be available, then you might as well not bother travelling.

The Milanello clubhouse, painted in the club's black and red colours, comprises rooms for the players, a billiards room, a TV room, a small bar and an excellent restaurant where, when the players have finished, the journalists can (sometimes) eat. All along the walls of the clubhouse are pictures, some in brilliant colour and others in grainy black and white, which recall the great Milan teams of the past. The atmosphere is hospitable, yet deadly serious. The visitor, and indeed newly arrived star players, cannot fail to have it impressed upon them that this is a club of a certain winning style, tradition and history.

Milan's great rival, Juventus, offers an intriguing comparison. For most of the last 20 years, Juventus have trained either at the Stadio Comunale or at sports centres normally used by Fiat workers. There is no plush-carpeted clubhouse, and interviews and press conferences are usually held in temporary Portakabins or tents. Not, mind you, that the Juventus results seem to suffer much.

At first, Berlusconi may have perceived AC Milan as one of many roads to furthering his already immense commercial success. As time went by, however, and as Italy underwent profound political changes in the wake of the fall of Eastern bloc Communism and the Tangentopoli scandal, Berlusconi came to understand that AC Milan could also help him down the road that would eventually lead to Palazzo Chigi in Rome.

Founded in 1899 by English industrialist Alfred Edwards and textile worker and team captain Herbert Kilpin, Milan Cricket and Football Club (the name changed to Associazione Calcio – AC – Milan in 1946) has long been an institution in Italian footballing life. In 1908, an internal club argument about foreign player quotas prompted the birth of a breakaway club called Internazionale, now better known to the English-speaking world as Inter Milan. That 1908 argument, of course, gave birth to one of the most famous and keenly contested derby rivalries of world football.

In more recent times, AC Milan blossomed in the 1960s, the era of Gianni Rivera, becoming the first Italian club to win the European Cup in 1963 and going on to win two league titles and a second Champions Cup in that same decade.

Milan fell foul of the infamous 1980 match-fixing scandal that also involved 1982 World Cup hero Paolo Rossi. The FIGC found that the then club president Felice Colombo and goal-keeper Enrico Albertosi had been involved in the match-fixing, pools-rigging scandal and relegated the club to Serie B. After immediately winning promotion back into Serie A, the club was again relegated at the end of the 1981–2 season, this time for purely sporting reasons.

By the mid-1980s, AC Milan was in deep trouble, a mid-table Serie A side burdened with debt and led by a club president, namely Giuseppe Farina, who eventually departed in something of a hurry for South Africa. When Farina announced his desire to sell the club on Friday, 13 December 1985, speculation mounted that Berlusconi might be tempted to buy it. Banners even appeared at Milan's Meazza stadium in San Siro, urging Berlusconi to step in and save the day.

Two months later, on 20 February 1986, after an inevitably complex 'on-off-on-again' negotiation, Berlusconi had acquired Milan and its debts for approximately £6 million.

From day one, the media tycoon had ambitious plans for his new club. For a start, he intended to go looking for the best talent around. Thus, when one of his staff at AC Milan showed him a video of the young Ajax Amsterdam striker Van Basten in May 1986, he sat up and took notice. The cassette had been sent to Milan by Van Basten's agent, Apollonius Konijnenburg, who had been frustrated by the failure of talks with another Serie A team, Fiorentina. When the Florence club failed to come up with the cash, Konijnenburg opted to try his luck with the newest club owner on the Italian block.

Legend has it that after seeing the fourteenth brilliant goal scored by Van Basten, Berlusconi turned off the TV and ordered his club director, Ariedo Braida, to immediately open negotiations with Ajax. That secret July 1986 rendezvous at San Martino sealed the deal, with Berlusconi persuading Van Basten to join AC Milan in twelve months' time, ready for the 1987–8 season, and for the bargain knockdown price of approximately £1.1 million.

One month after that first meeting with Van Basten, Berlusconi interrupted a relaxing Sunday at the Ligurian Riviera resort of Portofino to climb onto his private helicopter and go to watch his new club play Serie B side Parma in a pre-season friendly. This was to be an early test for his new team.

Having bought the club long after the midway point in the preceding season, Berlusconi had had to wait until this summer of 1986 before he could begin to assemble his 'own' team. In addition to buying Van Basten for the next year, he and his aides had also signed up a number of talented players for the new season, such as midfielder Roberto Donadoni, striker Daniele Massaro and goalkeeper Giovanni Galli.

So Berlusconi went to Parma, perhaps expecting to see his new-look side, coached by Swedish veteran Nils Liedholm, turn on an impressive display. Instead, it was Parma, a club just promoted from Serie C1, who gave a good account of themselves, forcing Milan to work hard for a flattering 2–0 win. Significantly, in his post-match comments to the press, Berlusconi praised the then unknown Parma coach, Arrigo Sacchi.

One month later, Milan drew Parma in a qualifying group phase for the Italian Cup. This time, Sacchi's side did even better, winning 1–0 at the San Siro. Given a freak draw, the two sides met again in a two-leg, second-round tie played in February and April 1987, with Parma eliminating Milan thanks to a second consecutive 1–0 win at the San Siro and a 0–0 home draw.

Berlusconi had seen enough. After the second home defeat by Parma in February, he sent Braida off again on his travels, this time with the order to hire Sacchi. At the time, it was an extraordinarily bold move. No one got to coach the major Serie A sides without having served an extensive 'apprenticeship', first as a top-rate Serie A player and then as a successful coach with minor Serie A sides.

Sacchi had been a shoe salesman, not a professional footballer. Prior to coaching Parma, he had cut his teeth with minor amateur teams such as Fusignano, Alfosine and Bellaria. Yet, as the years ahead were to prove, Silvio Berlusconi is a man of vision, boundless self-belief and considerable nous, be it political, commercial or footballing.

In that same February of 1987, Berlusconi laid another important foundation stone in the AC Milan success story. On a chilly winter's night, he boarded his private jet in Milan for Amsterdam. He was on his way to sign up the services of one of the hottest footballing properties then around, another Dutchman named Ruud Gullit.

Berlusconi invited Gullit to a meeting in a downtown, luxury Amsterdam hotel. He sat up late into the night using a characteristic mix of charm, flattery and determination to get his man. However, Gullit was not convinced and the two parties failed to arrive at an agreement.

Within the month, though, Berlusconi flew back to Amsterdam, his sights still trained on Gullit. In the end, the deal was clinched and the charismatic Dutchman was bound for AC Milan for a fee of around £2.8 million. With his dreadlocks, his Surinamese origins and his politically correct gestures – such as the dedication of his 1988 European Player of the Year award to the then imprisoned South African leader Nelson Mandela – Gullit was exactly the sort of mould-breaking image that Berlusconi wanted to bring to Milan. On top of that, he could play. Little wonder that Berlusconi subsequently described him as a player with 'the sun in his heart and dynamite in his muscles'.

Just one year after he had bought AC Milan, Berlusconi had now brought together three of the key elements – Van Basten, Gullit and Sacchi – that were to re-launch Milan and confirm it as one of the strongest clubs in European football over the next 20 years. The club already had one or two very important players, such as its captain, *libero* Franco Baresi.

One of the greatest defenders of his generation, Baresi was arguably the most quintessentially 'Italian' of all modern footballers. Elegant, and a sharp reader of the game, he was also awesomely fierce and sometimes cruelly cynical in the tackle. For many, he will be remembered for his heroic and superb performance in Italy's 1994 World Cup final loss to Brazil, less than three weeks after undergoing surgery for a knee cartilage problem.

Also in the side was a promising 18-year-old left-back called Paolo Maldini, son of the Wembley 1963 hero Cesare Maldini. Speaking to reporters after that July 1986 friendly with Parma, Berlusconi had said: 'I expect a lot of Maldini … and I can also tell you, keep an eye out for Costacurta.'

Nineteen years later, both Alessandro 'Billy' Costacurta and Paolo Maldini were still playing in Serie A and European competitions for Milan, Maldini having established himself as one of the greats of world football as well as the most capped Italian international of all time with 126 appearances to his credit. Proof positive, if any were needed, that Berlusconi knew his footballing onions.

From the start, Berlusconi talked the good fight, spouting the sort of optimistic management psycho-babble that he was later to use to great effect when persuading the Italian electorate to put him into government office. Speaking in May 1986, just three months after he had bought the club and at a time when his re-building plans were just beginning, he was not slow to highlight his own contribution to the construction process in *Corriere Dello Sport*:

> As a fan, I could say, well, I've put together the team, now I expect to win. But that would be a mistake …

we're not ready to win just yet … rather we've worked for the future. What we've got to do now is strengthen both the squad and the desire to win. For that reason, I myself will go with the team to their pre-season training camp at Vipiteno. The important thing is to initiate a winning cycle and, of course, to close the books in the black and not at a loss because we're not going to be mere benefactors here …

Ironically, while Berlusconi realised all his fondest dreams with AC Milan in terms of footballing success, he never did manage to keep the club out of the red. By June 2003, the accountancy firm Practice Audit estimated AC Milan to be €142.8 million in debt, while the club returned a €51.5 million loss for the financial year 2003–4.[3] Berlusconi, however, understood that, in terms of image, AC Milan was well worth the investment, and each year he came up with the cash to meet the club's debts. For someone with huge commercial and ultimately political ambitions in a country where football is encoded into the national DNA, four European Cup/Champions League trophies and seven Serie A league titles over the next 19 seasons were worth more than money could buy.

From the moment he took over AC Milan, Berlusconi was careful about the image projected by the club. When his own TV channels were covering games played by Milan (only friendlies in the early days since all the important TV rights then belonged to the State broadcaster RAI), he told his producers to focus on pretty female faces in the crowd so as to encourage the concept of the football match as a family occasion.[4] In that context, too, the combination of Van Basten and Gullit provided a perfect role model of racial harmony at work. Gullit, in particular, inspired huge enthusiasm amongst the fans in his early seasons at AC Milan. (Van Basten, injured for much of that first season, was later to overtake him in the fans' affections.) Such was the 'Gullit-mania' that many Milan fans took to wearing false dreadlocks and painting their faces black when they went to the Meazza stadium at San Siro.

Given that he was later to make a political bedfellow of the Northern League, a political movement not known for its love of the foreigner, it is intriguing now to look back on how Berlusconi then enthusiastically espoused Gullit's success to change the Milan fan mentality:

> I explained to them [fan clubs] that it was possible to support a club without being violent or intolerant. The Milan fans that I had inherited were the sort who held up banners with anti-Semitic or racist slogans written on them. That mentality had to go.[5]

The two Dutchmen – later joined by a third compatriot, Frank Rijkaard – were also fundamental elements in a technical revolution that the Sacchi-coached Milan team of Berlusconi's early years brought to Italian football. Berlusconi quickly made it clear that he wanted not only to win but to do so in a style hitherto almost unseen in Italian football. At least initially, he wanted his side to abandon the classic 'defend first, attack later' game, played until then by the best of Italian teams. He wanted a team that would go out there, take the match to the opposition, impose its own game-plan and do all this in winning style.

In players like the Dutch trio, aided by two of the greatest Italian players of all time in Franco Baresi and Paolo Maldini, Milan had the players. It was Berlusconi's intuition that put this formidable squad into the hands of Sacchi, a coach who believed, then and now, in attacking football and who, furthermore, argued that the old *catenaccio* (padlock defence) Italian game was outdated.

By the beginning of Berlusconi's second full season (1987–8) as owner of the club, the engines were getting ready to roar. Even if the side got off to a quiet start as it assimilated Sacchi's new ideas – for example, Milan were eliminated in the second round of the UEFA Cup by modest Spanish side Espanyol – the quality and quantity of its football soon had a telling impact. (After that Espanyol defeat, Berlusconi intervened personally to quell a dressing-room revolt against Sacchi, telling the players: 'I myself picked Mr Sacchi and therefore he will still be here next year. As for all of you, I couldn't be sure.')

The turning point in those early Berlusconi days at AC Milan came on Sunday, 1 May 1988 when the team travelled south for a decisive encounter with reigning champions and league leaders, the Maradona-inspired Napoli. From my Rome base, I had observed the Milan phenomenon from afar. Two weeks prior to the game, I had seen them win 2–0 at the Olimpico in Rome against a dull AS Roma, coached by Nils Liedholm, the man Berlusconi had offloaded in favour of Sacchi.

That win had been impressive enough, but to travel south to face Maradona and Napoli at the San Paolo was another proposition. Napoli, however, came into the match in less than ideal condition, at least mentally. There was a lot of internal squabbling, largely between the all-dominant figure of Maradona and the team's rather morose coach, Ottavio Bianchi, who had twice substituted and then dropped striker Bruno Giordano in the club's previous three games against Inter, Juventus and Verona. Napoli had beaten Inter but lost to Juventus and then been held to a draw by Verona. They had dropped three points in two games and, from a five-point lead, now went into the potentially all-decisive game with Milan just one point clear of Sacchi's side.

Maradona and other senior players, such as goalkeeper Claudio Garella, midfielder Salvatore Bagni and Brazilian striker Careca, all felt that Bianchi had got the call badly wrong with regard to Giordano and wanted him back in the side. Bianchi stuck to his guns and left him out.

Despite the internal tensions, though, Napoli gave a terrific performance in an epic game. Early in the match Pietro Paolo Virdis struck for Milan and things were looking distinctly bad for the Neapolitans until Maradona pulled one out of the hat with a superbly struck left-footed free kick just before half-time. It was 1–1 and all still to play for.

Milan had shown huge character and composure in the first half and any illusions that they might be intimidated by the Maradona equaliser were almost immediately dispelled with another goal from Virdis, brilliantly created for him by the sheer pace and power of Gullit down the right flank. With the home side committed to all-out attack in desperate search of a second equaliser, Milan struck again cruelly and somewhat atypically on the counter.

Gullit again did the damage, picking up a loose ball as a Napoli attack broke down on the edge of the Milan area, before making a majestic run almost the full length of the pitch. With the Napoli defence totally outflanked, Gullit then squared the ball for the easiest of goals from his compatriot Van Basten, a substitute that day and just back from an ankle injury that had cost him almost the whole season. That day also marked the *sorpasso* (overtaking) for Milan as they passed Napoli and went on to win the first major trophy of the Berlusconi era. Fittingly, the sporting Napoli fans gave the Milan team a standing ovation as they left the field at the end of a truly splendid game.

As I stood in my phone cabin in the San Paolo press room filing copy, I casually listened in to one half of an intriguing phone call. In the booth next to mine was Adriano Galliani, who asked to be put through to 'Dr Berlusconi'. When the media tycoon eventually picked up the phone, there was no denying Galliani's delight as he gleefully informed Berlusconi that 'things went really well' ('*E andato molto, ma molto bene, Silvio*').

Things were to get better. Next stop on the Milan winning run was to come one year later in Barcelona when Milan made the final of the European Cup where they faced Romanian side Steaua Bucharest. In those days, prior to the collapse of Eastern bloc Communism, Romanian sides did not exactly travel with many fans. Steaua's presence in the final was a potential disaster for UEFA, who risked seeing their biggest game of the year played in front of a less-than-capacity crowd in the massive Nou Camp stadium, with its 110,000 seats. To the rescue came Berlusconi, who oversaw the transportation of 26,000 Milan fans (thousands more Milan fans travelled by their own means) to the Barcelona game.

In the end, the club chartered one ship, 25 airplanes and 450 buses to get the fans to Barcelona. Along with those who travelled under their own steam, the Milan fans practically filled the mighty stadium, creating a San Siro effect in a Nou Camp where only one team had any supporters. In the circumstances, it was probably no surprise that Steaua kindly opted not to spoil the party, as Milan pummelled them 4–0, the goals appropriately being scored by the racial harmony team of Gullit and Van Basten. For Berlusconi, this night was a huge triumph. He told *Gazzetta Dello Sport* in 1991 that, of his first five years with Milan, this was the best moment: 'We celebrated winning our first Champions Cup in front of a 90,000-strong crowd most of whom had travelled from every corner of Italy. No one had ever seen anything like it before in football, and then too it was a splendid match.' In the same interview, Berlusconi also reflected on other satisfying aspects of his footballing success, commenting: 'I'll never forget the night when the San Siro stadium filled with fans, there to celebrate our first title win [in 1988]. Five years on, I can still feel the warm embrace of the fans and the public, an embrace made all the warmer by all the years of disappointment.'

And there we touch on an obvious aspect of the later Berlusconi-as-populist-politician phenomenon. It is stating the obvious to point out that Berlusconi's media empire, his wealth, ambition and, above all, political alliances with such as the late, disgraced Socialist Prime Minister Bettino Craxi were fundamental to preparing the way for his entry into politics.

Yet, somewhere along the line, the AC Milan factor weighed in heavily, too. As the silverware piled up on the club sideboard, it became obvious that Berlusconi was getting to enjoy the populist experience. Just try walking out in front of 70,000 people all shouting your name and bursting into applause at your very appearance and not be moved by the experience.

Prior to his purchase of AC Milan, he was already established as a heavyweight slugger in the Italian economy. Subsequent to that purchase, and independently of AC Milan, the growth of his commercial television empire gave him ever greater national visibility. Yet nothing quite plugged him into the psyche of the *popolo* as effectively as regular, spectacular success at the nation's favourite game.

Berlusconi used his football success to prove that with his energy and ideas (and important friends in places high and low), he could overcome any number of prejudices. If the *salotto buono* (literally, the good sitting room) of Italian high finance had at first tended to snub this ambitious ex-crooner turned builder, so what? He simply expanded from building into television and, in the process, became richer than all the regular patrons of the *salotto buono* put together.

When he took over at AC Milan, many football insiders expressed scepticism at his arrival on the football scene. Typical was this comment from Giovanni Trapattoni, coach to, amongst others, Juventus, Inter Milan, Bayern Munich, Fiorentina, Italy, Benfica and Stuttgart: 'Berlusconi has plenty of money, he says it himself, and if he wants to buy himself a Rolls Royce, that's his business ... But football is like a rose window; you need lots of hard stones and only a few that glitter.'

Within two years, Berlusconi was to prove him and others wrong. By 1994, just eight years after he had taken over the club, Milan stood proudly at the top of both Italian and European football, having lifted four Serie A titles and three European Cups in that period.

In a sense, it was hardly surprising that when Berlusconi opted to move into politics on the eve of the 1994 General Election, his carefully prepared entrance was heavily underlined with populist, football language. On the evening of Wednesday, 26 January 1994, in a nine-minute American-style presidential address from his study in Arcore, broadcast by both RAI and his own trio of commercial channels – Canale 5, Rete 4 and Italia 1 – Mr Berlusconi announced his entry into politics. To do so, he used a phrase that has become modern Italian legend: 'I have chosen to take to the field and involve myself in public life because I don't want to live in an illiberal country, governed by immature forces and by men [the ex-Communists] who are still closely linked to a past that proved both a political and economic disaster ...'

The key phrase is, of course, '*Ho scelto di scendere in campo*' (I have chosen to take to the field/pitch). This is a phrase that comes straight from the footballing lexicon since coaches and players spend half their lives telling us about what does or does not happen '*quando scendiamo in campo*' (when we take to the pitch).

Lest the Italian electorate fail to get the point, the Fininvest boffins came up with name of Forza Italia (Go On, Italy, or Up, Italy) for the newly formed centre-right Berlusconi party, while its parliamentary candidates were referred to as the *azzurri*. He even taunted economist Luigi Spaventa, the man who had the courage to stand against him in the Roma 1 constituency, by saying: 'Before running against me, go and win yourself two Champions Cups.'

In one bold move, Berlusconi had coined a brilliant slogan for his party while at the same plunging Italian football fans into existential crisis when it came to supporting the national team. After all, unless you are an avid Berlusconi supporter, it is a bit difficult these days to start shouting '*Forza Italia*' during Italy's World Cup games.

Political analyst Professor Ilvio Diamanti argued in an article published in *Limes* in 2005 that Berlusconi's footballing synergy had totally changed the face of Italian politics:

> Today, in the wake of Silvio Berlusconi's 'taking to the field' (a term that was certainly not used by accident by Berlusconi) it is hard to differentiate between football, the media and politics. That taking to the field transferred from football to political organisational models symbols and a sense of identity which pre-1994 politics had lost ... [6]

Curiously, within days of the Berlusconi General Election success in 1994, FIFA President João Havelange called on him to sell AC Milan and 'not mix sport with politics'. Given Havelange's own track record of consistently mixing FIFA sport with world politics, this was an interesting call and one which Berlusconi ignored, telling AC Milan fans: 'I will do everything in my power to hold onto Milan and I hope that this will not prove incompatible with my future obligations.'

And hold on he has. Even if he finally stepped down as president of the club in December 2004, that 'resignation' was more symbolic than real. Since the early 1990s, the day-to-day running of the club has been *de facto* in the hands of Adriano Galliani.

Ironically, Berlusconi formally renounced the Milan presidency in the wake of a new 'conflicts of interest' law passed by his own government in July 2004. Critics of Berlusconi had long called for him to address the serious conflicts of interests prompted by his twin roles of Prime Minister on the one hand, and that of the country's leading industrialist and head of a huge media empire on the other. The July 2004 legislation is a master-piece of its kind since it somehow manages to avoid dealing with these conflicts yet obliges him to offer his meaningless resigna-tion as AC Milan president. Rest assured that of all his various potential 'conflicts of interest', the one that least worried critics, political opponents and social commentators alike was that prompted by the presidency of his own football club.

Not, mind you, that you could spot the difference between Berlusconi the club president and Berlusconi the ex-club president. On 14 August 2005, talking to reporters after AC Milan had beaten Juventus to win the Luigi Berlusconi Trophy (a prestige friendly inaugurated by Berlusconi in memory of his father), he said: 'Football is so old-fashioned … I've always been an innovator but the problem is that you run into the mental block of most coaches. We want a more attacking game and new ways of playing it …'

Perhaps thinking back to Milan's embarrassing Champions League final defeat of three months earlier when his side surren-dered a 3–0 lead to lose the trophy to Liverpool, Berlusconi went on: 'When we're a goal up, our opponents shouldn't even see the ball. We should play it tight, short, square passes, even pass it back if necessary, but no long balls upfield. It didn't work out that way last season. I've been a football coach and I know what I'm talking about …'

Asked if he was in fact offering some tactical advice to the Milan coach, Carlo Ancelotti, Berlusconi reassuringly stated: 'These are just little dialectical darts to keep him on his toes. I did also tell him, though, that with a squad of players like the one he has, I could be the coach myself.'

Sounds very much like His Master's Voice speaking, be it president or ex-president. Curious, too, is the fact that Berlusconi repeats, almost word for word, his claim to a certain footballing expertise, as outlined in the 1991 *Gazzetta Dello Sport* interview. That much-trumpeted experience as a football coach had come in the early 1960s when he had acted as coach, manager, PR and laundry man for amateur side Torrescalla-Edilnord, a team comprising employees of his Edilnord company, including his brother Paolo and trusted aides Fedele Confalonieri and Adriano Galliani. The records show, too, that Torrescalla-Edilnord was an attack-oriented side that went unbeaten through the 1967 season and which won tournaments at youth and junior level.

Even if João Havelange might have expressed misgivings about Berlusconi's entry into politics in 1994, the Milan fans were not complaining. In May 1994, two months after Berlusconi's whirlwind election triumph, AC Milan routed Barcelona 4–0 in Athens to win the Champions League for the third time in five years, in the process giving one of the most glittering performances ever seen in a European final. Ironically, that Champions League win occurred on the very evening that the Italian Senate was passing a vote of confidence in the new Berlusconi government. '4–0 and 159 to 153, both Cruyff's Barcelona and Occhetto's centre-left were wiped out,' commented *Corriere Della Sera* next morning.

This was a period when everything appeared to be going swimmingly for Berlusconi. One month after that impressive Champions League triumph, he registered another success in the June European elections, his Forza Italia party picking up 30.6 per cent of the vote. That European election vote had taken place right on the eve of the World Cup finals in the USA where Italy, now led by Arrigo Sacchi (the coach discovered by Berlusconi), was about to blaze a trail of relative glory all the way to the final. But on 13 July 1994, with all the wind seemingly in his sails and the nation absorbed in the Italian team's World Cup progress, Berlusconi took a step too far.

On the very evening that Italy were playing Bulgaria in a

semi-final clash in New Jersey, Berlusconi's cabinet approved a decree law which basically put an end to the Tangentopoli corruption investigations. This was the first of many public confrontations between Mr Berlusconi and the magistrature. If he had hoped that Italians had taken their eye off the political ball, he was wrong. Despite the distractions of the World Cup semi-final and a hot July evening, the measure was greeted with public outcry and was subsequently withdrawn six days later.

Like other commentators, I have often wondered what would have happened to the public outrage if, four days later on 17 July, Italy had not lost the World Cup final to Brazil. Would the populist Berlusconi have ridden the tidal wave of national pride so successfully, immodestly pointing out his own role as Sacchi-inventor, as to have been able to push through any legislation he wanted? In the end, of course, Italy lost, and two days later the 'whitewash' decree was withdrawn. That defeat proved to be the first serious setback for a government that was due to last only seven months.

In all the years since then, Berlusconi football and Berlusconi politics have never again so dramatically crossed as they did on that July 1994 evening. From a distance, Berlusconi continues to follow Milan, taking great pride in the club's achievements. Only occasionally does he drop political business to intervene directly in the affairs of the club.

One such occasion came in March 2001, when he took time off from a fast and furious election campaign (election day was just two months away) to watch Milan's Champions League tie with Spanish club Deportivo La Coruña. Milan, then coached by Alberto Zaccheroni, needed a win to get through to the quarter-finals but were eliminated after a miserable, uninspired 1–1 home draw.

Berlusconi was disgusted, making it clear in a post-match TV interview that Zaccheroni's days as Milan coach were over: 'I'm going to have to get involved in the running of the club again. I didn't agree with many of the technical and tactical choices made – I haven't agreed with them for some time – but out of respect for the coach and the team director, I didn't intervene. Zaccheroni was defended by the press and by the fans, yet I'd have done many things differently. Tonight, we saw that I was not wrong.'

No sooner said than done. Zaccheroni's cappuccino was still warm in his breakfast cup when he received a phone call next morning confirming that he had been sacked. The summary dismissal of his coach, on live TV at that, was a clear reminder that Berlusconi cares deeply about his association with Milan's winning image. He had been hoping for a victory that would give his electoral campaign an added boost, but he had also gone to the match because of worrying signs of discontent amongst the Milan faithful. In the previous January, during a home game, fans had made fun of one of Berlusconi's nationwide election posters, which, alongside a picture of the smiling Berlusconi, read: 'To help those who have fallen behind.' To which some wit had replied with another poster that read: 'If you really want to help those who have fallen behind, why not start with AC Milan, dear president?'

Given his political responsibilities, Berlusconi's visits to the San Siro are much rarer now than they were 15 years ago. However, he still keeps an eye out for a chance to re-float the winning football-Milan-Berlusconi synergy. His current star striker, Ukraine bullet Andriy Shevchenko, offers fertile terrain.

In November 2002, on the day after Shevchenko scored in a Champions League win over Real Madrid, Berlusconi opted to celebrate the feat by summoning his player for a gala banquet held in Rome the following evening in honour of Ukraine President Leonid Kuchma, who just happened to be visiting Italy that week.

In September 2005, the christening of Jordan Shevchenko, the first-born son of Shevchenko and his American model wife Kristen Pazik, offered another splendid photo-opportunity. The christening was held in the little church of San Vincenzo, in up-market Cernobbio on Lake Como. Berlusconi arrived by motorboat, exchanged greetings and shook hands with passers-by before entering the church. Afterwards, he paused for the ritual picture of 'smiling politician with baby' before jokingly warning reporters not to write that he was the child's 'godfather' then going on to say that he felt he was 'a bit of a father figure' for Shevchenko and his wife.

The day before, speaking to a gathering of young entrepreneurs at Cernobbio, he had developed a similar theme, saying: 'For the good of Milan, I've even persuaded players to change their girlfriends, because they were having too negative an effect on them. A true leader must know about the lives of all his employees and collaborators. He must take care of all their family lives because if there's a problem at home, then the employee will not be happy and will not perform well.'

After the christening, he yet again touched on his role as the team's tactical maestro in reference to the 'advice' he had offered to his coach Carlo Ancelotti one month earlier: 'The other day I wasn't criticising Ancelotti but it is true that I said that with a squad of players like the Milan squad, I could coach them myself. But then, I have a very high opinion of myself; there are no limits to what I can do. I could have been a journalist or a parish priest. Indeed my old aunt used to say that I would have made a great Cardinal …'

In a country where the political debate is peppered with football-speak, Berlusconi rarely loses an opportunity to slip in a reference to football in general and Milan in particular. Likewise, wearing his government hat, he has occasionally intervened directly in football polemics.

In late August 2003, he cut short his annual holiday in his summer villa at Porto Rotondo on Sardinia's Costa Smeralda to return to Rome to chair an emergency cabinet meeting about Serie B regulations, a crisis which was threatening to delay the start of the football season. (This in spite of the fact that Russian President Vladimir Putin was due in Sardinia shortly.) Berlusconi's government decree legally obliged football clubs to accept both the FIGC's disciplinary rulings and also, as a final Court of Appeal, a Lazio regional court and the Council of State. It did not immediately resolve the crisis, but the decree, subsequently transformed into law, did set an important precedent.

The Berlusconi government also oversaw controversial legislation in March 2003 which introduced the possibility of some creative accountancy whereby Italian clubs can write off over a ten-year period the losses incurred in any one season with regard to player devaluation. AC Milan themselves used the benefits of this decree to the tune of an estimated €242 million.[7]

One year later, in March 2004, Berlusconi was tempted to push through another decree, this time allowing the clubs to pay off sums outstanding owed to the Inland Revenue, again over a ten-year period. On that occasion, opposition within his own governing coalition was such that Berlusconi quickly dropped the idea.

In football, too, Berlusconi has indirectly been responsible for a remarkable conflict of interests when his trusted aide at AC Milan, Adriano Galliani, was voted president of the Lega in early 2002. This inevitably led to some curious situations. For example, in the summer of 2005, Galliani ended up handling negotiations on behalf of the Lega for various TV rights in which the competing rivals were State broadcaster RAI and the Berlusconi-owned Mediaset. In the end, Galliani awarded the terrestrial TV highlight rights (the equivalent of the BBC's *Match of the Day*) to Mediaset, thus ending 30 years of RAI's celebrated *90th Minute* programme.

Not surprisingly, Galliani's decision stirred up a major political row with senior centre-left opposition figure Piero Fassino commenting: 'Given the fact that the Lega is led by Galliani, someone well known for his close links to the Prime Minister, it seems clear that he has operated so that Mediaset would win the TV rights.'

By January 2006, the issue was again causing concern with a number of smaller clubs in Serie A calling for parliament to amend the legislation governing the sale of TV rights, instituting 'collective' rather than 'individual' sales. In this way, the smaller clubs feel they will be better protected against the bigger ones (such as AC Milan) which can claim a much bigger slice of the TV cake on an individual basis. In a TV interview, Berlusconi seemed willing to help out the smaller clubs. Yet, one day later, his Forza Italia party blocked any attempt at amendments, ruling *de facto* in favour of Juventus, Inter Milan and, of course, AC Milan. So enraged was the Fiorentina owner, industrialist Diego Dalle Valle, that he called Berlusconi 'a liar'.

The rows about TV rights in the summer of 2005 and winter of 2006 were just further reminders of the extent to which Berlusconi dominated the Italian scene, be it political, sporting or related to the TV industry. It reminded me of my first close encounter with him, in the spring of 1988.

That happened when Berlusconi came to the foreign press club in Rome to talk business and, in particular, to spell out the details of an agreement that his Programma Italia advertising company had just stipulated with the Soviet Union. His upmarket sales patter, his charm, his sense of self, his vital energy, his desire to communicate and convince as well as his command of his subject were all immediately apparent. Typically, too, he was more than willing on that day to break off his press conference about Fininvest to take aside a small number of us who wished to quiz him about AC Milan. Here, too, his overall command of what was going on, not only at his own club and in Italian football generally but also in the European game, was striking.

I remember him telling us that the format of the then European Cup was old hat, arguing that UEFA should modify the tournament in order to guarantee that the big clubs made more than one appearance in a competition which in those days was sudden-death, knockout cup fare from round one, without the benefit of seeding. Berlusconi's remarks had been partly prompted by the fact that earlier that season, newly crowned Napoli, led by Diego Maradona, had gone out of the European Cup in the first round, eliminated by Real Madrid.

Perhaps the most curious aspect of that day, though, concerned the main news item, namely the Soviet Union contract. Given that Berlusconi's later political success was built on an outright condemnation of Communism, be it either the domestic Italian or the former Eastern bloc version, it is curious to note that he was happy to be doing business with the bad old USSR and Moscow. Describing the deal in a laudatory article in May 1988, the business pages of Rome daily *La Repubblica* commented:

> Programma Italia has won itself the exclusive right to sell advertising from Western European firms on Soviet television. This will be a major revolution for the peoples of Georgia, Latvia, Russia and Siberia who will now be faced with glamorous models wearing Benetton or the latest car from Renault. For Berlusconi, however, it is above all a very good deal that not only sees his advertising company handle the business of all big Western European companies but which also sets up his TV group to, one day, become a major supplier of programmes for Soviet television. For the time being, his company's image has gained. In time, Berlusconi's wallet will gain, too.

In 1988, however, the Communists – real, live Soviet Union ones too – were just more clients, good for business. It is hardly surprising then that, like many others, I have never really believed Berlusconi to have a true political creed or ideology. His only true credo is money: how to make it and how to keep it.

After that 1988 meeting, my next close encounter with Berlusconi came again at the foreign press club, where this time he was beating a rather different drum. This was November 1993, on the eve of his eagerly anticipated entry into politics. On this occasion, he said that if he had a vote in the forthcoming Rome mayoral electoral contest, he would use it in favour of former Fascist Gianfranco Fini, against the centre-left's candidate, Francesco Rutelli.

Berlusconi was still relatively new to the politics game in those days and he unwisely allowed himself to be conned into a violent exchange of opinions with militantly polemical left-wing Italian journalists. It provided a rare moment of truth, a moment when the smiling Berlusconi mask was lifted, as he lost his temper, venemously hissing '*Vergogna, vergogna*' (shame on you) at his critics. People had told me that Berlusconi had a vicious temper and would at times suffer fools most ungladly. Watching his performance that day as he completely lost it, I could believe it.

Silvio Berlusconi, like most humans, is a complex creature. It is tempting to conclude that his fixation with AC Milan was just another element in a well-laid cynical masterplan that saw him all the way to Palazzo Chigi. Yet his relationship to football and to AC Milan has always seemed to reflect the enthusiasm of a genuine fan.

In 2001, when running once again for office, Berlusconi himself paid tribute to the role of football in his political rise when dedicating space to his success with AC Milan in *Una Storia Italiana* (An Italian Tale), a glossy magazine-cum-picture story book that Forza Italia posted through the letterboxes of approximately eleven million Italians by way of electoral propaganda. The 'tale' in question concerned the life and times of Silvio Berlusconi. With regard to football, he wrote:

> I dreamed of winning the Champions Cup but I also imagined in what way we would win it, with what style this victory should be accomplished ... Our triumphs were not just the triumphs of a football team, it was the victory of those values in which we all fervently believed – commitment to the common cause, altruism, perseverance, willingness to sacrifice oneself for others, respect for your opponents and an obsessive attention to every detail ...

This is the winning political sales pitch, as applied to football, or to be more historically accurate, the winning football sales pitch, as applied to politics. Yet, it also touches on the sentimental and the personal by featuring a fictional letter written by Berlusconi to his late father Luigi in December 1989 in the wake of Milan's first Intercontinental Trophy success, beating Colombian side Nacional Medellin 1–0 in Tokyo. (It was originally published by *Gazzetta Dello Sport* both in 1989 and 1991):

> The sight of Milan as European and World Champions, as the club moves into its ninetieth year, for me blends in and gets lost with many of my childhood memories. Arguments with school-mates, long hours of study, waiting for my father to come home late from work and stand there at the door, smiling, it was as if a ray of sunshine had entered our house. My dear, sweet father. And then, after we had talked about school, we would talk about Milan, as if it were the very embodiement of our Utopian dreams – 'You'll see, Dad, we'll win, we've just got to win' – as if it were the two of us who would be lining out to play for Milan.

Then on Sunday morning it was off to Mass, followed by chat and comments on the sermon, and then off to the bakery to buy meringues for Mama waiting at home, in the kitchen preparing Sunday lunch, the only meal in the week that we ate in the dining room with an embroidered tablecloth and a vase of flowers on the table.

And I would be constantly checking the clock, impatient to be on our way and worried about being late. Then, at last, there we were, hand in hand, at the stadium entrance, the Arena, or later San Siro, and I'd bend down a bit to make myself small so that we would only have to buy one ticket. And then all the tension and excitement of the game, arms uplifted if we had won, sadness if we lost. And my dad would console me, 'Never mind, we'll do better the next time …'

What a sweet memory, Milan and my father … Tomorrow, we will be dreaming of other achievements, we will invent other challenges which will help us to realise what is good, strong and true in us, in all those of us whose lives have become entwined with a dream called AC Milan.

It is hard to believe that this is merely cynical electoral propaganda and not the expression of a genuine passion for the club. It is even harder to believe that such a public profession of a lifelong attachment to AC Milan would not strike a major chord with Italian football fans, whatever team they support.

The reality about Berlusconi and AC Milan is that, at the beginning, he almost certainly did not perceive of the club as an instrument to political success. That realisation dawned later, in correspondence with his own requirements. What seems sure is that AC Milan played a part in that political success, helping its owner on the road to becoming Prime Minister.

FIVE
TREVIGNANO

It was all down to a lack of footpaths, even if pollution and noise levels helped too. Or to put it another way, it was the effect of child-unfriendly Rome.

In the summer of 1989, Dindy and I moved out of Rome, leaving our flat in Via Col della Porretta, Piazza Sempione, and moving 50 kilometres north to the little village of Trevignano Romano on Lake Bracciano. In many senses, it was the best move we made in 20 years of Italian living.

Six months earlier, on 11 December 1988, Róisín, our first and only child, had been born. As everyone who has had children knows, life was never the same again. Never does the expatriate couple miss the extended family as badly as when you have just had a new baby. My late mother-in-law Marie Clare stayed with us for a two-month period before, during and after the birth, but after that we were on our own.

As the Commissario Tecnico appointed to relieve Mafeking by doing much of the baby walking whilst exhausted, breast-feeding mother tried to catch up on lost sleep, I soon came to a couple of earth-shattering conclusions. For a start, wheeling Róisín around our neighbourhood was no fun. Footpaths were few and far between. Bars where you could find the space to wheel in the pram, order your cappuccino and sit down to a quiet read of *Gazzetta Dello Sport* were even rarer. (When you did find one, rest assured that the little blighter would start to howl just as soon as your bottom hit the chair.) Worse still, I became convinced that car manufacturers in their dastardly way had designed and placed car exhausts precisely at baby nose level.

So, shortly after Róisín was born, we began a series of reconnaissance missions to the outlying areas of the Provincia di Roma. We already knew about Trevignano because we had been there to have lunch with friends, the late and talented Northern Irish writer Jack Holland and his wife Mary. It had immediately struck us as a very pretty and pleasant place.

Even though Dindy was very keen to move out of Rome, we hummed and hawed. I was the stumbling block. In the pre-Internet era, I felt it would put our precarious survival at even greater risk if I moved out from the centre of Rome, away from my established workbase at the foreign press club where, with all the main Italian news agencies spewing out stories by the minute, I felt 'in touch'. What if we found somewhere with no phone again? Furthermore, the choice of Trevignano meant a 100-kilometre round trip and sometimes daily commute for both of us.

By this stage in our Italian adventure, Dindy was still a teacher at the British Institute while I had a varied and expanding portfolio. Earnings were still modest enough, however, to make me question the wisdom of moving out of town. The freelance life can be precarious. Rome, though, was such a hard, unfriendly and unhealthy place that the choice in the end was easy. Trevignano won hands down.

There was another obvious consideration. Big cities, and not just Rome, can be lonely enough places for the foreigner. After three years in Rome, we really only had a handful of friends and acquaintances, nearly all from the foreign community. We did not get to know any of our neighbours in our condominium, nor did it seem that they were especially interested in getting to know us. Partly, this is the nature of the big city. Partly, too, it is the nature of the Italian big city and Italian living generally where social life is still, to a quite remarkable extent, ordered around the family. Having grown up in a small, rural village, I knew that village life was rather different. It is much more difficult to go unnoticed, for example. For some, this is a curse. For two foreigners, it is a godsend.

As always, there was the problem of finding somewhere decent to live. One of the Trevignano real estate agents, Signore Catena, took pity on Dindy when she went round to his office with the babe in arms. He found us a splendid apartment in the centre of the village, directly overlooking the lake.

The apartment was owned by the Zampaleta family, who had long since moved to Rome. Catena told us that Zampaleta *padre* had made good but that he had first appeared in Trevignano many years ago with just ten sheep to his name, on the *transumanza* to the Maremma lands by the sea.

What exactly was the *transumanza*? we wondered. It turned out to be an annual migration of literally millions of sheep, brought down from the Abruzzo mountains in the winter to graze along the Maremma (partly Lazio, partly Tuscany) coastlands, before turning back and heading up to the mountains again for the summer. The shepherds' homestead would be in the hills and they would set out for the lowlands usually in October or November, returning home in May or June. Trevignano was just one of many stops on the long march for the weary sheep and their equally weary shepherds (the *transumanza* was done on foot).

This was clearly a life of real hardship and one that put a huge strain on the family unit. When Trevignanesi recall the *transumanza*, they point out that often two widows would turn up for a shepherd's funeral. Given that he lived two almost separate lives – in the hills in summer and on the plains in winter – this was hardly surprising. Nowadays, of course, the practice of the *transumanza* has almost entirely disappeared, although it is still a common enough sight to see sheep grazing in and around the village, always with a shepherd and his dogs on guard.

That story served as a reminder that, until very recently, life had been not so much tough as positively feudal in Trevignano. Until 1870, the village had been part of the Stato Pontifico, the Vatican States, whose governorship was entrusted to Roman aristocratic families such as the Malaspina, Grillo, Torlonia, Conti and Del Drago. One of these governing families, the Conti, was officially awarded the title of Prince of Trevignano in a May 1899 judgement, which acknowledged that the title had been conferred on the family by Pope Gregory XVI in 1835.

These titles were much more than merely honorary. The Trevignano *contadino* (peasant) was expected to pay a whole series of tithes, including one on his catch of fish in the lake. It was only in 1954, in other words in living memory, that a decree from the Ministry of Agriculture and Fisheries finally abolished that feudal right, one that had been instituted in 1320. In truth, the feudal tithes had been the object of various violent protests by the *contadini* throughout the previous 50 years. Given that for much of the 1920s and 1930s, pay for a twelve-hour working day was the equivalent of 1p, it is not hard to understand why the *contadini* so bitterly resented the tithe system. 1954 was a good year for many Trevignanesi families for another reason, too, since many of them were awarded 'parcels' of land that had been 'expropriated' from the Del Drago family, the last family to 'govern' Trevignano. An idea of just how hard life was in even those relatively recent times comes from the following observation by Ofelio Maciucchi in his history of the village: 'For the new mayor ... his most important task continued to be provision of a daily supply of bread for the poor and humble people of the village ...'

Clearly, the Trevignano that we arrived into had moved on. It had become a prosperous village in which fishing and farming were losing out to daytripper tourism from Rome and to building speculation, as more and more Romans saw it as an ideal spot for a weekend house. Even though the village population is now officially estimated at 5,000, we can still claim 30 or more restaurants, nearly all of which do a roaring weekend trade.

Within hours, almost, we got to know people. It was a huge luxury to be able to wheel the pram up and down the lakefront in the fresh warm June air. Given that Róisín was never a great sleeper, we would often be out even late at night, bouncing her up and down on the cobbles of the *centro storico* or whizzing along the lakefront in the hope that she would finally go to sleep. In the summer, when she was a little baby, we put her out in the lake in her *ciambella* (rubber ring), the rhythmic sway of the water sending her to sleep.

Shortly after our arrival, Dindy was out with Róisín when a young woman, also with a baby, stopped her to ask about the baby book Róisín was holding. The woman was Lucia, whose baby Lucrezia had been born just two days after Róisín. She and Dindy quickly became friends and she has remained a friend ever since. Likewise, shortly after we arrived, Jack and Mary Holland introduced us to neighbours of theirs, Simona and Corrado, then busy renovating a house. They, too, are still good friends. Village life is like that.

In the context of Róisín's childhood, Trevignano proved a godsend. This was clearly a baby-friendly environment. For a start, when you walked into a shop, a bar or a restaurant, people were always delighted to see a baby. Italians, as a race, are good with babies. They make baby, and by extension baby's parents, feel good. Every baby is *bellissimo* or *bellissima*. In those days, we often ate out at the Miralago restaurant where little Róisín spent half the evening being carried around by the proprietor himself, much to the relief of exhausted parents.

When we returned to Ireland, passing through France, in

those early summers with Róisín, we always got a major culture shock when confronted with the extent to which French, British and Irish public life left no place for baby. Restaurants in France, England and Ireland tended to look at you as if you had brought in a diseased, stray dog when you walked in with a baby and buggy. In contrast, Italians always make space for babies.

Through Lucia, we found an afternoon babysitter in the person of Manuela, one of her relatives. She and her husband, Dado, lived a life that was still linked to the tough, thrifty *contadino* past of their parents. Even though Dado worked hard as a builder's labourer, he still found time every night for his *orto* (fruit and vegetable garden). He supplied his table (and often ours) with lettuce, tomatoes, onions, courgettes, aubergines, eggs and much else besides. He was and is part of an older generation of Trevignanesi who also made their own wine and olive oil (as recently as the 1960s, there were five olive mills, or *frantoio*, in and around Trevignano) and who might even kill their own pig, curing their own ham. Mimmo Perconti, a village real estate agent now in his fifties, once told us he could remember taking his family's own flour to the baker, flour ground from wheat they had grown themselves. In turn, the baker kept a record, decreeing that X amount of flour equalled Y amount of loaves for the following winter. You would go down to baker, ask for bread and it would be ticked off in his magic book.

Things, obviously, have changed and continue to do so. There is a younger generation of Trevignanesi more interested in having a pair of Gucci shoes, Armani jeans and a SmartCar than in gathering around a long table loaded with tomatoes on a hot August afternoon to make jars and jars of *sugo* (pasta sauce) for the following winter.

Yet, the village still preserves many aspects of what might be termed village life. We still have a band that marches up and down enthusiastically on civic occasions. The roads are still decorated with flower petals on Corpus Christi. There is still a ghostly Easter procession complete with chained, hooded and barefoot figures carrying a cross, and we still have a splendid *Ferragosto* (15 August) celebration during which the Madonna is taken out on the lake in the evening to bless the village and villagers. She travels on the little ferry that normally takes tourists around the lake and is followed by a fleet of small fishing boats all carrying flickering Chinese lanterns, creating a magical effect when viewed from land, like a hundred little stars glittering around the Mother of God. After this spectacle, the whole thing is rounded off with a firework show.

In recent years, too, the Commune has taken to organising a beach barbecue on the night of San Lorenzo, the night of the falling stars. I remember walking along the beach during one of these nights, looking at the succession of blazing wood fires stretching into the distance and thinking that this must have been how an army on the move would once have looked, with everyone gathered around the fires, keeping warm and cooking food. Not, mind you, that you need a fire to keep warm on an August night in Trevignano, at the end of a day when the temperature was probably well over 30 Celsius.

The Trevignano summer, too, is enriched by the open-air cinema run by Fabio Palma, whose father had to ship stones across the lake to build the original village cinema back in the late 1940s. (In those days, the roads around the lake were so poor that it was easier to transport heavy materials by boat than by road.) The village now has two cinemas, a permanent indoor one for year-round use and an outdoor one (called L'Arena) which is splendidly sited on a rocky promontory overlooking the village and functions for the two hot months of July and August. Watching films here is a mesmerising experience, a case of a film within a film. For a start, if you lift your eyes above the huge screen, there is the moon shining brightly, illuminating the shimmering lake below. For a second, on hot and sultry nights, the film's soundtrack often has to compete with the drone of the *cicada*s.

I remember once, back in the early 1990s, before L'Arena had been built, watching an open-air screening of Fellini's masterpiece *Amacord* on a huge white sheet hung up on a wall in the *centro storico*. Half the village, it seemed, had turned out. There they all were, walking up and down, finding seats, observing and being observed, as they watched a film in which village folk walked up and down, saluted one another, observed and were observed. Where did reality end and art take over?

Summertime in Trevignano is occasionally enlivened by a snake sighting. You could be doing your own impersonation of Lance Armstrong on a downhill descent when you glimpse a short, sharp flash of bottle-green on the asphalt. This is probably Mr Snake also heading downhill, looking for a drink on a hot day. There are two types of snake in these northern Lazio parts – the wood snake or *frustone,* which is often impressively long (up to 10ft) but is almost totally harmless, and the little viper (18in), which may look less dangerous but can in fact be deadly.

The summer in Trevignano has always been good. With the football season finished, things are quieter journalistically and there is time for daily swims in the lake and even the occasional long, hot afternoon down at Quinto's clubhouse sitting in the shade under the trees by a sandy little beach. (Old Quinto is now dead but that only serves to remind us how long we have been here. He used to fish the lake himself while he also worked hard as a market gardener, regularly getting up at four in the morning to make his deliveries to Rome's fruit and vegetable market. In the afternoon, he too would stretch out under the tree and, exhausted, fall fast asleep.)

When the first *temporale* (thunderstorm) of August comes, it always prompts a moment of melancholy. I am loath to give up the many and varied rituals of summer living, when all I ever wear are shorts, T-shirt and sandals, and when the evening concludes with a glass of *prosecco* in front of Jollo and Leonella's bar, La Vela, on the lakefront.

Summer, too, is the time when much of the waking night can involve a losing battle against the heat. Take a walk down to the lakefront any July or August night between midnight and 1.00am and you meet half the village, complete with babies, all looking for a cool breeze or a cool drink, having long abandoned the idea of sleep.

Then, too, village life lends itself to privileged work habits. When I do not have a news conference, interview or meeting in Rome, my working day nearly always begins with a bike ride down the hill into the village to the *edicola* to pick up the papers from Giancarlo, prior to heading on for the morning cappuccino and cornetto in La Vela. There I sit, along with pensioners and the young mothers who have just dropped children off at school, 'working' at my initial daily read.

After that, it is back up the hill and on with business. Over the course of the year, a great deal of time is spent at Jollo's bar, sitting out on the little jetty in the summer evenings or looking out through the full-length front windows on winter days, philosophising about the most recent decline and fall of Roma and Lazio or, more likely, the most recent Juventus success. (Jollo is a Juventus supporter, but we still love him.)

Life in the village takes on a human dimension. Be it Alberto the baker or Lino the mechanic or Brunella the butcher or Fabio at the petrol station, people are flexible, helpful and available as you go into the daily battle of Italian life. Not for nothing, one of the great Italian real estate trends of the last decade has been the move out of the city in search of the 'provincia' with its more relaxed lifestyle.

All of this, of course, paints an extremely rosy picture of village life. Yet there are obvious down sides. For a start, the more work has intensified for both of us, the more we have to commute by car back and forth to Rome. In 16 years, the bus timetable has not changed. Admittedly, there is now an improved train service from the village of Bracciano across the lake, but it is totally inadequate for the area's commuter needs, while, such is the lack of an all-encompassing underground system in Rome itself that the train is useful only if you are going to specific central places. Even something as simple as getting Róisín to school on Rome's Via Cassia has become a huge problem, and Róisín can spend four or more hours of her day making a trip which, with even minimally decent transport infrastructure, should really take only 40 minutes each way.

When we first moved to the village, Romans warned us that Trevignano was nice but the commute was a disaster and the schools were worse still. Beware, they said. They were right. Recently, just to be sure, we went to check out a local *liceo* with a view to saving Róisín all that travelling.

We arrived at the school at about ten-thirty in the morning. We walked in the front door and into the main concourse where we found plenty of activity. Students were walking up and down the corridors shouting at one another, classroom doors were open with teachers standing on the threshold, while other students were shouting out the window to their mates, ordering pizzas and cokes. The overvall noise level was deafening.

We looked around for a moment, then I said to Dindy, 'Let's wait until the break is over before we go looking for the head-master.' So we walked up and down the corridors, noting that in some of the classrooms, a few students were at their desks apparently studying. Just then, we walked into the headmaster's secretary, who just happened to be an ex-student of Dindy's from the British Institute.

She was surprised to find us in the school and asked us what we were doing. When we told her we were considering enrolling Róisín, she expressed a certain perplexity. We said that, anyway, we would like to talk to the headmaster but that we would wait until the break is over. 'What break?' she said. 'The students are in class now. Well, at least they're meant to be.'

With that, we turned on our heels and never again considered an Italian school for Róisín. Obviously, all Italian schools are not like this one and the quality of education clearly varies from region to region and from town to town. In particular, northern regions like Lombardy, Piedmont, Emilia Romagna and Veneto are home to excellent schools. Yet friends who teach in the Italian secondary school system, especially in Rome and further south, tell similar tales.

Even allowing for the problems of schools and commutes, however, we still considered Trevignano a valid option and for another rather obvious reason – the price of Roman real estate. Put simply, if we were ever to buy a house, then it would have to be somewhere outside Rome, an expensive city where real estate values have never known a 'crash' in the market, even during both world wars.

Thus it was that after the usual protracted bout of huffing and puffing on my part, in 1994 we bought a modest, one-floor house in its own grounds on a hill outside the village, overlooking the lake. We went to see the house one Sunday morning and put in an offer for it within 40 minutes.

The purchase of a house is inevitably closely followed by plans for improvements, conversions, adjustments and general tinkering. That was how we got to know Bruno Paris, brother of Dado, our babysitter's husband. We engaged him to do some minor changes to the house itself and, above all, to carry out a major conversion of the garage into an office for me.

Watching him build was remarkable. Apart from a couple of

drills, a cement-mixer, modern bricks and cement, he used only the tools and materials that people here as far back as ancient Rome have used – hammer and chisel, his plumb line, *pozzolana* sand and chestnut wood. When he was putting in the chestnut beams for the studio roof, he had me stand under them at one specific point just to be sure that I would not bang my head. In that sense, I have to be just about the only working journalist in the western world with an office that is literally made to measure.

The first time I recall noticing Bruno at work was on the occasion of a village funeral. The deceased was a relative of his and it fell to him to 'wall in' the coffin, i.e. literally closing off the coffin's cemetery wall slot with bricks and cement at the end of the funeral service and with most of the family mourners still present. Such was the speed and accuracy of his work that we immediately vowed that if ever we needed any building done, then we would look no further.

We often joked that if ever we were to be stranded on a desert island, then Bruno would be the ideal companion. He was very much in tune with his northern Lazio environment and was so intimately familiar with the winds and movement of sun, moon and clouds that his weather forecasts had to be taken very seriously. He was also such a good vegetable gardener that, from a half-acre plot, he was able to meet much of the fruit and vegetable requirements of the restaurant run by his wife, Mirella.

He knew where and when to go looking in the woods above the village for gastronomic treats such as wild fennel, asparagus or mushrooms, not to mention snails. He also knew where to find Etruscan tombs, at one point becoming a regular night-time 'tomb raider' dealing in 'recovered' Etruscan artefacts, most of which he gave away as wedding presents. He abandoned this (illegal) activity when a local policeman tipped him off, remarking how busy Bruno was, having to work 'by day and by night'.

He was intimately familiar with the Lago di Bracciano,

following its currents closely and knowing where and when to fish. Once when we asked him how much he had paid for some splendid ancient Roman steps that he had 'acquired', he told us that the price had been 300,000 old lire, plus 20 fish.

When the time came in 2000 to rebuild the house, Bruno was again the obvious choice. Sadly, he contracted cancer shortly after the work began, but even though he was far from well, he struggled to come up to the building site most evenings and look over what had been done. Impishly, he would then complain about this and that and tell us it should have been done another way. Like a lot of cancer patients, he seemed to make a good initial recovery. Only one month before his death, he spent his last two mornings before his final hospitalisation fishing on the lake. At his bedside in hospital, one neighbour recalled her incredulity at his apparently sudden and terminal ill-health. Unable to sleep, she had woken early a few mornings previously and gone for a walk. From out in the middle of the lake, she had heard Bruno and another fisherman singing bits of an old local song at one another from their respective boats.

Born into the poverty of post-war Trevignano (he was 62 when he died), Bruno had an instinctive curiosity that prompted him to travel to some exotic destinations in later years. He used to say that he was the first person in the village to get a passport, claiming that when he went to the village carabinieri to find out how to obtain one, they looked at him in bemusement, not knowing what it was.

Brazil, China, Germany and Poland were just some of the places he visited. He returned from China to make an indelible impression on a (then) very small Róisín, by recounting how he had eaten eggs boiled in horse urine.

Naturally thrifty and hardworking like many of his generation, Bruno was totally disinterested in the consumer icons of designer-label, conformist modern Italy. He was more than happy driving around in his beat-up old Fiat Panda. A superb craftsman, an incurable gossip and story-teller, an enthusiastic drinker (in his atypical way he preferred beer to wine) and a life-long Communist, he was the embodiment of a Trevignano that is fast heading for extinction.

Before Bruno's illness we had set out on the *ristrutturazione* of our house with all the necessary planning permissions but with only a very basic set of architect's drawings. For the day-to-day, indeed hour-to-hour, decisions that building involves, we had intended to rely on Bruno's experience.

When he became sick, in the winter of 2000, the roof had been taken off the original house and some of the walls knocked down. What were we going to do? We had rented the empty house next door, moving backwards and forwards through a hole in the hedge. At first we waited to see if Bruno might recover quickly.

After almost two months of inactivity on the site, though, we had to do something. Via the local Polish community, a builder called Andrea arrived from Poland and, along with another Pole, Dario, and Bruno's original labourer, a Romanian called Giorgio, the work resumed, following Bruno's traditional building methods, but with Dindy running the whole enterprise.

Throughout this period, I continued to work in my studio, which had now become the site foreman's office and tool parking zone, while Dindy was always out on the site, marching up and down and measuring heights, widths, depths. (For Valentine's Day that year, I gave her a professional measuring tape; she was delighted with it.) I spent a great deal of time in the local builders' merchants, as I was often hastily summoned, nearly always in mid-article, to get an urgently needed bag of cement, or screws, or taps, or handles or sand. As for the noise, there was obviously plenty of that when plasterers, carpenters, painters, plumbers, electricians and the *marmista* (the marble specialist) all got going. Regularly, I would have to climb up on the scaffolding and shout at the lads not to use their drills for the next five minutes because I had a radio interview on the way. This particular request was always carefully respected.

Another abiding memory was the overall quality of the work done by the specialists, all of them from Trevignano. Without Bruno, we had recruited Gianni, a one time enthusiastic footballer, who did some very skilful work with tiles, floors and beams.

Dindy shouldered 99.3 per cent of the entire building project (she was the mastermind who knew what she wanted) and that in itself meant that she toured a thousand different builders' yards and various antique dealers as she searched for old roof tiles, old bricks, old nails for woodbeams and much else besides.

After many vicissitudes, but within the space of less than a year, the house was finally built. Dindy received a handsome compliment, too, from one of our neighbours who told her: '*Complimenti*, you've built a house just like the ones my grandparents built, in the old style ... *bellissimo*.'

From the football viewpoint, Trevignano offers no particular advantages, other than that of watching at close quarters the eternal Lazio versus Roma rivalry that grips fans in the greater Rome area. On one of the first days we travelled to Trevignano, we introduced ourselves to the then mayor, Rolando Luciani. Years later, his son, Andrea, managed briefly to break into the Lazio first team when coached by Sven-Göran Eriksson. Andrea's football story is unusual in that it, thus far, has gone from an immediate high with Lazio down to the more humble surrounds of Serie B and Serie C1 with clubs such as Salernitana, Cosenza, Fermana, Sora and Martina.

Described as the 'new Nedved' (the great Czech midfielder at the time played for Lazio), Andrea played in two Champions League games against Anderlecht and Sparta Prague in the 2000–1 season as well as in friendlies against Barcelona, Bayer Leverkusen and Eintracht Frankfurt. After that, in the time-honoured Italian fashion, he was sent off to learn the business with smaller clubs with the idea being that, when he was ready, he would be recalled to base.

Of course, it did not quite work out that way, Andrea finding his career blocked by everything from injuries (ankle and back) to the cash crisis that has bitten hard into lower level football. For example, he had the misfortune to find himself on the books of Serie B side Cosenza when the club president Paolo Fabiano Pagliuso was arrested in March 2003 on Mafia charges of 'criminal association' and 'extortion', related to alleged money laundering. By the end of a confusing season, Cosenza had collapsed and Andrea had had four different coaches but only two months' salary payment. (Three years later, he was still in litigation trying to get the money owed. At one point during his, so far, six seasons in the lower divisions, Andrea had been paid his not exorbitant salary for one year out of three.) Even when he got his wages, Andrea encountered plenty of other problems. For instance, in his first year out on loan at Salernitana (south of Naples), he was dismayed to discover that the club did not have adequate medical infrastructures to deal with an ankle problem. In the end, he resolved matters by returning to Lazio for treatment.

Likewise, training facilities are not always what they should be, especially where southern clubs are concerned. In his season with Sora (near Frosinone in southern Lazio), he and his teammates would sometimes meet up at the club and then have to drive themselves 60 kilometres to an improvised training ground where, on at least one occasion, the gates were locked, forcing the players to change in their cars and then climb over the wire fence to get into the training ground. Life in a lower division is no fun, but Andrea's career is far from over and we may yet hear more of him.

As for Trevignano, as we sit and look into the log fire on a winter's evening (we do have snow here occasionally and the temperature is often below zero in January and February) we wonder about the future of the village. Given its proximity to Rome and its current attractiveness, it runs the risk of becoming too quickly and too shoddily over-developed, in the process losing the charm that attracts people here in the first place.

In the meantime, as I walk up the road alongside the wood behind the house and hear the dogs bark in terror as they come across another wild boar that has come down the hill looking for whatever it can find to eat, I often think to myself that this is no bad place to live.

SIX
ERIKSSON AND THE MEDIA

On a bright Tuesday morning in January 2001, I set off for the Lazio training ground at Formello, north of Rome. Formello may not be high on the 'must-see' list for the average tourist but for me it has the splendid advantage of being less than half an hour from home in Trevignano, just down the Cassia B on the way into Rome.

As a rule, rushing out to cover sports news stories is not my average lot. Most breaking sports stories in Italy have a limited news value for the Anglophonic world. That morning at Formello, however, was different. There was a very English angle on events here since Lazio's Swedish coach, Sven-Göran Eriksson, was also the England manager-elect, due to take up the England job in July.

Ever since Eriksson had announced in October 2000 that he had accepted the job, the English media – in particular, the infamous English tabloids – had put Eriksson under close surveillance. Interest in a new England manager is logical enough, but when results started to turn sour for Eriksson, then the English media weighed in heavily with speculation that Eriksson was about to resign from Lazio or be sacked.

On the previous Sunday, Lazio had picked up their seventh Serie A defeat of the season when losing 2–1 at home to relegation battlers Napoli. That defeat had come hot on the heels of a pre-Christmas fortnight when Lazio pulled off an unenviable hat-trick by losing to Leeds in the Champions League, being knocked out of the Italian Cup by Udinese and then, most painful of all, being beaten 1–0 by AS Roma in the Rome derby.

On the Monday morning after the Napoli defeat, the Italian sports dailies were screaming headlines such as ERIKSSON FOR THE SACK. When he was summoned to an emergency meeting with club owner Sergio Cragnotti at Formello that morning – remember, Monday is usually a day off for Italian footballers and coaches – we all presumed that resignation or sacking was on the cards.

When that resignation failed to materialise, we all wrote our 'Eriksson still hanging on in there' pieces that Monday night and moved on to the next story. Except that, the next morning, whilst filling his car with petrol on the way to training, Eriksson himself there and then decided that the time had come to throw in the towel. Within minutes, he was at the club grounds, had communicated his decision to Cragnotti, and a news conference had been hastily called.

For once, I had been listening to the right radio station at the right time. As the ten o'clock news announced an imminent press conference at the Lazio club grounds, I was already reaching for the tape recorder, counting my blessings that Formello was just down the road.

After the press conference finished and I had done a series of snap radio interviews with BBC Five Live, TalkSport and others, I finally caught up with Eriksson as, in the company of some of the regular Lazio press corps, he walked across from the club's palatial clubhouse to the dressing room and training grounds.

By some fluke, the British tabloids, after having staked out the joint for months, had missed the final act when it unexpectedly broke that morning. Their absence gave me the freedom to wish Eriksson good luck with the following words: 'Best of luck in England, Sven, but watch yourself with the tabloids. You do know what they're like, don't you? They're not *Gazzetta Dello Sport* nor *Corriere Dello Sport* neither ...'

By way of an answer, he just nodded and smiled. Over the last few years I have often thought that if Eriksson did not know then how the British tabloid press works, he certainly knows now. From the infamous *News of the World* 'sting' in Dubai in January 2006 and on to revelations about his private life – his affair with former Football Association employee Faria Alam, for instance, or tensions between himself and his partner, Nancy Dell'Olio – Eriksson stories have kept the tabloid press busy. By now, he will have got the point. *Gazzetta Dello Sport* is one thing, but the *Sun* is quite another.

I had met and interviewed Eriksson on many occasions over the previous years and had always found him refreshingly straightforward, honest and easy to deal with. Back in his Roma days in 1986, he had come round to the foreign press club and sat with a few of us chatting easily and without reserve about how things were going in a season in which his Roma side almost overhauled the Platini-led Juventus.

Years later, in 1992, on a train on the way from Stockholm to Malmö during the European Championship in Sweden, I had run into him again. He had been out of Italian football since moving to Benfica in the summer of 1989. Far away from the clamour of Italy, I was curious to hear him reflect on his Roma and Fiorentina experiences. (He coached Roma from 1984 to 1987 and Fiorentina from 1987 to 1989.)

Even though I hardly knew him, having had but fleeting encounters at post-match news conferences, Eriksson invited me to sit down and have a coffee. He was open and friendly as usual, amused at my questions about the famous Roma–Lecce debacle towards the end of that 1986 season. (Roma had inexplicably lost at home to little Lecce in the second last match of the season and just at the very moment they might have overtaken Juventus.)

He recalled that if he could do it again he would have handled the build-up to that game entirely differently, above all taking the Roma squad far away from Rome and the pressures created by the Rome-based battery of private TVs, radio stations and local papers as well as the national media. He recalled, too, that perhaps the worst pressure of all had come from the then Roma owner, the late Dino Viola, a man not shy about poking his nose into the dressing room.

Later, when he was in charge of Sampdoria (1992–7), I occasionally came across him. I remember him explaining, on the phone, just how he had backed out of an agreement to move to Blackburn Rovers in the Premiership in order to stay in Italy and move south to Lazio. He related details of his negotiations with the late Jack Walker (then owner of Blackburn) and recalled – very honestly, it seemed to me – both his embarrassment at having to back out on his agreement and Jack Walker's less than enthusiastic reaction to his decision.

During his three and a half seasons with Lazio, I had come across him a great deal more regularly. This was not because Lazio happen to train just down the road, but rather because, by this time, I was involved in regular Champions League-related TV interviews for the US sports channel ESPN.

Working for ESPN often meant a linguistic tour de force for the good reason that their producers believed interviews should, as far as possible, be done in the player's native language. There is plenty of sound logic behind this practice. For a start, if the player is going to say anything interesting, controversial or unexpected, he will more likely say it if he is talking in his own language. For a second, ESPN International does big business in South America and it does not make much sense to offer Argentines a TV interview with an Argentine speaking to them in Italian.

So it was that, for ESPN purposes, Paolo Maldini would be interviewed in Italian, Hernan Crespo in Spanish, Cafu in

Portuguese, Zinedine Zidane in French and so on. For me, French and Italian were no problem, Spanish was just about feasible, but Portuguese was a language too far. If the player spoke good English, of course, then ESPN were always happy with an English-language interview. The problem was that, then and now, the number of Serie A players or coaches with good English was extremely limited. They were usually Scandinavian, Dutch or German. For years, my bi-annual visits to AC Milan featured interviews with Dane Thomas Helveg and German Oliver Bierhoff. Both players were smart, articulate and usually had plenty to say, and, what is more, they were able to say it in excellent English.

In that context, I often had reason to be grateful to Eriksson during his Lazio days. When Sinisa Mihajlovic or Marcelo Salas or Pavel Nedved, for example, could not be persuaded to do an interview (as far as I am concerned, players are always entitled to say no) then Eriksson would step into the breach.

I recall one occasion at Formello when, after hanging around for half a morning, in spite of the best efforts of the Lazio press office, a player had failed to present himself for interview. Doubtless, he had had to go to physiotherapy, to the doctor, to his sick mother, his sick wife, his visiting parents, to the dentist, take the car to the garage or whichever of the myriad excuses presented by players who, in the end, are just fed up with interviews. On this particular occasion, we were packing the camera and gear into the back of the car when Eriksson came round the corner in his trademark Volvo. I immediately flagged him down. Even though he was on his way to a business lunch (in his case, this was more than probably true), he still stopped, parked the car and got out to do an interview with me, in his excellent English.

The pettiness of those English critics who complain or joke about his command (or lack of) of the English language says much about their own myopic Little England worldview, not to mention their lack of linguistic skills. I am always amazed, too, by the nonchalant ease with which some colleagues, arrived in from Blighty, will ask you to translate interviews or newspaper articles for them. It is as if all the hubble, bubble, toil and trouble that you have gone through to understand the language, its context and its Italian football-speak contortions, has no significance for them. Yeah, well, if that's the case, translate it yourself.

From those days, too, I recall a two-hour chat with Eriksson in the autumn of 1999 in his less than swanky office in the underground section of the Formello training complex. I was writing a piece commissioned by Swedish soccer annual *Fotboll* which needed more than just the usual ten-minute chat. Eriksson told me to come round after training, in the evening, since that would be the only moment in the day when he would have both time and peace to sit and talk.

By this stage, Lazio was fully ensconced in the *salotto buono* of Italian fooball, thanks in part to Eriksson. In the previous two seasons, they had won the Italian Cup and the Cup Winners' Cup. Lazio had become '*di moda*', the Olimpico in Rome becoming one of the many places where the shakers and makers of Italian society liked to meet and, above all, to be seen to meet. At the time, too, Lazio was the first Italian club to be floated on the stock market. In short, the club was hot stuff, seeming to embody the brave new world of footbiz, with Eriksson playing a key role in its transformation.

Under Eriksson, and payrolled by the millions of financier Sergio Cragnotti (whose Cirio food empire subsequently went belly-up), Lazio had regained an elite status last experienced during the Fascist era. Those had been days when Lazio was one of the few institutions in Italian life that could thumb their noses at Benito Mussolini and live to tell the tale. Take the famous Sunday when Lazio received a message from government house informing them that they were to suspend that afternoon's game for a short period in order for a speech from Il Duce to be broadcast over the stadium's loudspeaker system. The club refused. In the end, the speech was transmitted, but at a greatly reduced volume, while the match played on.

Lazio owed this independence to the man who then ran the club, Giorgio Vaccaro, a senior officer in the Fascist military hierarchy who was, in fact, more a sportsman than a soldier. For most of the 1930s he was in charge of both FIGC and CONI. Vaccaro was a man who, within the constraints of the time, went his own way. When Mussolini oversaw the foundation of Lazio's modern day rivals, AS Roma, in 1927, the original plan had been for the new Roma club to absorb all other clubs in the capital city, including Lazio. General Vaccaro defended Lazio's autonomy, angrily insisting that if any new club were to be formed in the city, then it should be called 'Lazio'. Such was Vaccaro's prestige, and his good relations with Il Duce, that he won his case.

Lazio remained a largely free agent during the Fascist years and one that could use its charisma to attract one of the greatest players of that period, Silvio Piola. In the meantime, General Vaccaro went on to head FIGC for a highly successful period in the 1930s when Italy won both the 1934 and 1938 World Cups as well as an Olympic gold at Berlin in 1936.

Since Vaccaro's time, when Lazio's best showing was a second-place finish in 1937, the club had won little, with the exception of a three-year period in the early 1970s when a team inspired by striker Giorgio Chinaglia won Lazio's first ever *scudetto* in 1974.

From then until the arrival of Eriksson and Cragnotti, however, times had been hard, and none harder than five seasons in Serie B in the 1980s during which the club sank to an all-time low in the 1986–7 season when only a play-off avoided relegation to Serie C1.

That autumn night, Eriksson recalled his initial contacts with

Cragnotti and reminded me of how he had had to get out of his commitment to Blackburn and Jack Walker. He also spoke of Cragnotti's astonishment when he told him that he wanted to bring the then 33-year-old Roberto Mancini with him from Sampdoria.

For Eriksson, Mancini was a key factor in guaranteeing overall performance quality. Outrageously talented and much respected by his fellow players, Mancini guaranteed that Eriksson's ideas would be quickly assimilated by the Lazio dressing room. One might be tempted to see a parallel between the Mancini choice then and that of David Beckham at the heart of the current England team. The principle may well be the same, the only problem is that Mancini was probably a more talented player than Beckham.

Eriksson was, of course, lucky in that he had inherited a talented Lazio squad with players like defender Alessandro Nesta, Croat striker Alen Boksic, Argentine midfielder Matias Almeyda, Yugoslav midfielder Vladimir Jugovic and Czech midfielder Pavel Nedved. Add Roberto Mancini and Eriksson's own coaching skills and a league title was simply a question of time. (It duly arrived in May 2000, six months after our chat in the Formello bunker. In truth, Lazio should have won the previous season's title too but their nerves failed them when the pressure came on.)

Looking back over his career that night, Eriksson conceded that he had changed. Once, he considered the '4–4–2' lineout to be 'the Bible'; now he had learned to be more flexible. Shortly before our interview, he had said after a 0–0 draw with Juventus that he had wanted to win all right, but had added that it was 'more important not to lose'. More Italian than the Italians themselves. After the Euro 2004 finals in Portugal, and perhaps again at Germany 2006, those words might mean something to England fans.

As always, I found Eriksson interesting and informative that night. He tried to talk honestly and directly, if, obviously, without revealing professional secrets that best remained within the dressing room. He talked about the stress of Italian football, the constant media scrutiny. He also talked about the improvised, daily chaos of life in Italy, from traffic jams to the university system his daughter was going through in Florence. Not every coach at one of Europe's biggest clubs is willing to sit into the night chatting frankly about his projects, past and present.

Even on the January 2001 day when he announced his resignation at Lazio, Eriksson was especially helpful. Swedish colleague Kristina Kappelin and I happened to share the same Rome-based TV crew. Both of us needed to interview Eriksson, she in Swedish and myself in English. The problem was that Kristina had been taken by surprise by the short notice of the press conference and could not get to Formello in time, so, in order to do her and the crew a favour, I asked Eriksson to do two interviews for me, one after the other, in Swedish and English. No problem. I asked him a question, he gave me an answer in English, then he paused and gave me the same answer, word for word, in Swedish. Time and energy saved all round.

As Eriksson headed off to England, I wondered if he could possibly remain quite as affable and available while holding down the hottest management job in the land. I remember picking up *Gazzetta Dello Sport* one morning some weeks later to find that he had already been the victim of a hoax radio interview when a presenter pretending to be Kevin Keegan (his immediate predecessor in the England job) had got him to talk about his plans for the England team. However, by comparison with the row prompted by the *News of the World* 'sting' in Dubai, it was mere chicken feed.

Eriksson and his agent Athole Still were lured to Dubai by a *News of the World* undercover reporter acting as a wealthy Middle Eastern businessman and expressing an interest in investing in English football. It was reported that after being wined and dined, Eriksson became ill-advisedly eloquent, spilling beans on his future plans (leave the England job), criticising some of the England players (defender Rio Ferdinand was described as 'lazy') and also making allegations of widespread corruption in English football.

Watching the fall-out from this side of the water, it was curious to note that it was Eriksson, rather than the *News of the World*, who emerged as the villain of the piece. The vast amount of media attention focused on Eriksson's comments, with only a minority of commentators interested in questioning the *News of the World*'s methods, which, while probably not illegal, certainly raise serious moral and ethical questions. Typical was this reaction from Brian Alexander, a presenter with BBC Radio Five Live and a former sports editor of the *Sun*: 'What is amazing is that as a public figure, earning a huge salary and having been in the news before for the wrong reasons, Eriksson was caught out like this. He knows only too well what the English tabloids are like and must have heard of their "fake sheikh".'

People will always say that someone as highly paid as Eriksson (the world's highest paid national team manager at a reported £4 million per annum) has to expect plenty of media flak along the way. Flak, yes, but duplicity and tricks?

Perhaps the most amazing thing about the Eriksson and England saga is that he got the job at all, given the aura of Little Englandism that surrounds the England team and its supporters when they take to foreign fields. Seen from afar, the treatment afforded to England's first ever foreign manager by sections of both the British media and the English football community hardly seems edifying.

Of course, commentators and fans alike will point out that had Eriksson won the 2002 World Cup with England on his first tournament outing, the story would have had a very different ending. It is the results that do the talking. In all probability, victory in 2002 would have kept any number of 'fake sheikhs' off his back.

For better or for worse, the tabloid school of journalism has largely bypassed Italian football reporting. *Gazzetta Dello Sport* in Milan, *Corriere Dello Sport* in Rome and *Tutto Sport* in Turin are three broadsheet sports dailies, usually featuring up to 30 pages and 70 per cent football. *Gazzetta Dello Sport*'s circulation stands at around 450,000 to 500,000 copies, making it one of the most popular dailies in Italy. These papers offer match reports, interviews, profiles and general news coverage of just about every aspect of Italian and, to a lesser extent, European and world football.

With regard to Serie A, every player's performance the previous weekend is not only analysed, but is also given a *pagella* or mark in which the impossible score for a performance of total perfection would be ten. The reporting, however, remains very much football-oriented. A player will be endlessly questioned as to why, just at that moment, he opted to hit a square pass to his left when there was a completely unmarked team-mate on his right. He will not be asked (or certainly not formally and in print) if he was the player seen entering a certain local nightclub at three in the morning, in the company of two glamorous ladies of the night.

In my early years in Italy, there was an incident which emphatically underlined the radically different modus operandi of the Italian and British sports media. When he first arrived at AC Milan, Dutch footballer Ruud Gullit struck up a relationship with a colleague of mine, Licia Granello, who in those days covered AC Milan for Rome-based daily *La Repubblica*. Like a lot of other newly arrived players in Italian football, he was a bit lost in a strange new environment and, at first, he spoke no Italian.

Licia was good-looking, smart and spoke English, making her one of the few reporters with whom Gullit could communicate. To cut a long story short, the pair had an affair, which was soon well known to some in the football media. Yet, remarkably, no TV channel, radio or newspaper discussed the issue, which only became public after the affair had ended. In a British context – if a female reporter from the *Daily Mirror* were to have an affair with David Beckham, for example – this silence would be hard to imagine.

In Italy, so long as a player is 'doing the business' on the pitch, his private life remains his own affair. Sometimes, as in the case of Maradona at Napoli, too much leeway is extended. The *omertà* that reigned over Maradona's extra-mural activities in Naples, in the end, probably did him no good. Yet he was, in every sense, an extreme case in a very special context.

When I first arrived in Italy, I was forcibly struck by two aspects of the football industry. Not only did the media eschew the tabloid penchant for reporting players' private lives, but football reporting was deadly, upmarketedly serious, enjoying a cross-class, cross-party, cross-gender following. In the Ireland and Britain of the 1960s and 1970s, football was a hugely popular sport but not many perceived it as 'sexy', 'cool' or 'fashionable'. It still had a strongly working class, anti-intellectual, down-to-earth aspect about it.

In the mid-1980s, it was the quality more than the quantity of football reporting that surprised me. I had expected wall-to-wall TV and radio coverage as well as the huge volume of words turned out by the sports dailies. What I had not expected was the level of detailed, technical analysis carried especially by the print press.

In those days, the guru of football writers was the late Gianni Brera. His observations and his elegantly written columns were considered compulsory reading for everyone, from heart surgeon to football fan. His words seemed to command more respect than cabinet ministers or university professors.

Even today, I find it hard to believe that there is a better football daily in the world than *Gazzetta Dello Sport*. Certainly, Paris-based *L'Equipe* is a broader-based sports paper and one with an admirable campaigning bent when it comes to the issue of doping in sport, yet it is not as consistently insightful or stimulating with regard to football. Likewise, there are few more original, literate or engaging football writers anywhere than my colleague Gianni Mura of *La Repubblica*. I should also add that throughout 20 years of football reporting in Italy, my Italian colleagues, from a whole variety of papers, have been unfailingly helpful.

These days I get the impression that perceptions of football have changed greatly in the Anglo-Saxon world. During the Mantova Festival of Literature recently, I found myself sitting in a little square not far from the town's celebrated Palazzo Ducale in the company of family friend, the novelist Colm Toibin, and two of his colleagues, novelist Roddy Doyle and poet Carl Phillips.

Over a late-night drink, much of the chat was about football. Carl was especially curious to know how the former Arsenal player Frenchman Patrick Vieira was getting on at Juventus. Likewise, he told a fascinating story of a recent visit to Ghana where he had sat in a bar along with young Ghanaians watching the English Premiership on TV, noting how they knew more about all the Premiership stars than about their own local teams. Roddy Doyle, for his part, was able to give me a sharp and detailed account of Ireland's recent 1–0 World Cup defeat in Dublin by France. It struck me forcibly that in the post-Nick Hornby, sexy-Beckham, millionaire-monied Abramovich era, the Anglo-Saxon football-loving intellectual no longer has to hide his *Fever Pitch* football interests. In Italy, in contrast, you take it for granted that the intellectual is football-loving in the first place.

Further proof of this theory came from the 25 November

edition of *Gazzetta Dello Sport* which carried a front-page photograph of Daniel Harding, the conductor due to preside over the traditional Sant'Ambrogio, 7 December opening night at La Scala. The point about Daniel Harding was that he was photographed sitting in La Scala's splendidly refurbished theatre wearing a Manchester United shirt. He is, for better or worse, a Man U. fan. Twenty years ago he would have kept that dark secret to himself. Now that the Anglo-Saxon, football-loving intellectual is out of the closet, he is positively flaunting it.

There are still other serious differences between English and Italian views on football. Put simply, while a majority of Italian football commentators have a pretty upbeat view of English football (especially in the age of the Premiership), some of their British counterparts still tend to talk of Italian football in the manner of the late Brian Clough, who infamously commented, 'Fucking, cheating Italians,' in the wake of Derby County's European Cup elimination in the 1972–3 season.

For example, the Anglo-Saxon prejudice against the intrinsically defensive nature of Italian football has always amused me, especially now that the wheel has turned full circle with the England national team, under Eriksson, and leading English Premiership sides, such as Chelsea and Liverpool, playing a very Italian-style game. A couple of years ago, English friends and colleagues were telling me that there could be nothing more boring than a Champions League final between Juventus and AC Milan. Nowadays, they may have to admit that a clash between Chelsea and Liverpool (to the neutral eye) is even more boring. After watching Liverpool versus Chelsea in the Champions League in the autumn of 2005, former Juventus and Chelsea striker Gianluca Vialli commented in a piece in *Gazzetta Dello Sport*:

Once, it was an easy enough business to play against an English team. There were no surprises, the stadium was full, the atmosphere fantastic, the team played a traditional 4–4–2 and the players were tough but fair. Bit by bit, however, the arrival of foreign coaches in English football has changed things, making the English game more varied and less predictable.

These days, Premiership managers are less involved in buying and hiring players and have more time to concentrate on training, they are more coaches and less managers, concentrating on the tactical and technical aspects of their team's football ...

Jose Mourinho and Rafael Benitez are two very shrewd coaches who know that in certain games, what matters above all is not to lose. That way, they transformed a game that once would have been a breathtaking, end-to-end spectacle into a game of chess.

The only thing more boring than Italian *catenaccio* is English *catenaccio*, of course.

There are thousands of examples of the unreasoning anti-Italian prejudice that used to dominate the British media, but the one that always amused me was the treatment reserved for AC Milan and Italy striker Filippo Inzaghi.

Although Inzaghi, at his best (before his recent injury problems), had a skyscraper-tall reputation in Italy, many English critics seemed not to rate him. I recall stepping into the lift at the San Siro after Inzaghi had scored a hat-trick in a vital European Championship qualifying 4–0 win over Wales in September 2003 and being amazed to hear English colleague Ian Ridley mutter about the absurdity of a 'player like Inzaghi' scoring a hat-trick in such an important game.

I was genuinely surprised, partly because Ian is a thoughtful, observant and talented football writer. Mind you, that surprise was mitigated by the fact that, over the years, I had noticed

Inzaghi had been singled out for unfavourable treatment by many British football writers and commentators, a treatment that was officially sanctioned when Netherlands and former Manchester United defender Jaap Stam (ironically now his team-mate at AC Milan) wrote an autobiography in which he pointed an accusatory finger at Inzaghi, suggesting that he did not always play by Marquess of Queensberry rules.

But what did such criticism make of his goal-scoring record? After all, wherever he went and at whatever level he played, Inzaghi scored goals – 21 for Italy; 47 in European club competitions; and 113 in Serie A (including 24 in a single season for relegation battlers Atalanta; 15 for Piacenza in Serie B; 13 for Leffe in Serie C1). Even if it was often easy to score goals for Juventus and AC Milan in Serie A, what about his record with Leffe, Piacenza or Atalanta, clubs which are hardly international world beaters?

That track record notwithstanding, English colleagues have often suggested that 'SuperPippo' was nothing more than a 'poacher' and a 'six-yard line merchant', with a marked penchant for taking a 'dive' to boot. It is, of course, undeniable that Inzaghi is and was one of those opportunist strikers who lurk in and around the six-yard line, whilst at the same time consistently playing the offside line so tight that he regularly gets caught out. Yet, by the standards of the modern game, he never struck me as any more of an opportunist or a diver than many of his colleagues in the English Premiership, Saint Michael Owen, Ruud Van Nistelrooy or Wayne Rooney included. 'Diving' is just part of the game, in England too, like it or not.

The point is, of course, that notwithstanding the rampant globalisation of the world game, parochial loyalties hang on in there. Critics and fans still tend to be wary of players they do not see playing regularly. Had Inzaghi moved to Arsenal or Manchester United rather than to AC Milan, then English critics would doubtless have been hailing him as the 'outstanding opportunist of the modern game'.

In that context, what does one say to the ardent Arsenal fan who, during a phone-in on London's TalkSport radio, asked me indignantly how anyone in his right mind could give the European Player of the Year award to Andriy Shevchenko, ahead of Arsenal's 'own' Thierry Henry? I did gently reply that maybe our listener had not seen Shevchenko play.

Mention of Thierry Henry, though, is a reminder that parochial prejudices work on a worldwide basis. It reminds me of an occasion, while watching Roma play Arsenal in a Champions League tie at the Olimpico in November 2002, when a Roma stadium steward in the press box came across to ask me who was the black striker playing for Arsenal. I was amazed by the question since, then as now, Henry was one of the best-known players in world football. Indeed, that night he went on to score a memorable hat-trick in an impressive 3–1 win for Arsenal. Like Eriksson getting to know the British tabloid press, if my Roma steward was unaware of Thierry Henry before, he certainly knew all about him now.

SEVEN
BEHIND THE CAMERA

One Friday afternoon in January 2006, on his popular radio programme, the talented singer, showman and comic Fiorello interviewed Juventus star Alessandro Del Piero. Fiorello is nothing if not brilliantly original.

Thus it was that his 'interview' was *not* the usual, gushy-gushy, nice-to-have-you-in-the-studio chat. No, Fiorello engaged in a wickedly funny game whereby he asked Del Piero the sort of questions that journalists ask him three times a week. The difference, however, was that Del Piero had to give not one but two answers. For example:

FIORELLO: How would you react if coach Marcello Lippi does not pick you for the World Cup squad this summer?

DEL PIERO 1: Well, there are a lot of good strikers in Italy and the boss has to make his choice, pick whoever is in form. I hope to be called up for Germany, but if that isn't to be, then I'll be Italy's number one fan in front of the TV.

DEL PIERO 2: If Lippi doesn't call me up, then I'll slash his tyres, sink his yacht, support all of Italy's opponents and go round writing on the walls 'Lippi is Gay'.

FIORELLO: What did you feel the other day when [Romanian Adrian] Mutu came on instead of you and scored the winning goal?

DEL PIERO 1: I was delighted for Adrian. We all play for the team, not for ourselves.

DEL PIERO 2: It was a real pain in the balls. You run your ass off for 80 minutes, then this guy comes on and scores a goal. And what a pathetic goal. Anyone could have scored that goal.

FIORELLO: Last week, you scored a hat-trick. Tell the truth, were you more pleased about the three goals or the three points?

DEL PIERO 1: The three points, of course. You don't win a game for yourself, you win for the team.

DEL PIERO 2: The three goals, of course. What do I care about the three points? If I hadn't scored those three goals, we'd have never won the game.

Anyone who has ever spent any time interviewing footballers will appreciate the point. Serie A footballers tend to be pleasant and courteous when faced with a microphone but often end up trapped by clichés, the sort of FootballSpeak used by Del Piero in his No.1 answers. Rarely do they give you a No.2 type, a straight-from-the-chest, this-is-how-I-feel-about-it answer.

The players have plenty of good reasons to resort to FootballSpeak. For a start, not all of them are articulate – they are valued for their ability to play football, not to talk. For a second, anything they say may be slightly exaggerated and used against friend or foe in next day's *Gazzetta Dello Sport*. Even without a tabloid press, Serie A footballers (more the Italians than the foreigners) tend to be careful.

When footballers talk to footballers, however, it is a different matter. In the summer of 1997, for instance, I worked as a 'fixer' for the BBC presenter and former England star Gary Lineker, then preparing a World Cup series for the following year. This was an enlightening experience, in many ways.

For a start, Lineker was thoroughly professional and wanted to do the job as well as possible. Secondly, he and the crew were up for just about every laugh you could have, and we had lots of them. For me, though, the most revealing thing was the interaction between Lineker and the people we wished to interview, a cast of living legends that included 1982 Italy World Cup hero Paolo Rossi, the former Inter and Italy midfielder Sandro Mazzola, the 1982 Italy coach Enzo Bearzot, and the 1990 Italy coach Azeglio Vicini.

Without exception, all of our interviewees were delighted to meet Lineker. All of them had stories to tell him about various matches in which they had seen him play. If I had not worked it out before, I certainly would have understood it during that week's filming that there exists a special relationship between footballers. They do not need a special masonic handshake nor do they need to speak the same language to recognise and understand one another. The rest of us, especially the journalists, are on the outside looking in at them. Theirs is a world which can only be understood by those who, like them, have lived through it, trained through it, been injured, tried, tested, criticised, adored, exalted, rewarded and celebrated by it.

In particular, I remember the interview we did with Paolo Rossi, at the suitably panoramic site of the baroque basilica of Monte Berica, which looks out over Vicenza. Rossi had played for Vicenza and when he retired he had adopted it as his home.

From the moment Lineker and Rossi shook hands, there was an obvious, immediate empathy between them, although Lineker spoke no Italian and Rossi no English. My main role was to act as interpreter for Lineker. Yet, in some senses, the pair of them were able to talk to each other immediately. They were both life members of the players' brotherhood, a club that is forever closed to the rest of us.

Those interviews, too, prompted an amusing technical

problem. All of the interviews were done by me. Yet, for obvious TV purposes, it had to seem as if Gary was doing them himself. This meant that I would sit to the side and ask a question and then remind the interviewee that he should look at Gary, who was sitting straight in front of him, rather than at me. Most of the time it worked OK, but Enzo Bearzot, in particular, could not get it at all and insisted on addressing all his answers to me.

On the day we interviewed Bearzot, it just so happened that our rendezvous was in a Milan hotel which was doubling up as an out-of-season football 'hiring fair' where contacts are made and players (never the famous ones) are signed up for the new season. When Bearzot arrived, I went to meet him at the hotel's main door. As we crossed the lobby to our interview point, we came across Gabriele Oriali, then working as a team sports director but, of course, one of the key figures in Bearzot's 1982 World Cup winning side. The two men greeted one another like lovers from a distant but never forgotten past, embracing one another. The affection and the warmth was tangible.

'It's good to see you, Mister,' said Oriali. (Italian players alway refer to the coach as 'Mister', an inherited habit from the early days when many of the coaches were English.) 'I have so much to be grateful to you for ... What days they were, back in Spain. Only you could have got us to win that World Cup.'

Bearzot smiled broadly but shook his head. 'No, no, I didn't win anything. You lot won it, you were the players out there.'

In Italy itself, an aspect of that 1982 World Cup win much referred to is always the sense of group spirit, 'us against the world', created by Bearzot and his squad. In that context, a press blackout after the Italian media had savaged the team for its disappointing first-round performances proved especially useful. Watching Bearzot and one of his players 15 years later was to experience, even in a mild way, that sense of team spirit so vital to the Italian success. The more the team were criticised, the more united they became and the better they played. Furthermore, Bearzot said in his formal interview, when his players perceived that the criticism did not change Bearzot's ideas one jot, he rose in their estimation.

Most of my TV interview work, of course, has been done not as a fixer but as the journalist interviewing today's Serie A stars. Here, too, I have always felt privileged, especially when doing interviews at the private training grounds of the biggest clubs in Serie A. You always feel as if you have infiltrated an inner sanctum. Even if the club, and football generally, needs the media just as much as the media needs it, I still always feel like an intruder, or at best an uninvited guest.

You set up your camera – in the car park beside the old Stadio Comunale in Turin (Juventus), in the clubhouse at La Pinetina (Inter Milan), alongside the swimming pool at Trigoria (AS Roma), in front of the training pitch at Formello (Lazio), outside the dressing rooms at Collechio (Parma), or under the vines at Milanello (AC Milan) – and then you stand and wait and watch until the interviewee finally emerges from dressing room, dining room, physio's room or wherever.

Fortunately, not all interviews produce monologues of FootballSpeak. The two most recent Italian national team coaches, Marcello Lippi and Giovanni Trapattoni, are both willing to talk if the time and place are right.

I first met and interviewed Lippi back in the 1992–3 season when he had done especially well with little Atalanta. After that, for ESPN, I had interviewed him a number of times during his second period with Juventus (2002–5), and always found him stimulating. In particular, I remember one half-hour interview in the absurdly spartan Portakabin alongside the Stadio Comunale that Juventus then used when he spoke of his sense of satisfaction at having returned for a second stint as coach to the 'Old Lady'. During that conversation, he outlined his belief that clubs sometimes do well to break up a winning team in the off-season, selling players who might be short of motivation for the following season and replacing them with 'new boys' who would clearly be 'hungry' and desperately anxious to establish themselves. By and large, that policy has been one of the many winning factors in the ongoing Juventus success story.

Lippi also spoke of his respect for and friendship with Manchester United manager Sir Alex Ferguson. He made the point that if Sir Alex were to make the sort of slow (and not very winning) start now with Manchester United that he made back in the late 1980s, no big Premiership or Serie A club of today would have the patience that Manchester United showed then.

Since then, of course, Lippi has moved on to take charge of Italy, leading them to the Germany 2006 World Cup finals. No coaching job in Italian football is more subject to nationwide pressure, ill-informed criticism and endless media speculation than that of the 'CT' (*commissario tecnico*) or national team coach. Doubtless in Germany, the Lippi temper will reappear on occasions as it did in the autumn of 2005 when, miffed by criticism of his side's 1–1 World Cup qualifying draw with Scotland at Hampden Park, he remarked to the press that 'the day that I find myself in agreement with you lot, is the day I start worrying'.

Lippi had been preceded in the Italian hot seat by Giovanni Trapattoni, an immensely successful coach who comes from the 'old school' of that generation that grew up in the tough black and white days of post-World War Two Italy. Although I had often encountered him at post-match press conferences and training sessions, it was only in March 2002, prior to the South Korea and Japan World Cup finals, that I actually sat down to talk at length with him.

The occasion was, again, a TV interview. Usually, these interviews are done in an institutional place such as FIGC's training centre at Coverciano, Florence, or its Rome offices in Via Allegri.

I was therefore a little surprised when FIGC press officer Antonello Valentini told me to get myself and my crew up to a place called Cinisello Balsamo, an industrial hinterland of Milan, which apparently was 'Il Trap's' private hideaway.

We had the precise address but a typical Milanese March downpour made it just about impossible to recognise the car in front, let alone street signs that would lead us to Trapattoni. As we drove up and down the nondescript back streets of industrial-ised Greater Milan, I became convinced I had got it wrong. As the 'hired gun' for the Sunset and Vine TV production company, the man who would not only set up the interview but actually do it with Trapattoni, I was getting worried. Never before had I missed an interview by failing to find the agreed rendezvous.

Eventually, we pulled in at what we thought was the right address. Surely there was some mistake. We had stopped in front of a busy garage, where some expensive-looking Mercedes and BMWs were up on jacks, having their toenails polished. At least the people in the garage would be able to direct us onto the right road. In we walked and headed for the little office, complete with hatch-window, in the corner. And there he was, behind the hatch-window, Giovanni Trapattoni in person, smiling broadly and patiently waiting for the foreign journalist.

So, what was a living legend of Italian football doing sitting in the office of a busy garage? It turned out that the garage in question was owned by Franco, a buddy with whom Trapattoni once formed a business partnership and with whom he has retain-ed a lifelong friendship, still keeping his own private office there above the workshop. (During the subsequent World Cup, when his handling of the Italian team brought fierce criticism, 'Il Trap' was regularly on the phone to Franco, checking out both what the papers were saying and the national mood.)

Trapattoni is that type of person. '*Buono come il pane*', good like bread, as Italians like to say. Notwithstanding a 34-year coaching track record so full of league titles (seven in Italy, one in Germany, one in Portugal) and cups (Intercontinental, European, UEFA etc.) that it fills half a page of the *Annuario Del Calcio Mondiale*, Trapattoni remains faithful to himself and his Cusano Milanese background.

Before we sat down to do our interview, Trapattoni showed us around his own trophy room and then insisted on ordering coffee and biscuits for us. His old-fashioned good manners, his easy-going attitude (he did not seem much upset by the fact that we had arrived late for the interview) and his obvious warmth struck a strong contrast with the tough, often agitated coach who had stomped up and down the most famous touchlines of Italy, aiming his ear-piercing, two-fingered whistle of warning at famous names such as Michel Platini. (The great Frenchman once joked that he spent much of his first year at Juventus pretending he could not hear that infamous whistle.)

When, later that year at the South Korea and Japan World Cup, Trapattoni was spotted with a little bottle of Holy Water on the Italy bench, I was neither surprised nor scandalised (unlike some sections of the Italian media). That is the way he is, a man from another generation for whom good manners, saying the rosary and putting dubbin on your boots held serious sway.

Trapattoni, of course, was a gift for those in the Anglophonic media world who insist that Italian football is exclusively defensive. Against South Korea in the 2002 World Cup finals and against Sweden at Euro 2004 in Portugal, Trapattoni gave his critics plenty of fodder when making defensive-looking substitutions in both key games at a time when Italy were leading 1–0 (midfielder Gennaro Gattuso on for striker Del Piero in South Korea; midfielders Stefano Fiore and Mauro Camoranesi on for strikers Del Piero and Antonio Cassano against Sweden in Portugal). In the end, of course, both opponents came back into the game, South Korea eliminating Italy with a 2–1 golden goal win and Sweden earning a late 1–1 draw that effectively cost Italy a place in the quarter-finals. That, however, is another, longer story.

Interviews with players and coaches can sometimes be useful even when the subject does not seem to say much. The car that a player drives and how he drives it out of the car park, the way he stops (or does not stop) for a photo with a fan, the chat-up routine he lays on the glamorous lady at the front desk, the way he says hello to the club staff – generally how he behaves when he is in a familiar, relaxed environment.

I remember watching Andriy Shevchenko, in his first winter in Italian football, asking team-mate Billy Costacurta about the expensive JC Blancpain Swiss watches, which were being featured in a special promotion and award ceremony at the Milanello training ground that day. Swiss watches were probably hard to come by in the Ukraine, while these particular ones were handmade little miracles of engineering genius that retailed at anything from £3,500 to £350,000.

Then there was the day at Inter Milan that I saw Brazilian Ronaldo turn up late for training. When he was informed by coach Gigi Simoni that he would be fined for being late, his obvious annoyance said volumes about his potential for being less than fully committed to team training, something that Real Madrid have learned to their cost in the meantime.

Dutchman Clarence Seedorf helping his little daughter eat an ice cream at Milanello; Alessandro Del Piero's wary look as he walked past our camera at the Stadio Comunale; the softly-spoken, self-effacing tones of Zinedine Zidane. These are just some of the hundreds of little snapshots that can sometimes tell you something you might not otherwise have known about a player.

For 15 years, however, my TV work has been focused not on interviews but on match commentaries. That began one day in

March 1991 when I received a phone call from a colleague who told me that RAI were looking for someone to do live English-language commentaries on Serie A. I was told to get in contact with a woman called Adrianna Ricucci.

I did as suggested and a few days later found myself sitting in a huge, empty TV studio doing a test commentary off a small TV screen. I knew the teams pretty well and after I had blathered on for about ten minutes, somebody shouted down at me, '*Va bene*, that'll do.' Adrianna later told me that the technicians recording my little audition had convinced her immediately, telling her that 'he knows the players better than some of our own guys'. The technicians were obviously a charitable, kind-hearted lot. I had lots to learn.

Within days I was at work, commentating on a 1–1 European Cup quarter-final draw between AC Milan and Olympique Marseilles. From then until now, I have worked with RAI's affiliate, Raitrade, the body which sells RAI programmes, commentating on literally thousands of mainly Serie A games. (I usually do three or four per weekend.)

One of the most intriguing aspects of working for Raitrade's worldwide audience is the delayed drip feedback that comes to me from the most unexpected of sources, from Irish Augustinian priests in Nigeria, to colleagues working in Singapore, to friends on holiday in Bali. Then, too, there is my brother-in-law Colm in Winnipeg, Canada, who, along with his Italian barber, regularly gives me a raincheck on performance standards.

What about Italian TV coverage of football itself? Friends and visitors to Italy often express their bemusement when watching some of the prime-time Italian TV football shows. For them, the problem is usually that, while the programme does indeed have plenty of football action, it nearly always also contains a glamorous female presence. Sometimes, the woman in question is a competent presenter. Sometimes, though, she is asked to read out the results and little else, or to be part of the studio's discussion panel, being more presence than participant. Some of these programmes are clearly the expression of a macho Latin culture into which feminism and political correctness have made but limited inroads.

If the printed press in Italy reflects an obviously educated, literate and middle-class football readership, there is no denying that Italian TV coverage of football tends to touch a more populist chord. In this regard, it was perhaps the now celebrated Monday night show (still going) *Il Processo Del Lunedi* (*The Monday Trial*) which set the tone.

When I arrived in Italy in 1985, it was an absolute 'must-see' for football journalists. Every Monday evening it put the main protagonists of the previous day 'on trial' for their various failings or successes. It did so with that typically democratic Italian TV production practice whereby a cast of thousands of experts are invited to sit on the panel, with nearly all of them seemingly determined to shout down anyone with an opposing viewpoint (or team loyalty) in an atmosphere of cacophonous bedlam. *Il Processo*, inevitably, featured a glamorous woman who might occasionally read out a news item or the results – or not. To some extent, *Il Processo Del Lunedi* has proved to be the template for a host of Italian football chat shows that have followed in its wake.

Yet, fortunately, this is not the full story. In spite of Italy's macho culture, women have always managed to carve out a serious role for themselves in Italian television coverage of football. Twenty years ago, Marina Sbardella, daughter of a famous referee, was a regular football news and magazine programme presenter on the commercial channel TeleMontecarlo. Today, presenters like Simona Ventura, Paola Ferrari and Ilaria D'Amico (RAI and Sky Italia) know their football, while another pundit, Carolina Morace, nowadays coach of the Italian women's team, was one of the first women anywhere in the world to take up the position of coach to a professional side when she handled Serie

C1 side Viterbese, albeit for an admittedly brief spell (June to September 1999).

One of the trailblazers in carving out an ever larger role for women in football coverage on Italian TV was Alba Parietti. During Italia '90, she fronted a very successful World Cup programme which, in turn, led to her presenting a Sunday night chat and analysis programme, *Galagoal*, both on the (now defunct) commercial channel TeleMontecarlo. The opening sequence to *Galagoal*, in which Alba pulled on (and off) the various team shirts of Italy's most famous clubs, was not quite *Match of the Day*, however. During the commercial break, too, Alba would promote some forgotten product, smiling broadly and wearing a dinner jacket – and nothing else. Writing in the Italian weekly *Panorama*, Giampiero Mughini commented: 'From the day that Alba Parietti appeared in a television programme on football, television programmes on football are not the same ...'

Such was the Alba phenomenon that I too was prompted to write a piece about her. I remember travelling out to the dark hinterland of northern Lazio, where *Galagoal* was recorded, one Sunday night to interview her. Along with a dozen friends and admirers, she sat in her dressing room as her make-up artist and hairdresser tugged, powdered, tweaked and generally glossed up her glamorous TV look, and her producer gave her last-minute instructions. 'One of the things I have done,' she told me, 'is to attract a large number of female viewers to my show, women who empathise with my "woman in the street" view of football.'

Her success may, at first, have seemed like nothing more or less than the confirmation of all the worst stereotypical, chauvinist, Latin male views of women, yet Alba's programme also poked fun at players, coaches and club directors. To an extent, a female presence has been a constant of Italian football coverage ever since.

At the 1994 World Cup I had my own experience of dealing with that curiously splendid Italian cocktail of football, glamour, song and dance in another programme presented by Alba, this time on RAI (Alba's star was on the rise). The occasion was afforded by the fact that Italy started their 1994 World Cup finals campaign at the Giants Stadium, New York with a game against Ireland.

As the *Irish Times* man in residence, I was invited on to the show for the pre-match warm-up and the half-time chat. The basic idea, repeated when Italy were playing other countries, was to focus on the Irish expatriate community in Italy. I went along, armed with a photocopy of my column from the previous day's *Irish Times*, which began with the pompous words: 'Next Saturday night in New York, Ireland will beat Italy in their opening World Cup game ...'

That prediction might have sounded daft but it was based on the calculation that Italian coach Arrigo Sacchi, with his theories, his megaphone and his high-volume training sessions, might have confused his players beyond any hope of reasonable football. In contrast, Jack Charlton's Ireland might have had a limited game plan but it was one with which they could prove singlemindedly effective.

Co-presenting the programme along with Alba was Fabrizio Maffei, now head of RAI Sport. In between chats with soccer pundits, including Carolina Morace and the former Sampdoria player Beppe Dossena, the programme was enlivened by a song and dance routine in which the 'star turn' was a certain Valeria Marini (later to become involved with cinema producer Vittorio Cecchi Gori, owner of Serie A side Fiorentina at the time of its financial collapse in the summer of 2002). Valeria was large and blonde; Alba was large and brunette. Both wore distinctly glittery clothing of the revealing kind. What any of this had to do with a World Cup first-round game is a mystery that can only be explained in the byzantine workings of the Italian (male) mind.

Then and now Italy remains a country where the politically correct agenda re. the use of women and their naked or semi-naked bodies in all manner of promotional, televisual and advertising contexts has thus far failed to catch on. Twenty million plus people watched the programme that night and, with all due respect to Alba and Valeria, I think we can take it for granted that the main attraction was the football match.

On arrival in the studio, a member of the Irish delegation had immediately spotted a large stash of *prosecco* on a table in the corner. The studio, it seems, was expecting an Italian win. In the circumstances, no one was much interested in my little column with its Doomsday predictions for Italy. Indeed, when one of my compatriots – there were about half a dozen of us there to represent the nation – had the temerity to suggest on air that Ireland would win, he received a withering look from Alba.

The rest, of course, is history. Italy were sunk by an eleventh-minute Ray Houghton goal. Carolina Morace, as an act of goodwill, had crossed the studio during the game to watch the match with the Irish contingent, and immediately became involved in all manner of good-natured banter. Listening to her analyse the game, however, was an eye-opener, since her knowledge and awareness of football was indeed serious. Long before the final whistle, she too had predicted an Italian defeat.

It was then that tragedy struck. Just when the Irish contingent were preparing to party, in strode the studio crew and whisked away all the bottles of *prosecco*. So outraged were my compatriots that I was delegated to make enquiries. After all, went our reasoning, even if you lot do not want to celebrate, just slip us a couple of bottles and we will have a good time ourselves instead. No such luck.

On the way out of the studio, I brandished my column to Maffei. Told You So. Not, mind you, that it did Ireland much good. They were soon on the plane back to Ireland whilst Italy went all the way to the final in Pasadena and that penalty shoot out loss to Brazil.

Carolina Morace, the studio pundit who had watched the game with the Irish camp, was later to write her own little page in football history when, as aforementioned, she was appointed coach of third division side Viterbese.

The appointment was made in June 1999, but within three months she had already resigned from the job. Before the male chauvinists of this football-loving world jump up to say, 'Told-You-So, Football's-A-Man's-Game,' it had best be pointed out that she was sacked by the then Viterbese owner, Luciano Gaucci, a man with a penchant for sacking coaches.

Three years later during the South Korea and Japan World Cup, Mr Gaucci earned himself his own quarter hour of worldwide fame by sacking his South Korean player Jung Hwan Ahn, scorer of a dramatic golden goal that had eliminated Italy. At the time, Ahn was a (largely unused) player with Mr Gaucci's then Serie A club Perugia. The South Korean's World Cup heroics did not much please his erstwhile employer, who commented ruefully: 'That gentleman need not come looking to join up with our team again ... I have given orders that we exclude any possibility of extending his contract. I am simply outraged. Ahn became a good player only when he had to play against Italy. I am a patriot and I consider his behaviour not only an affront to Italian pride but also an offence to the country that threw its doors open to him for the last two years.'

Put simply, Mr Gaucci was not an easy employer. At the time, media reaction was kind enough to Carolina, concentrating more on Mr Gaucci's vulcanic nature than on the shortcomings of a Viterbese side that had just lost 5–2 away to Calabrian side Crotone.

It may be that, in time, people will look back at Carolina Morace's three-month rise and fall at Viterbese as a significant event both in itself and as an indicator of the changing times in modern soccer. Her appointment may have been a European first but it would be a brave pundit who predicts it will be a European last.

Football is indeed a predominantly male world but it is one that is changing even with regard to sexual stereotyping. From the English Premiership to Serie A and, especially, on to World Cup and European Championship finals tournaments, the female fan presence is ever more felt. Female Argentine, Brazilian, Colombian, Danish, Dutch, Portuguese, Spanish and Nigerian fans (to name but the most obvious) at France '98, Euro 2000, South Korea and Japan 2002 and Portugal 2004 all brought much welcome fun, glamour, family atmosphere and fiesta to the finals.

What about the dismay of those French TV advertising executives who during France '98 had opted to withdraw a whole range of women-only products from the World Cup prime-time schedules? Within days, they were cursing their own decision since, by the end of June 1998, surveys showed that the French TV audience for the World Cup was 40 per cent female. Anyone out on the streets of Paris on the night of 12 July, the night that France lifted the trophy by beating Brazil, would probably agree. As Paris went football mad for a night, it was all too patently clear that this was football fervour, male and female, big time. That trend, too, is confirmed in Italy where a recent survey found that 31 per cent of women consider themselves fans and closely follow a specific team.[8]

As for Carolina Morace, I remember meeting her at the European Championship in Holland and Belgium, one year after her sacking by Luciano Gaucci. Had she any regrets about her short time at Viterbese, I wondered?

'No, no, I had no choice … but to tell you the truth, Gaucci, you know, is a bit difficult …'

Which was putting it diplomatically.

Returning to the matter of TV coverage of football, it is also true that Italian television has developed its very own style of football-cum-variety-cum-chat show that goes on for three or four hours on a Sunday afternoon, mixing song, dance, comedy and Hollywood stars with up-to-the-minute information on football. It is equally true that the success or failure of such programmes commands huge media interest. When Mediaset parted company with Paolo Bonolis, presenter of its prime-time Sunday evening football show *Serie A*, in November 2005, the matter was front-page news and ran in every radio and TV news bulletin. (Some reports even suggested that Bonolis's departure came after the direct intervention of Mediaset owner Berlusconi.)

Given the huge ratings claimed by shows like this, presenters tend to earn good money. Bonolis, for example, claimed to have been on €8.5 million per annum. Given the popularity of these programmes, too, there is a recurring debate about the correctness of allowing politicians to appear, given that they will inevitably use the forum to reshape their not always very attractive public image.

Occasionally, these programmes find themselves at the centre of the political debate. During an edition of RAI's Sunday afternoon football programme *Quelli Che Il Calcio* in December 2001, an audibly furious Minister for Communications, Maurizio Gaspari, rang up to complain. On air, his phone call was passed to presenter Simona Ventura. The minister wanted to complain about the programme's use of satire, much of it directed at himself, arguing that it was not satire at all but rather 'defamation'.

Minister Gaspari's comments came within the overall context of a Berlusconi government which systematically attempted to silence critical voices such as the current affairs presenters Michele Santoro and Enzo Biagi, and the comedienne Sabrina Guzzanti. Two years later, in November 2003, intellectuals such as the Nobel Literature prize winner Dario Fo and pianist Nicola

Pavini expressed their concern about media freedom in Italy. Then, the full-frontal attack by Minister Gaspari on Simona Ventura and her programme prompted days of political rumblings about 'Fascist thuggery'. (Mr Gaspari is a member of Alleanza Nazionale, formerly the Movimento Sociale Italiano, inheritor of Mussolini's political mantle.)

Can you imagine Jack Straw or Gordon Brown ringing up *Match of the Day* to make an important point on behalf of the government? The viewers would think they'd lost their marbles.

EIGHT
SEVEN MINUTES IN SERIE A

It is 25 May 1997, the second last day of the season. Fiorentina are at home to Reggiana, a side already relegated from Serie A. After an hour of the game, the contest is over with Fiorentina cruising home 3–0 thanks to two goals from Argentine ace Gabriel 'Batigol' Batistuta and one from striker Anselmo Robbiati.

With just six minutes of normal time remaining, Reggiana coach Francesco Oddo is about to make his third substitution of the afternoon. With the match lost beyond recall, it is hard to see what point there is in bringing on a third player. Even stranger is the fact that as Oddo prepares to send on the substitute, another player on the bench, experienced midfielder Fernando De Napoli, angrily intervenes.

Even if he now has problems with his knees and is coming to the end of his career, De Napoli is the sort of player who commands respect. In a 15-season career, he not only picked up 54 caps for Italy but was also a key figure in the Maradona-led Napoli side that won the league title in 1987 and 1990. De Napoli is a heavy dude.

He and Oddo are shouting at one another. In the end, De Napoli makes his point. Oddo changes his mind about the substitution he was about to make and instead brings on his reserve goalkeeper, Ettore Gandini, in place of first-choice Marco Ballotta.

For 28-year-old Gandini, this is the realisation of a lifelong dream. This is his belated Serie A debut, the moment he has worked towards since he joined his first club as a madly enthusiastic eleven-year-old. After ten years as a professional player, laboriously working his way up from Serie C2, he has finally made it to top of the greasy pole. He has made it into Serie A.

Gandini was not to know it but the following seven minutes of football were to constitute his total career in Serie A. Within 18 months, he was out of football, injured in mind and body, disillusioned by a world that had promised much but delivered little.

Sports editors and football journalists tend to be an elitist lot. If we are going to interview someone, then, by and large, he has to be a big shot. That way, you find yourself standing in the mixed zone area outside the dressing rooms after a match, microphone in hand, crudely screening the players as they file past.

Each player is quickly assessed as to his 'interview value'. If it is Del Piero, Maldini, Kaka or Zidane, great. If it is the guy who scored that night's hat-trick, even better. If it is some bloke, perhaps a talented international, who spent the night on the subs' bench, forget it.

I have lived and worked in Italy for all of Ettore Gandini's not-so-famous football career. During my peregrinations from Serie A grounds to Champions League games to World Cups and European Championships, it would never have occurred to me to interview Ettore. He was never front-page news, never made the sort of headlines that would have prompted ESPN or the *Irish Times* to send me looking for him.

I came across Ettore by chance after he turned up in one of Dindy's English classes at the Italian golf federation's Scuola di Golf in Sutri, just over the hills behind our house. By that stage, for him, football represented the past and he was fully launched into a fledgling career as a golf professional.

His story is neither sensational nor controversial. It is, however, a reminder that there is another football world out there. Football is not just about the Beckhams, Del Pieros, Rooneys, Maldinis and Zidanes, even if media coverage inevitably concentrates on such players. Obviously, these superstars are the talented ones. Sometimes, they are also lucky. When a promising 17-year-old badly damages a knee (Ettore had knee problems from the age of fourteen) and has to kiss goodbye to any idea of a career in football, the superstar might do well to remember that there, but for the grace of God, goes he.

Ettore's experience is worth telling for at least two other reasons. It shines an unflattering light on life in the lower Italian divisions, and it serves as a reminder that craft, guile, political savvy and a good agent (all elements missing from Ettore's story) can also help promote and prolong a career.

During the 2000–1 season, doyen coach Carlo Mazzone, then at Brescia, was asked about his experienced striker Dario Hubner. In that year, the 33-year-old Hubner was defying his age to have an excellent season with Brescia, scoring 17 goals in Serie A. The reporter wanted to know why such an obviously talented player had only had one previous season in Serie A (1997–8) in 13 seasons of professional football. 'Probably Dario made the mistake of not having an agent,' came the candid Mazzone reply.

Ettore Gandini was born on 1 May 1969, just three months after a boy called Gabriel Omar Batistuta was born in the town of Reconquista, Argentina. Ettore's story begins with a night to remember, a night of the most overwhelming emotions, on Sunday, 11 July 1982. Along with just about the entire Italian nation, he and his family gathered around their television to watch Italy face West Germany in the World Cup final at the Estadio Santiago Bernabéu in Madrid.

For Ettore, the match was doubly intense not only because

he wanted Italy to win but also because he desperately wanted his hero, the Italian goalkeeper and captain Dino Zoff, to do well. However, the game did not exactly go to plan, at least initially, with Italy's stylish left-back Antonio Cabrini missing a first-half penalty.

'When Cabrini missed that penalty in the first half of the final, I ran out of the house and climbed up a tree and remained there for a quarter of an hour,' Ettore recalls. 'I still remember that, just as if it was last night. Eventually my brothers came out looking for me and persuaded me to come down ... After a while, I relented. I climbed down and went back in to see the second half. Good job that I did ... After the match, it was fantastic, my brothers and their friends took me with them and we drove around Varese, waving flags, blaring horns and creating a rumpus. That was a night I'll never forget.'

When ten-year-olds pick a kick-around team amongst themselves, nobody ever wants to go in goal. Not Ettore. He just loved throwing himself around, diving at the other kids' feet and going up for the high ball. If there was nobody to play with, he would spend hours kicking a ball up against the wall or the garage door at his parents' home close to Varese, 70 kilometres north of Milan near the Swiss border. When his brothers and their friends met up for a kick-around game, jackets rolled up as goal posts, Ettore always insisted in joining in, too, playing in goal, of course, even if the other kids were six or seven years older than him.

Long before that magical July night, Ettore had made up his mind. He wanted to become a professional footballer. Two years earlier, he had started playing for the eleven-year-olds team at a local club, SA Bosto, a club that traditionally functioned as a 'feeder' for Varese, then a serious club playing in Serie B, or – if the kid was really promising – for nearby giants AC Milan and Inter Milan.

Like a lot of kids, too, Ettore's football passion was of the self-starting kind. Throughout his subsequent professional career, a journey that took him from Serie C2 to Serie A, Ettore's parents left him to his own devices. He now recalls that his mother once saw him play in a friendly against AC Milan but his father never saw him play at all.

At the age of 13 he did his first *provino* (trial) with Varese. He was one of maybe a hundred kids who turned up at the Varese training ground on a Thursday afternoon. If things went well, you got to play for 45 minutes in a proper match. If things were running late, you got maybe half an hour in which to impress the talent scouts.

'Varese in those days was ... properly organised and with their own scouting system,' Ettore explains. 'Basically, the word had gone around, the scouts knew who they wanted ... [but] even if the scouts had already identified the promising players, they still gave everyone a try out, just to keep all the small clubs happy. Those trials used to go on for two hours, every Thursday ... Even then my left knee was giving me problems and I didn't play especially well in the trial. I was lucky though because we had a coach at Bosto, Giuseppe Majorca, who really believed in me and he insisted that they give me another chance.'

Reluctantly, Varese agreed and, after having seen Ettore in action again, invited him to play for their Under-14 team in a tournament in Turin, playing against youth teams from some of the biggest clubs in the land, including Atalanta, Inter and AC Milan. The tournament lasted six days and, by the end, Ettore had won the best goalkeeper of the tournament award. If he knew anything now, it was that he was definitely going to be a professional footballer: 'I was 14 at the time but that's the age at which you begin ... I gave it everything, body and soul ... I was totally concentrated, totally focused on the one thing – football. I remember, too, watching the other goalkeepers in the tournament and thinking to myself that, with the exception of one of them, the rest were nothing much ...'

The one guy who impressed him was AC Milan's 14-year-old goalkeeper Francesco Antonioli, a player still keeping goal in the 2005–6 season in Serie A with Sampdoria and who won Italian league titles with both AC Milan and AS Roma. Ettore's 14-year-old eye was clearly not bad.

That tournament settled matters. Varese definitely wanted him. He played his way up through the various youth teams at the club for the next two years before, at the age of 16, he was called into the first team squad. Even if Varese had by that stage slipped down to Serie C2, Ettore could not quite believe it. He thought he was on the threshold of a rocket-quick start to his professional career. He was wrong.

For three full seasons, from 1987 to 1990, Ettore worked hard, trained hard, spent a lot of time watching the other goal-keepers in training and generally improved, but he never got to play in a league game: 'In those days, Serie C sides were full of experienced players, Serie A and Serie B players finishing their careers. Youngsters didn't get a chance. You were always coming across coaches from the old school who simply preferred to play their more experienced players ...'

For three seasons, he was caught up in this Catch 22. Eventually, as so often in football, one man's misfortune was his opportunity. At the beginning of the 1990–1 season, the first-choice goalkeeper, Claudio Fadoni, broke his nose playing in a pre-season friendly against Inter. It gave Ettore his first break. He was brought into the side for a handful of Serie C Italian Cup games as well as three league games. Soon, however, Fadoni recovered from his broken nose and reclaimed his place in the team, relegating Ettore once more to the subs' bench.

In time, Ettore's self-motivation began to pay off. At the end of the 1990–1 season, the season in which Ettore made his professional debut, Varese was involved in a relegation play-off against Empoli. Varese lost the game, and was relegated to Serie C2. Fadoni had played badly, making a couple of serious mistakes. Varese decided not to renew his contract but rather to trust their No.2 goalkeeper for the 1991–2 season in the fourth division. Ettore did well, playing in all 38 league games, and at one point even going more than a thousand minutes without conceding a goal. By the end of the season, 'people' had noticed him. Word on the football grapevine was that a number of Serie B and Serie C1 sides were interested in signing him.

I would not have noticed either Ettore or Varese back in 1991–2. I was much more interested in that season's batch of Serie A 'new boys', a batch which included Englishman David Platt (Aston Villa to Bari), German Thomas Doll (Hamburg to Lazio), Frenchman Laurent Blanc (Montpellier to Napoli), German Jurgen Koehler (Bayern Munich to Juventus) and, perhaps the most exciting of the lot, Argentine Batistuta (Boca Juniors to Fiorentina for £2.2 million).

Batistuta's impact on Italian football had been almost immediate, as he had scored in his first full Serie A game for Fiorentina at home to Genoa in a 3–1 win. By the time he and Fiorentina came to play Roma at the Olympic Stadium in February 1992, he had already earned the nickname 'Batigol'. Writing a column for the *Irish Times* after watching him score two goals for Fiorentina in this 3–1 away win against Roma, I could hardly have been more enthusiastic: 'A new star has entered the international soccer firmament. Twenty-three years old, Gabriel Omar Batistuta is his name, and scoring goals in the most defensive league in the world is his business … Players can come and go and Batistuta may hit on hard times further down the road. Yet, having watched him on Sunday, we would suggest that this is a player who will be among the best in the world for some time to come. Class is not water, as Italians would say, and this boy has lots of it.'

Batistuta did, of course, live up to those predictions. In the summer of 2003, he left Italian football after twelve seasons, having scored 183 goals in Serie A for three clubs: Fiorentina, AS Roma and Inter. He was, quite simply, one of the best strikers ever to play in Serie A.

By the time the paths of Ettore and Batistuta crossed in that Fiorentina versus Reggiana game in May 1997, the Argentine was at the very height of his formidable powers. In his last year of Italian football, Batistuta declared pre-tax earnings of €8.74 million. In his only year in Serie A, Ettore earned €60,000. Perhaps Ettore should have used a good agent.

One day in the summer of 1992, a phone call came through to the club from Ancona, newly promoted into Serie A. They were looking for a reserve goalkeeper and had heard good things about Gandini. Could they meet up at the Calciomercato (literally, an annual football hiring market) being held that year at Cernobbio on Lake Como? He drove over to Cernobbio, but no one from Ancona showed up. So he stayed put, having another good season the following year. At this point, however, things took a turn for the worse at Varese with the club opting for 'self-relegation' to amateur level because of pressing financial problems.

Ettore was now a free agent but without a club. Gigi Piedimonte, team director at newly promoted Serie A club Reggiana, had long rated Ettore and contacted him now, persuading him to join the club even if that entailed being 'farmed out' for experience at a lower division club. For Reggiana, Ettore represented a bargain since Varese's relegation out of professional soccer meant that his contract was no longer valid and he could be picked up on a free transfer. Even if he was to be farmed out, this was a big break for Ettore.

* * *

After three months, Reggiana agreed to loan Ettore out to Serie C1 team Barletta, in Puglia, southern Italy. The boy from Varese was now for a major culture shock.

Ettore's home town of Varese, with its neat houses, organised traffic and cycle lanes, has plenty in common with nearby Switzerland. This is a part of the world where people have been coming and going for centuries, passing in and out of Italy via the nearby Alpine passes, Sempione and Gottardo. Life here has a sense of order and organisation largely missing in great tracts of *il Mezzogiorno.*

Southern Italy is still one of the poorest zones of Europe, a region where, according to ISTAT, Italy's national institute of statistics, infant mortality (5.7 for every 1,000 births) is four times higher than in northern Italy. In the south, 24 per cent of school children have already left school by the age of 14 and 7.3 million people earn less than €531 per month.

Above all, the south is the land of organised crime, plagued by four different Mafia organisations – Cosa Nostra in Sicily, the 'Ndrangheta in Calabria, the Camorra in Naples and the Sacro Corona Unità in Puglia. According to a 2004 report by independent research body EURISPES, they command up to 40,000 foot soldiers, men responsible for 666 Mafia killings in the period between 1999 and 2003.[9] A recent survey by Fondazione BNC and social research institute CENSIS estimates the Mafia costs southern Italy €7.5 billion per annum in economic development. Racketeering, corruption, market control and killings tend to discourage investment and growth.[10]

For all of these criminal organisations, drug trafficking is the core business. Yet, to varying degrees, they all run vigorous sidelines that include infiltration of public works contracts (of every sort, but building and waste disposal are favourites), prostitution rings, racketeering, arms trafficking and illegal betting rings, in which, of course, football is often the focus of Mafia 'interest'.

In October 2004, that interest took on an unusual turn when two amateur teams in Calabria – Strongoli and Isola Capo Rizzuto – observed a minute's silence before a keenly contested local derby. The observation of a minute's silence in memory of the dead before football games is in itself nothing new. The difference here was that the dead man was not a former team player but Carmine Arena, a Mafia godfather who had been 'taken out' the previous evening in a bloody shoot-out. It sounds implausible, but it happened. In Calabria, there are estimated to be 112 organised crime families counting on one 'soldier' per 345 citizens, and the homicide rate is 17 times higher than the national average.

Carmine Arena, 45 years old and cousin of the president of the Isola Capo Rizzuto team, Pasquilino Arena, had been a figure well known to local police authorities and to anti-Mafia investigators alike. Nephew of 'Ndrangheta boss Nicola Arena, Carmine had served a six-year sentence for Mafia membership, being released from prison in 2000.

On a Saturday night, he had pulled up in front of the family villa in Isola Capo Rizzuto in his bulletproof Lancia Thema. As he waited for the automatic gate to open onto the driveway, he was shot down in a hail of deadly fire by a command of rival mafiosi who had been waiting for him. The weapon used was a 'RPG 7' bazooka, a combat weapon normally used against armoured cars, tanks and helicopters. For good measure, his killers then peppered the car with several rounds from Kalashnikovs and shotguns.

In a region beset with gangland warfare, the killing commanded little or no space the next day in Sunday news bulletins. It was only when the minute's silence was observed at the game that afternoon that the national media latched onto the story.

The match was handled by an 18-year-old referee, Paolo Zimmaro, who later claimed that he had been misled, adding that he was unaware of the killing of Arena the previous evening and saying: 'We were lined up on the centre circle, when one of the directors from the Isola team shouted across at me, asking me if we could observe a minute's silence in memory of one of their lads, who had died.'

Whether or not the young referee was genuinely unaware of the gravity of his action, or had in fact been intimidated into calling the minute's silence, is, in the end, of only relative importance. Crotone public prosecutor Franco Tricoli probably spoke for many of his colleagues in the magistrature and the police force when commenting on the Monday after the incident: 'From the legal viewpoint, no crime was committed, but from the moral viewpoint? ... It takes more than policemen and soldiers to beat the 'Ndrangheta, it also requires the participation and the strength of civil society, things that in this case were absolutely missing.'

This minute's silence was no isolated incident. In March 2003, Paolo Fabiano Pagliuso, president of Serie B side Cosenza, was arrested on charges of 'criminal association' and 'extortion'. (In effect, Pagliuso was accused of using the club for money laundering purposes.) Speaking after the arrest, investigator Vincenzo Macri told reporters: 'We had become aware of the fact that the 'Ndrangheta seems to be especially interested in lower-level football. For them, it's more about winning consensus in the local community than about making money.'

In November 2005, speaking at a seminar on the socio-economic problems affecting young people, Don Pino Demasi, a priest in the Calabrian town of Polistena, warned: 'Many of the club presidents around here are mafiosi and they put in their own trusted guys to run the club. That way, sooner or later, a lot of young lads will end up working for the Mafia.'

Just before Christmas 2002, a banner appeared on the terraces in Palermo's La Favorita stadium during a Serie B game, demonstrating against the '41 Bis' legislation then going through parliament aimed at making prison sentences tougher for convicted mafiosi.

Even where organised crime does not interfere, such is the socio-economic context in southern Italy that football tends to weigh heavily on day-to-day life. For the ordinary, honest fan, football can become very important. Looking back on his experience in Barletta, Ettore now says that football in the south is '*un po strano*' (a bit strange). By some standards, his experiences were relatively 'normal', but they still testify to the climate surrounding the game.

'I remember playing a friendly against Potenza [another southern club],' he recalls, 'where our fans burned the bus of the Potenza fans by way of welcome. Up here [in the north] people have other things to be thinking about, but down there, they spend the week thinking about the game on Sunday ... They killed you down there if things went wrong for you ...

'I remember another time, when we went to play Juve Stabia, in Castellamare di Stabia [just down the coast from Naples] ... There were maybe 200 metres between where the bus dropped us and the stadium but in those 200 metres, you had all sorts of things happening. People shouting insults at you, spitting at you, and all of this two hours before the game was due to begin. But that's the way it was down there ...'

It needs to be pointed out, too, that lower-division football in Italy is played on a regional basis, with Serie C1 and Serie C2 divided into broadly defined northern and southern groups. This means that lower-division football has a viciously local aspect with every second game being some sort of bitterly contested derby.

Ettore was lucky because little went wrong for him at Barletta. He had an excellent season and did not fall foul of the fans, unlike his predecessor. The club, like a lot of clubs, was very ambitious, and when Ettore arrived in October 1993, all the talk was of winning promotion to Serie B. In the end, though,

Barletta ended up that season struggling to avoid relegation to Serie C2.

Ettore's worst memories of his nine-month stay at Barletta are not so much about organised crime as about boredom. Such was the club's ambition that the team spent three months locked up in a hotel from Wednesday to Sunday every week for the pre-match *ritiro*: 'We were shut away like monks in a monastery ... it gets to you, being locked away all week. The same faces, the boredom, in the end it was counterproductive ... You weren't allowed out, you weren't allowed to sleep in until midday or anything like that, they got you up early ... I was a single guy, I got married the following April, but for the married lads with wife and kids at home, it was hell.'

The passion of the Barletta fans, the jeering his team-mates got if they were seen about the town in the week after a defeat, and the exaggerated ambitions of the club were all reminders of just how seriously the football was taken. In some senses, Ettore fitted in just fine: 'I was always one of those players who really felt a game, who lived it out in a very aggressive sort of way, who shouted a lot, got behind my team-mates, and for that reason I was well suited to the south. Football at that level in the south is like that; it is perhaps less technically accomplished, they run harder, they're meaner and you see some really nasty tackles. You could get clubs in the north that might well prefer players who are a little bit calmer, less hot under the collar, but down south, the hotter the better ...

'The strange thing, though, is that your own personality changes in that sort of situation. If, like me, you are the sort of player who can become very aggressive anyway, then it works you up down there. It's more a man's game down there. A lot of teams anywhere have one player who can be really tough, who kicks players, who goes in over the top. Down there, each team seemed to have five of them ...

'Mind you, I got on fine with the fans because I was playing well and also because I was one of those keepers who was never afraid to come out of goal, throw myself at a striker's feet, knocking over three or four players. The fans down there loved that sort of thing. You could bring off a really difficult save but it would mean less to them than if you were throwing yourself about the area, knocking defenders over ... That's the way they lived their football ...'

Ettore, by this stage, was doing quite well, so far as his salary was concerned, earning about £22,000 per year plus expenses, which included his living accommodation. It was a long way from his millionaire Serie A colleagues, such as Batistuta, Baggio et al, but for the Italy of the early 1990s it was acceptable. Furthermore, along with many of his team-mates, he had chosen to live in Trani, a pretty, quiet little town, 15 kilometres from Barletta.

In other circumstances, it could have been a really nice time in Puglia, but, as Ettore puts it, the off-pitch stress and tension meant that it was hard to relax. Lest he and his team-mates had any doubts about the peculiar nature of football in the south, a small, seemingly innocuous incident towards the end of that season reinforced the point.

'We were playing against Nola, I think. It was a big game for the club, that was for sure. We were doing our best but getting nowhere. At half-time, it was 0–0. When we came back out for the second half we found 15 or 20 fans on the pitch, waiting for us. They were very very aggressive, very threatening, calling on us to get stuck in, to try harder. I don't know what exactly they thought was wrong about the way we had played in the first half, but they were certainly very threatening. Several of them had knives; they weren't brandishing them about but they made sure we saw them and the implication wasn't reassuring. The message was along the lines of "who knows what'll happen after the match if you don't win".

'The amazing thing was that the police did nothing, just watched them and let them stay on the pitch for two or three minutes until the second half was ready to start. Afterwards, the guys who had been on the subs' bench told me that, at half-time, the club president had come down from the grandstand and, rather than going straight to the dressing room, went down to the Barletta fans' *curva* [kop], stopped there for a minute or two and then went to the dressing room. I always imagined, afterwards, that the pitch invasion by our fans started with the president, because after that he came into the dressing room, shouting and roaring, followed by the fact that the police just stood there and did nothing about it. The whole thing seemed like a stitch-up ...

'In the end, we played our bollocks off in the second half, but Nola held on against us. We were very apprehensive after the match but, in fact, nothing happened, no one was threatened ... What I do know is that other players and people close to the club told me afterwards that five or six of the fans, the best-known ones, were actually on the club's payroll. They got paid to travel to the away matches, got their tickets from the clubs ... That was normal, I think, for the south ... mind you, it happens with plenty of clubs in the north, too ...'

When the season with Barletta ended, Ettore was more than happy to travel back north to Reggiana.

Curiously, that 1993–4 season had also seen Batistuta 'demoted' because Fiorentina, for the first time in their history, had been surprisingly relegated the previous season. 'Batigol', however, had a happy time in Serie B, scoring 16 goals, and was allowed to leave before the end of the season to join Maradona and the rest of the Argentina squad then preparing for what was to be a dramatic and shortlived stay at the World Cup finals in the USA. (This was the competition marked by Maradona's positive dope test and subsequent suspension,which effectively killed off Argentina's interest in the competition.)

Back at Reggiana for the 1994–5 season, Ettore had rather more mundane concerns. The club wanted to farm him out again so that he could gain further experience. This time, he was sent to Crevalcore, another Serie C1 club, but a bit closer to home, just north of Bologna.

'I had a good year there, played in 30 or so league games,' he remembers. 'The number two goalkeeper in the squad was Matteo Sereni [who went on to play for Sampdoria, Brescia and Lazio in Serie A as well as for Ipswich Town in the Premiership]. He was a funny player, even then, because he would do really well in training, make fantastic saves, and then in a match, he would do a howler. I used to think that, technically, he had problems with his upper body, but you'd have to know what coaching he had had as a youngster …

'We had a good group of players there, though. Another team-mate was Alessandro Pistone [who later played for Inter in Serie A and for Newcastle and Everton in the Premiership], and then there was Vittorio Mero, who was killed in a car crash years later, when he was playing along with Baggio at Brescia in Serie A …

'My best memory of that season, though, was when we played Bologna in two derby games. Bologna had dropped all the way down to Serie C1 but it was obvious they would be going back up again. We normally would play in their stadium, the Dall'Ara in Bologna. It was like playing in an empty quarry; we might get 3,000 spectators in a stadium that can hold nearly 40,000. When we played the two derbies, though, the stadium was packed, the atmosphere was a real derby one and we had two great games – even if we lost both of them.'

By the time that season was over, Ettore felt his wandering days of apprenticeship up and down the peninsula should come to an end. Fortunately, Reggiana agreed. The fact that the club had, in the meantime, dropped back down to Serie B perhaps made the decision easier.

The 1995–6 season at Reggiana promised to be interesting, if only because the club had appointed an intriguing debutant coach in the person of Carlo Ancelotti. An influential player, first with AS Roma and then with Arrigo Sacchi's AC Milan, as well as 26 times capped for Italy, Ancelotti came with an aristo-cratic pedigree.

As a player, he had been the classic 'player-manager', bossing his team-mates around and generally running the show from a central midfield berth in a manner not dissimilar to Ireland and ex-Manchester United (now Celtic) midfielder Roy Keane. Like Keane, too, Ancelotti had a fierce appetite for winning. As some-one who came with a track record of European Cup and league title wins, he was also likely to gain the respect of his players.

When he retired as a player in 1992, Ancelotti made an immediate start on a career as a coach, and at the highest level, too. Arrigo Sacchi, who by that time had moved from AC Milan to take over the Italian national team, called him in as his number two. His job with Reggiana for the 1995–6 season was his first as a coach and it came after three seasons of apprenticeship along-side Sacchi in the Italy job.

From the start, Ancelotti was straight with Ettore. He would start as the reserve goalkeeper behind first-choice Marco Ballotta, who had played for three seasons in Serie A with Parma, two of them as the reserve. Ballotta, however, in his season as first choice at Parma, had won a European Cup Winners' Cup medal. He was a player with a certain pedigree, too, and it was going to be hard to get him out of the team. (Ettore was not to know it then but Ballotta was to prove himself a survivor, still playing in Serie A ten years later at the age of 41, keeping goal as the reserve keeper for Lazio in the 2005–6 season.) All that would be left for

Ettore were a couple of games in the now extinct Anglo-Italian Cup and, maybe, in the Italian Cup as well.

Yet, Ettore says they got on well none the less: 'When you are a goalkeeper, you have to get on with the other goalkeepers because you do your different training, together, side by side, day by day all year long … I looked on him as someone from whom I could learn, but the more I trained with him – maybe I was a bit presumptuous – the less I felt I had to learn from him.

'He didn't have much of a physical presence, he never came off his line, he never went for the cross; that way you never take any responsibility onto your own shoulders. Coming off your line, going for the high ball, it's not a spectacular thing, it's not the instinctive save that everyone sees, so when you come out for the high ball, you're on a hiding to nothing.

'The more I saw him train, the more I got the impression that I could play as well as him … Looking at him, you say to yourself, what's he got that I haven't got?

'I knew how things were. I went there as the second choice but hoping to play my way into the side. In the end you hope that the guy out there doesn't play well and that you get your chance. I didn't want to be there, at 26 or 27 years of age, having worked my bollocks off to get there, and finding that the other guy is going to play and play badly for five games in a row and I still won't get my chance … And yet, that's exactly what happened in Serie A the following season …'

For Ettore, the only hope was the generally ignored Anglo-Italian Cup. By the mid-1990s, this was a tournament featuring Serie B Italian clubs and Division One English teams. In the 1995–6 season, the clubs playing in Reggiana's group were Ipswich Town, Stoke City, Southend United and West Bromwich Albion for England, and Foggia, Salernitana, Brescia and Reggiana for Italy.

The competition was usually played over a period of months

in the first half of the season, and Reggiana's group section was coming to an end in October 1995 when, from out of the blue, it seemed that Ettore might be about to get his big break. Down at Lazio in Rome, first-choice goalkeeper Luca Marchegiani had picked up an injury that would rule him out for some time. Lazio were apparently looking for an experienced replacement and had Ballotta in mind for the job. At Reggio Emilio, the local press quizzed Ancelotti for his reaction to the news that he might lose his goalkeeper.

'Ancelotti,' says Ettore, 'gave the sort of answer that coaches give in that situation, saying that it would be a pity to lose a good goalkeeper like Ballotta but adding that, all the same, he was happy enough because the Anglo-Italian tournament had allowed him to try out his reserve keeper and he was well satisfied with Gandini. I don't need another goalkeeper, he told them. By way of precaution, the club would look for a new reserve goalkeeper [Armando Pantanelli], he said, but that was only for cover … Francesco Dal Cin, who was the club's managing director, wanted Ancelotti to go looking for another, more experienced goalkeeper, but Ancelotti said no …

'On the final week before the transfer window closed [in those days, in Italian football, there was a short October transfer window as well as the January one] we were due to play our last Anglo-Italian tie, against West Bromwich Albion. That game was on a Tuesday with the transfer market due to close on Thursday night. Everyone seemed to take it for granted that Ballotta was off to Lazio. Ancelotti's number two, Giorgio Ciaschini, who was actually listed as the team coach because Ancelotti didn't at that time have the full Serie A/Serie B coach's licence, came to me before the game …

'Ciaschini said to me, "Look, Ettore, so far you have done well, but this will be different because now we want to see how you play tonight, because you know that this is a game that can change the entire season for you." He was right, too, because it's one thing to play as the reserve keeper, with less responsibility. It is something very different to play knowing that your future can depend on the game.

'Ciaschini said to me that the Anglo-Italian tournament didn't really matter in itself but that for me it could be all-important. It's like this, if you play well, then we have no doubts about what to do when Ballotta leaves. If, on the other hand, you play badly then a certain amount of doubt sets in … We lost 2–1, but we were winning 1–0 until ten minutes from the end and I was making impossible saves …

'That is one match report cutting that I probably still have at home. I had played well and I knew it. After the game, Ancelotti told the Reggio journalists that Gandini was "the hero of Birmingham" because I had saved the unsaveable. [It is a common Italian journalistic cliché to link a player's feats to the actual place of the achievement.] I was absolutely delighted. Ballotta was on his way to Lazio, and Ancelotti, Ciaschini and everyone else at the club were pleased for me because I had come through the test really well. Finally I had my chance to make it into the big time as the first-choice keeper …

'Next morning, we arrived at Linate [Milan airport] at about midday. We were loading our bags into the bus when Ancelotti gets a call on his mobile. Ballotta was joining Lazio. It had been confirmed, and the first-team place was mine. I was euphoric, I couldn't have been happier. It was all working out. When I got on the bus, the other guys were coming back down to me, giving me slaps on the back and high fives and saying well done. You can just imagine how good I felt. Ballotta was delighted, too, because Lazio at that time were a really good team and he was glad to make the move …

'So off we set on the journey down the *autostrada* for Reggio Emilio. We were getting close to Reggio when another phone call came through. It was all off. The Lazio club president, Dino Zoff, had wanted Ballotta but the club coach, Czech Zdenek Zeman, apparently didn't fancy him, preferring instead to go for Francesco Mancini, a player he had already coached at Foggia ... I didn't say anything but I was devastated ... The phone call came through to Ballotta himself. Zeman wanted Mancini at all costs, and that meant Ballotta was going nowhere. My career as the first-choice keeper lasted less than an hour, from one phone call to another ...

'From then on, I hardly got a game. I didn't play in a single Serie B match. There was the chance that I might play in a cup match against Bologna, all the papers had me in the side, but even there Ballotta asked if he could play because he comes from near to Bologna and he had begun his career there ...

'In the end, we won promotion back into Serie A that season. If it hadn't been for that, I would have probably left the club at that point. When I had got back from Crevalcore the previous summer, I said to myself, well, I will sit this one out on the bench and see how it goes. If we hadn't gone up to Serie A, probably I would have asked to move to another club rather than spend another season on the bench. But, once we won promotion, I opted to hang on in there. I was 27 years old.'

By this stage, too, Ettore was dealing with a growing problem that had dogged him practically all his career, namely, trouble with his left knee. Once the season was underway, he was fine, but he tended to have serious problems during pre-season training when the regime usually involves two tough sessions of training per day. If he trained hard, the knee would swell up. These were days when he spent half his life with an ice pack wrapped around the knee, immediately after training, in the car on the way home, and while sitting watching television at night.

'The knee was beginning to give me trouble all right,' he recalls. 'I could see the way it was going. This was clearly going to be my first and last chance at Serie A. I kept thinking to myself, you never know, maybe I'll get a break, maybe the other guy will get injured.'

Ettore, however, was in for a major disappointment. Ancelotti had moved on to pastures new, taking over at Parma and being replaced at Reggiana by Romanian Mircea Lucescu. The team, however, was playing badly. Halfway through the season, Lucescu got the sack. On the day he was fired he said that the worst thing that had happened to him on his return to Italian football (he had previously coached Brescia in Serie A) had been to find himself stuck again with Ballotta as his goalkeeper.

Lucescu was replaced by Francesco Oddo, father of Italy and Lazio defender Massimo Oddo, but he stuck with Ballotta.

That Reggiana side was not without talent. Amongst those on the club books that year were Russian striker Igor Simutenkov, Romanian midfielder Ioan Sabau, Belgian defender Georges Grun, former Napoli and Italy midfielder Fernando De Napoli, former AC Milan defender Filippo Galli and midfielders Gianluca Sordo and Max Tonnetto, who was still playing in Serie A with Sampdoria in the 2005–6 season On paper they were good enough to avoid the drop. In the end, they were relegated long before the end of the season, finishing last with a miserable record of just two wins, 13 draws and 19 defeats in their 34 Serie A games.

As the season came to an end, with Reggiana obviously headed back down to Serie B, Ettore began to wonder if he would ever get his chance. He had become friendly with De Napoli, who kept telling him to approach the coach, Oddo, and ask for a chance. But Ettore was too proud. He had been part of the club for four years. He had played two full seasons with small clubs like Barletta and Crevalcore and had done it willingly, as part of the business, as preparation for his big chance. He had worked hard, trained hard and never said a begrudging word to anyone. Furthermore, whenever he had been given a chance, he had kept goal well. Why, after all that, should he go begging for a team place?

Things came to a head towards the end of the season when Reggiana were already mathematically relegated: 'All of a sudden, all sorts of guys started getting games. All these kids from the *primavera* [youth team] were given their chance. Some of them came from Conigliano Veneto, which was a club where the son of our managing director, Michele Dal Cin, worked ... The club these youngsters came from would get extra money if the player made a Serie A debut.'

The record books confirm Ettore's story. In games against Cagliari, AC Milan, Inter Milan and Perugia, *primavera* players Christian Araboni and Luca Ariatti, both 18, Massimo Minetti and Paolo Coppola, aged 19, and 20-year-old Fabio Faso all got a game, usually as substitutes.

Then came the game against Fiorentina on the second last day of the season. Ettore recalls: 'It wasn't much of a match. Batistuta scored in the first ten minutes and another guy scored a second after 20 minutes and we were struggling. As was now usual, Oddo brought on a couple of the reserve players as substitutes [Araboni at half-time and the splendidly named Ivano Casanova in the seventy-fourth minute].

'We were well into the second half and Oddo decides to make his third and last change. He calls up another of the young reserves and tells him to get ready. At that point, De Napoli lost his temper, right there on the touchline in front of everyone. He started shouting at Oddo. He went up to him and he said, "That's it, that's enough. For fuck's sake, give Gandini his chance. Does it seem right to you that this lad here should work his balls off all year long and then he has to sit here and watch all these youngsters get their chance and he gets nothing? Come on, give him a chance." Oddo was shouting back at him and I was sitting there on the bench feeling sort of awkward and embarrassed ...'

De Napoli's words had the desired effect, however. Oddo changed his mind, sending on Ettore to replace Ballotta. Recalling that day eight years later, Ettore thinks he got about a quarter hour of football. The *Almanacco Illustrato Del Calcio* begs to differ, recording that Gandini came on in the eighty-fourth minute. In other words, he got to play for six minutes, plus one minute of extra time.

'I remember hoping the referee would add on about 25 minutes,' he says now. 'In the end, it wasn't much, was it? Mind you, I've an impeccable record in Serie A. I'm unbeaten, no goals conceded!

'After the match, Ballotta came to me in the showers and he said to me that I would be playing in the final game of the season away to Atalanta. I just said that I hoped so, that I'd be ready if they let me play ... Next week, though, same as usual it was Ballotta who played ... Looking back on it now, that was the moment when I lost my love for football ...

'As the years went by, too, my knee was giving me more and more problems, but the worst thing for me was the realisation that, after all those years of hard training, after working my way to Serie A bit by bit ... I wasn't going to get the chance to play even two or three games ...'

By the previous December, Ettore had seen the way things were going. He was convinced that he could do better than Ballotta but knew that he was not going to get his chance. When the club asked him to sign a new contract, he declined. Other players in his situation might have reacted differently. After all, he was on relatively good money for a reserve – £35,000 plus an apartment and expenses.

'When they wanted me to lengthen my contract, I said no and told them that I felt they didn't rate me and that I preferred to go back down to Serie C rather than continue there ... For three months now Ballotta has been playing badly, I said to them, and you won't give me a chance ... I was stupid. I could have shut up and signed a new contract but I was sick of it ...

'The following year there were a lot of clubs from the south looking for me but I didn't want to repeat that experience and I had the chance of going to Carpi [near Modena]. That year they were into the play-offs for Serie B and I had met the club president and we had agreed for me to join if they beat Monza in their play-off. But they lost to Monza and that was the end of that ... There were clubs like Cosenza, Acireale from the south looking for me, but I didn't want to go again ...

'In the end, I went to Novarra in Serie C2; it was close to home. But, frankly, I had lost almost all motivation. A couple of years earlier I would have been more ambitious ... I still played well enough, though, and Alessandria from C1 came looking for me in November but Novarra wouldn't let me go ... Then people in the Reggiana set-up told me that Reggiana wanted me back. Mind you, these were only rumours, if well-founded ones ...'

Then, one week after Alessandria enquired about him, Novarra had a game against Solbiate Arnese, a club from a small townland just down the road from the AC Milan training complex of Milanello. Early in the game, Ettore went out to pick up a bad backpass from one of his defenders. He and the opposing centre-forward got to the ball at the same time. It was one of those 50–50 balls, when 99 times out of a hundred the two players crash into one another, the ball gets cleared and they both get up, a bit sore and bruised but no worse for the experience.

This was the hundreth time. With the centre-forward steaming down on him, Ettore opted to clear the ball in the direction of the touchline. In other words, rather than running straight at the centre-forward, he was sideways on to him as he attempted to clear the ball. His opponent smashed into his right knee, his good knee, at full force. Ettore went down in vicious pain, with his posterior cruciate knee ligament snapped.

'I could have just blasted it at him,' he recalls, 'but that was dangerous because you never know where the ball will go, it might rebound anywhere, so I was sideways onto him when he crashed into me. All I remember is the bang of the impact and then the searing pain ...'

Eight years later, as Ettore recalls that autumn day in 1997, the memory still hurts. Tears come to his eyes and, for a moment, he stops talking.

Ettore was not to know it but that injury, picked up playing in the fourth division in front of maybe 300 spectators, was to end his career.

Within six months, his right knee had healed and he felt keen, despite everything, to get himself back to full fitness and continue playing. When he started to train seriously again, however, he was in for an unpleasant surprise. His other knee, the left, which had been occasionally problematic, had now got much worse. Perhaps because of the enforced inactivity and the four months spent on crutches, it had worsened to a point where it was almost impossible for him to train.

He did come back to play a couple of games at the end of the season for Novarra but he was a long way short of full fitness. During the summer of 1998, at the end of the season with Novarra, he received an offer to play for a club in Malta. He does not even remember now which club. All he recalls is that he was not interested. And so, at the age of 29, Ettore's football career was pretty much over. Partly through habit and partly because he could not think of anything else to do, he agreed to play for another Serie C2 club, Fiorenzuola, near Piacenza, again in the north, for the 1998–9 season. By now, though, thanks to his knee, he was a part-time footballer. He could only train twice a week, on a Tuesday and a Friday, because if he pushed it any more than that, his left knee would swell up 'like a melon'.

'I still played well on the Sunday,' he says, 'but then experience and 15 years of coaching help you to get by when you are playing at that lower level ... At the end of that season, though, I knew I had come to the end. Either I do it well or I give up, and so I gave up.'

At the age of 30, like a lot of footballers before him, he now had to invent a life for himself. Given his relatively low-profile career, options such as being hired by major Serie A or Serie B clubs were out.

Four years later, at the age of 34, even Batistuta had to bow to the inevitable, slipping out of Italian football for a brief career coda in the tranquil and well-paid surrounds of Qatar in the Middle East. His final seasons in Serie A had been marked by a sharp decline. He still scored six goals in each of those two seasons but, by his standards (he once scored 26 goals for Fiorentina), he was a long way short of his best.

Such was his immense class, however, that at the age of 31 and with huge mileage up on the clock (he was always a very physical player), Batistuta was still able to make the difference when he moved to Roma from Fiorentina in the summer of 2000. Playing brilliantly well for the first half of that season until injury problems slowed him down, he scored 20 goals and was a key factor in Roma's title-winning year. (Remember, that title win marked only one of two seasons since 1992 when either AC Milan or Juventus have not won the title. The other season had been the previous year when Sven-Göran Eriksson's Lazio had lifted the trophy.)

For Batistuta, as for Ettore and every other footballer, age and the physical stresses and strains eventually caught up with him. He finally and definitively retired in the summer of 2005, returning to Florence in January 2006 to be presented by Mayor

Leonardo Domenici with the keys of the city as a mark of respect (he had played for the Florence club for nine seasons). Batistuta, too, had a sound commercial reason for returning to his favourite hunting ground since he was also there to present a fashion show of clothes bearing his name and the logo 'GB', designed by the Chinese stylist Xu Qiu Lin for the fashion house Giupel of Prato. 'I'm not a fashion designer, I just give my approval to the designs. I've retired from football and I've got to concentrate on other objectives,' commented Batistuta.

In the summer of 1999, Ettore, too, had had to concentrate on other objectives, but without quite the same range of options open to him as those available to a world-famous star like Batistuta. Fortunately for Ettore, a couple of friends had invited him to play golf a couple of years earlier. He was a complete beginner but enjoyed the experience. Varese has a splendid golf club, not far from his home, sited in the renovated and handsome grounds of a twelfth-century monastery, complete with cloisters. Ettore soon became a regular player. In time, he developed the idea that he could work towards a career in golf, a relatively late-developing sport in Italy where there might be space to carve out a future.

Football, for him, now belongs to the past. He rarely watches matches on television and never goes to the stadium. When I met him in October 2005 for an interview, to talk through his career, it was just after Italy had qualified for the 2006 World Cup finals by beating Slovenia 1–0 in a qualifier played in Palermo. Ettore had not even bothered to watch it.

These days, his life is focused on a career in golf. He considers himself relatively lucky. By lower-division standards, he earned well for a number of years and was able to contribute to a players' pension fund. With his wife, Alessia, and two small children, Adrianna and Ilaria, he still lives in Varese, in a family complex, with other members of the extended family sharing the condominium.

He came through the dark night of 'life after football' and got out the other side, thinking positively. Football has left him a legacy of hopeful intensity that went sour, a feeling that he never quite got a fair rub of the green. It has also left him the legacy of a left knee that may one day require replacement surgery in order to avoid chronic arthritis. For all that, Ettore bears football no grudges.

'At first I missed football a lot, it was very hard ... but those days are behind me now. These days, I don't even watch football; I'd prefer to watch a game of basketball ... Bit by bit, I've let go of football. You can't go on for the next 50 years thinking about those sort of things ...

'I like to coach the kids at Verbana but the professional football world, I simply don't want to know about it any more ... Even when I go to watch the kids play, I stand on the sidelines and keep away from the dressing room, well clear of all those tensions ... The idea of never playing football again costs me nothing, but if you told me that I couldn't play golf, that would be bad ...'

Still, when Ettore looks back at his football career, he can always tell his grandchildren that he once played in Serie A – and against the great Batistuta, too. He can gloss over the seven minutes detail ...

NINE
JUVENTUS ON TRIAL

JUDGE GIUSEPPE CASALBORE: Tell me, do you remember this business about the ten pills, about which you have already spoken?

ALESSANDRO DEL PIERO, JUVENTUS PLAYER: Yes.

JUDGE: Just before the 1998 Champions League final?

DEL PIERO: Yes.

JUDGE: And what do you remember about it?

DEL PIERO: That they were vitamin pills that would help us recover and recuperate from the strains of a season that had been very tough for us since we had gone all the way in both the league championship [Serie A] and in the Champions League.

JUDGE: You are on the [court] record as having declared, 'That year in May' – this statement was made in 1998 – '20 days before the Champions League final, the team doctor advised us to take pills. I think they were Enervit pills, containing vitamins, carbohydrates and maybe amino acids. They were a little packet of ten pills that we had to take in the morning. The pills were all different. We were told to take them every second day, according to the doctor's instructions, although each of us dealt with them according to his own physical condition. The doctor also told us that in the last few days we were not to take two particular pills that we could tell from the others because of their colour. One of them was yellow, I

don't remember what colour the other was.' Do you confirm
that you said this?

DEL PIERO: Yes.

JUDGE: What does it mean, 'in the last few days we were not to
take two particular pills that we could tell from the others
because of their colour. One of them was yellow'?

DEL PIERO: I think because at the end of the treatment, we
didn't need those particular vitamins any more. That's what
I think, anyway. I'm not 100 per cent sure of the reason.

JUDGE: Tell me, that year you were also in the Italian national
team, is that not so?

DEL PIERO: Yes.

JUDGE: At the World Cup finals [France '98]?

DEL PIERO: Yes.

JUDGE: Did you ever have occasion to take those pills in the
Italian national team?

DEL PIERO: Yes.

Testimony, Tribunale di Torino, 21 July 2003

JUDGE: How often did you have recourse to this intravenous
drip of Esafosfina? Once a month? Once a week?

GIANLUCA VIALLI, FORMER JUVENTUS PLAYER:
Probably once a month. There was a period when we were
playing on Sunday, then on Wednesday and then again on the
following Sunday, and I felt that I needed something that
would help me recover and absorb all the toxins, so I took it,
but I didn't make a habit of it; it was an occasional thing and
it depended on the particular moment of the season.

JUDGE: Did you make much use of anti-inflammatory
products?

VIALLI: Well, let's say I used them.

JUDGE: What did you use? Voltaren?

VIALLI: Voltaren, yes. Sometimes before a match, I'd get an

Sergio Cragnotti's fortune plus Sven-Göran Eriksson's coaching skills equalled Lazio success. But when poor Lazio results followed the announcement that Eriksson would leave to coach England, pressure from both the Italian and British media forced Eriksson's resignation.

The proliferation of TV channels in the Berlusconi era has not always helped the quality of the programmes – a slightly bemused Giovanni Trapattoni seems a little out of place among 2003 Miss Italy contestants.

In the summer of 2005, the Italian league's Disciplinary Commission found Genoa owner Enrico Preziosi (left) guilty of having paid €250,000 to Venezia sports director, Giuseppe Pagliara (below) so that Venezia would 'throw' their Serie B game 3–2, thus ensuring Serie A promotion for Genoa.

Angry Genoa fans demonstrate after the match-fixing verdict, which saw Italy's oldest club demoted to Serie C and handed a points penalty.

© EMPICS

Juventus team doctor Riccardo Agricola (left of picture) celebrates with his lawyer after his conviction for administering banned substances to Juventus players was overturned in 2005.

Juve's Alessandro Del Piero gives evidence in the original trial, in a scandal that began with comments in the media about the 'muscular explosion of certain Juventus players'.

The famous and the not-so-famous: Roma's Francesco Totti marries showgirl Ilary Blasi in 2005 (above); Paolo Di Canio's widely condemned 'Fascist' salute to Lazio fans, which saw Di Canio – an unrepentant admirer of Mussolini – banned in 2005 (below); Ettore Gandini, whose ten-year professional career as a goalkeeper resulted in just seven minutes in Serie A for Reggiana (right).

True fanatics: A car carrying some of Italy's national team is attacked by supporters who expected their players to bring home the 1966 World Cup.

A living legend of Italian football, Dino Zoff brought home the World Cup in 1982 as captain (left) and nearly took Italy all the way in Euro 2000 as coach (right), but quit following an astonishing personal attack by premier Berlusconi after the defeat.

The weight of expectation is too heavy for Roberto Baggio as his miss sees Italy lose to Brazil on penalties in the 1994 World Cup final.

© EMPICS

© GETTY IMAGES

Fans gather by a big screen at the Piazza del Popolo in Rome to watch Italy's 2002 World Cup clash with South Korea, which ended in defeat and yet more disappointment and recriminations at home.

© GETTY IMAGES

© EMPICS

Again, expectations are high as Italy coach Trapattoni faces another barrage of media speculation at Euro 2004 (above), while the tifosi soak up the atmosphere in Portugal (left).

The ugly sight of banners displayed by the Fascist and Nazi supporters at Livorno, and still endemic in Italian football (right) – Fans display flags of Mussolini and make Nazi salutes (below).

Inter Milan ultras lighting flares, just one of the tactics hardline fans employ to create an intimidating atmosphere.

Roma and Lazio captains Totti and Mihajlovic in discussion with an official after ultras invaded the pitch during a 2004 Rome derby and appeared to threaten Totti, leading to the match being abandoned.

Referee Anders Frisk called it a day as a result of this coin-throwing incident in Roma's Champions League tie with Dynamo Kiev.

injection of Voltaren and I'd take it with something that helps your stomach absorb the anti-inflammatory.

JUDGE: Like a protection for the stomach?

VIALLI: Yes.

JUDGE: What did you use? Mepral?

VIALLI: No, I used Maalox.

JUDGE: And how come you made such ample use of Voltaren?

VIALLI: I used Voltaren because when I had a little problem, a little pain, something that I knew wasn't serious, I preferred to play without having to think about it and, in that sense, Voltaren helped me play through the pain so that I could take to the pitch without any problems.

JUDGE: For …

VIALLI: No, it's like this. There comes a moment maybe when your ankles give you problems, that sort of thing, not serious but from the mental viewpoint they can interfere with your performance, so every now and again before a game …

JUDGE: In other words, the very thought that you might be in pain, you say, could condition your performance? What exactly would it do to you?

VIALLI: It could be a distraction, the idea that I might have some small problem that would stop me concentrating on the match.

Testimony, Tribunale di Torino, 17 October 2003

JUDGE: Did you also use intravenous drips?

ZINEDINE ZIDANE, FORMER JUVENTUS PLAYER: Yes.

JUDGE: You did intravenous drips, but drips of just vitamins?

ZIDANE: Yes, just vitamins.

JUDGE: Just vitamins, nothing else? But, what are you smiling about? … When did you take it? I mean, if you were taking an intravenous drip, when did you do it?

ZIDANE: I took it, the drip, before the match.

JUDGE: Before the match, and how often did you take it, do you remember?

ZIDANE: As I've said, that depended on the number of games we were playing.

JUDGE: You mean, when you were feeling tired?

ZIDANE: Yes, if we were playing three times in the week, I would take it …

JUDGE: You would take it, and if you weren't playing three times per week, you didn't take it? …

PUBLICO MINISTERO, STATE ATTORNEY FOR THE PROSECUTION: Tell me something, how can you say and how can you know that there were only vitamins in the drip?

ZIDANE: Because when you're in a big club like this … with the team doctor who tells you …

PUBLICO MINISTERO: One thing that you said earlier really struck me. When you gave evidence [at the preliminary inquiry] you said, 'The drips are useful for us, otherwise how would we manage to play 70 games per year?'

ZIDANE: Yes.

PUBLICO MINISTERO: What does that mean?

ZIDANE: Only that we need vitamins to play 70 games per year.

Testimony, Tribunale di Torino, 26 February 2004

The above extracts of testimony, given by three of the best-known footballers of the last decade, come from transcripts of the so-called *Processo Juve,* or Juventus trial, in Turin.[11] In November 2004, at the end of a trial that had lasted nearly three years, the Juventus team doctor, Dr Riccardo Agricola, was given a 22-month suspended sentence for sporting fraud. Just over a year later, that sentence was reversed in a Turin Court of Appeal, which acquitted Dr Agricola.

It might seem perverse to hark back on a trial that ended in an acquittal. Yet, the eight-year saga of investigation and two subsequent trials merit serious consideration if only because they represent a rarity in modern jurisprudence. Namely, that this was the first time a top-level European football club was hauled before the State judiciary and asked to explain its modus operandi, especially with regard to medical practices. The trial provided a remarkable insight into the workings of a modern club, in some senses prompting more questions than answers.

Juventus are an institution in Italian football. In recent years, only Berlusconi's AC Milan has been able to match their remarkable strike rate. The most successful side in Italian football with 28 league titles (six in eleven years since 1994) and finalists in four out of ten Champions League finals between 1996 and 2005, Juventus are a team of awesome effectiveness, industrial efficiency and usually gracious style, both on and off the pitch.

Many of the world's greatest players, such as Welshman John Charles, Argentine Omar Sivori, and Frenchmen Michel Platini and Zinedine Zidane, have donned their famous black and white shirts. When Italy last won the World Cup in 1982, six of the eleven players who started the final were Juventus players.

As someone who has been a regular visitor to the club over the years and who has always admired its sheer professionalism, I found it bewildering even to consider the idea that a four-year period of success between 1994 and 1998 might owe something to illegal substances. Everything about Juventus implies tradition, high standards and a seriously professional, no-frills attitude, as if reflecting the club's northern European, hardworking industrial ethic.

Founded in 1897 by a motley crew of Turin, English and Swiss youngsters, Juventus took its name from the Latin word for youth. The original club strip was a splendid pink shirt, complete with cap and tie. In time, though, the pink shirt was considered too female a colour. Legend has it that one of the club's English players, John Savage from Nottingham, disgusted with the pink, sent back to his native city for some 'real' sports shirts. Savage, however, apparently forgot to specify the colours he required and, in the end, his suppliers in Nottingham sent him the Notts County black and white strip, which is still used to this day.

Juventus first made waves when winning the 1905 league title, ending a Genoa run which had seen the Ligurian club win six of the first seven Italian championships. Popular myth suggests that Juventus 1905 was a side of poets, painters, clerks and factory workers. In those days, football goal posts did not have nets attached and the Juve goalkeeper, a certain Luigi Durante, used to make much of this by protesting vigorously whenever a goal was awarded against him. Durante, apparently, would argue that the ball had not really passed between the posts and then he would run across to the small collection of spectators and dramatically declare: 'I appeal to the people.'

It was an otherwise unremarkable Juventus left-back called Antion Bruna who, allegedly, re-shaped the club's destiny. Bruna was a factory worker at automobile giant Fiat who, in 1924, got into an argument with the factory foreman because he wanted time off to train with the team. The argument rebounded all the way up to Giovanni Agnelli himself, the man who had founded Fiat in July 1899.

Agnelli senior not only decided that football was a good thing, allowing Bruna to take time off, but he also encouraged his son Edoardo to take a direct interest in club affairs. From that year to the present day, a member of the Agnelli family has been involved in the running of the club, which, for most of that time, has been owned either by Istituto Finanzaria Industriale (IFI), the Agnelli family holding company, or by Fiat itself. Even today, when Juventus is a publicly quoted club, the Agnelli family retain a 60 per cent majority shareholding via IFI.

If Fiat was the flagship for Italian industry for much of the last century, so too was Juventus a standard-bearer for Italian football. Like Barcelona in Catalonia, Manchester United in England or Real Madrid in Spain, Juventus is much more than just a football club. To suggest that Juventus had been systematically cheating was not only mindboggling, it was also to tilt your lance at a very imposing windmill.

The Juventus trial concerned a remarkably successful four-year period between 1994 and 1998, during which the club had won three league titles (1995, 1997, 1998), one Champions League title (1996), one Intercontinental Cup (1996), and one Italian Cup (1995). In those same four years, they also reached two other Champions League finals (1997 and 1998) as well as a UEFA Cup final (1995). Not bad going. Coached by the current Italy coach, Marcello Lippi, the side distinguished itself by the quality of its aggressive, tough, hard-running and intelligent football.

The complex case first began back in the summer of 1998, the year when the ill-fated Italian cyclist Marco Pantani (he died of a cocaine overdose in February 2004) had just won a controversial stage of the Tour de France. That Tour, of course, had been sullied by the 'Festina Affair', a doping scandal related to the Festina team, which saw team managers, doctors and cyclists arrested by French magistrates for trafficking in illegal substances.

In late July, in an interview with Rome-based daily *Il Messaggero*, the then AS Roma coach, Czech Zdenek Zeman, commented: 'Football is changing, and for the worse, I'd say ... I just wish football would get out of the chemist's laboratory ond out of the financial controller's office and just remain a sport and fun ... But football is every day more an industry and every day less a game.'

The taciturn Zeman is a man who uses three words where three hundred might be required. At the age of 21, with the Soviet tanks about to roll into his native Prague, he had made his bid for freedom, helped by his uncle, Cestmir Vycpalek, a former successful coach to, ironically, Juventus, but who was then living in Palermo, Sicily. His first job in Italy had been as coach to the Under-12 team of local club Palermo, a job that paid less than 40 cents per coaching session.

From the Under-12s, Zeman worked his way up the greasy pole, starting off in professional football with Serie C side Licata in the 1983–4 season. From there, his career had been on a constant upward curve. He had done especially well with little Foggia, taking them into Serie A in the 1991–2 season. After that, he had gone on to coach both Rome clubs, first Lazio and then Roma.

I had met him a number of times during his Lazio and Roma days. He had always struck me as a cool customer and an intelligent coach. He certainly did not seem the sort of guy who would opt for the 'whistleblower' role just for a bit of cheap publicity.

In early August, in an interview with Italian news weekly *L'Espresso*, Zeman expanded on his earlier remarks, suggesting that pharmaceutical malpractice was widespread in Italian football:

The problem is that players are motivated by short-term considerations and do not worry much about their health. Then, too, club directors think only of exploiting them to the full, without being remotely subtle about it … I get the impression that recently things have got out of hand. Players are under ever greater pressure and it gets harder and harder for them to resist the temptation of the magic little pill … I'm sure that many players in Serie A, probably even in my own Roma side, have difficulty giving up on certain substances.

Zeman did not say it, but his words seemed to imply that some Italian footballers were making a systematic use of illegal products, perhaps amphetamines, cortisone-related drugs, anabolic steriods, even EPO (Erythropoietin, a glycoprotein hormone which increases the oxygen-carrying capacity of the blood). Furthermore, he suggested, there might be long-term health implications related to the use of multi-vitamin cocktails, so-called 'restoratives', such as creatine.

Why was nobody confronting the issue of doping in football? *L'Espresso* journalist Gianni Perrelli asked Zeman. He replied:

> Because football is too big a business and it suits everyone's interests not to look too closely at the negative aspects. I'll cite one emblematic example. People were talking about Maradona's drug problems when he was bought from Barcelona [in July 1984] ... Yet, I'd like to point out that if people had not looked the other way, if someone had tried to deal with his drug addiction, Maradona could have been saved from his squalid decline and fall. But, at this stage, business considerations dominate everything. Football is controlled by the world of high finance, as well as by pharmaceutical products.

At one point in the interview, Zeman was asked specifically about Juventus. Was it not true that on many occasions he had expressed his 'surprise' about the 'muscular explosion of certain Juventus players'? 'My amazement starts with Gianluca Vialli and goes all the way to Alessandro Del Piero,' he responded.

Zeman's comments inevitably signalled the start of a media Blitzkrieg with both Del Piero and Vialli emphatically denying any malpractice, arguing that their physical progress was the fruit of intensive and specialised training methods. A spokesman for

Del Piero spoke of the 'unacceptable damage' to his reputation, while Vialli branded Zeman a 'terrorist'.

In the meantime, Juventus chose to reply to the apparent allegations about the two players. At a news conference in Turin, Dr Agricola, the club's chief medical officer, denied that his players took performance-enhancing drugs but admitted openly that they used legal 'restoratives' to recoup energy, adding: 'Confusion breeds ignorance ... Restoratives – that is to say, amino acids, creatine, vitamins, mineral salts and water – are legal and, indeed, it woud be a crime not to use them because the body needs to regain equilibrium after heavy exercise.' Juventus president, the late Vittorio Chiusano, then confirmed that Juventus would be suing Zeman for what he described as an 'underhand and ambiguous form of defamation which cannot be tolerated'.

Zeman was summoned to appear before the anti-doping panel of CONI, the overall authority for all Italian sport. After his hearing, he told journalists: 'There are some substances that are considered doping and others that are not, even though they maybe should be because they enhance performance. If a player is given creatine because he's injured and because he needs it, that's one thing. If it's given to a player who clearly does not need it, that's another.'

The case might have ended there were it not for the intervention of a Turin-based public prosecutor, Raffaele Guariniello. Investigative reporter Marco Travaglio happened to be in the office of the prosecutor in the Pretura di Torino on the morning of 8 August when he was intrigued to find a copy of *L'Espresso* on the desk. Just professional curiosity, replied Guariniello, when asked if he was thinking of opening an investigation.

The next day, however, a policeman turned up at Roma's training ground Trigoria, close to Rome, with an 'invitation' for Zeman to present himself in Guariniello's office on 12

August. Thus began what is undoubtedly the most serious judicial investigation of modern times into alleged doping practices in Italian football.

Zeman was just the first of a Who's Who of international football to give evidence to Guariniello. Coaches, club doctors, club directors and, above all, Juventus players past and present were soon 'invited' to his office. First up was Del Piero on 14 August, followed three days later by Vialli. Over the following weeks other players, including Roberto Baggio, Didier Deschamps, Zinedine Zidane, Paolo Montero and Fabrizio Ravanelli, were called to give evidence. When the Juventus case finally came to trial, no less than 18 Juventus players testified in court.

Guariniello's next move was to send health inspectors to 'requisition' the Juventus 'medicine cabinet' at the Stadio Comunale in Turin as well as to seize the club's medical records. The search revealed a well-stocked arsenal of no less than 281 medicinal products. In his '*motivazioni*' (the Judge's written explanation for his November 2004 verdict, made public in February 2005), Judge Casalbore was to write: 'The State Attorney's consultant has suggested that, in truth, 281 medicinal specialities of various type and nature, like those kept by Juventus, represent the normal stock of a small-sized hospital.'

Following a lead, Guariniello then extended his inquiry to CONI's dope-testing laboratory at Acqua Acetosa in Rome, where footballers' samples were tested. It transpired that tests were carried out in a chaotic manner, if at all. Steroids were looked for in only 20 per cent of tests and diuretics in only 5 per cent of tests. (Diuretics can be used to mask steroids.) In late September, *La Repubblica* reported the following testimony given to the Guariniello inquiry by an unnamed CONI employee:

Often it is the very doctors who are collecting the urine sample who themselves pee into the test tubes of players 'at risk', and they do so at the request of the club in question. Of course, everything then disappears afterwards. If you looked into it in depth, you'd discover that the urine samples didn't come from any player at all but rather from the usual four or five obliging doctors.

Another unnamed laboratory technician allegedly told investigators that on those occasions when tests had proved positive (be it for amphetamines, steroids or cocaine, for example), they were simply '*insabbatti*' (buried in sand). The technicians also suggested that often samples taken from players arrived at the lab in a condition which made them unusable – sometimes, it had been conveniently forgotten to seal them properly, or to conserve them at the right temperature.

By early October 1998, the head of the Acqua Acetosa lab, Dr Emilio Gasbarrone, had been sacked, CONI president Mario Pescante had resigned and the IOC (International Olympic Committee) had been forced to revoke the Acqua Acetosa's testing licence, given its manifest operational incompetence. (The licence was restored by the IOC one year later in October 1999.) There was clearly plenty of smoke about now, but was there real fire, in the sense of systematic doping in Italian football?

In December of that year, I went out to Trigoria, the Roma training ground, with an ESPN crew to interview Roma players and coach Zeman. Given all that had happened in the wake of Zeman's original interview in *L'Espresso*, I was less than convinced that he might want to again talk about the matter of doping, especially on camera. Sitting by the Trigoria swimming pool alongside the clubhouse, Zeman, however, had no problems explaining his views. 'I give a lot of interviews and I've given a lot about doping, but I don't mind giving another one just as long as the question is dealt with seriously,' he said. 'People think that I have found myself ostracised by the football community but the truth is that the vast majority of people in this [football] world are with me on this issue ...

'For me, sport has its own morality. If you want to improve your performance, you do an extra lap of the pitch or an extra circuit in the gym. You don't take a pill and sit in the sun for an hour. That's the morality of sport ... I'm not worried about people who died ten years ago or last year; you can't do anything for them now ... I'm worried about the future, and it seems to me that the time has come for the whole football movement to admit to the problem ... and do something about it.'

After we had finished filming, Zeman offered me a coffee at the clubhouse bar. Over the coffee, I asked him what, in his opinion, was the scale of the phenomenon of doping in professional football. Zeman thought for a while – he is never a man to say anything in a hurry – and then replied: 'I don't know about the size, the dimensions of the problem, but I do know that doping practices have been around for years in sports like athletics, swimming, cycling, weight-lifting and so on. Do you really believe that they haven't moved into football, too?'

In the end, after years of complex investigations, inevitably involving the contrasting opinions of medical experts, the Juventus case came to court on 31 January 2002. In the dock were three people: Juventus managing director Antonio Giraudo, Juventus club doctor Riccardo Agricola, and the Turin-based pharmacist Giovanni Rossano, who was charged with running an illegal pharmacy, in that he had supplied Dr Agricola with medicinal products without the necessary medical prescriptions. Dr Rossano opted to plea bargain rather than go to trial and was given a five-month suspended prison sentence.

Over the following two years, the trial attracted a blaze of publicity as some of the most famous names in football turned up in Turin to give evidence. There was tension in the courtroom, too, with the Juventus defence angrily contesting the findings of the two independent medical experts – Dr Giuseppe D'Onofrio and Professor Eugenio Muller – especially regarding the alleged use of EPO.

On several occasions, Dr Agricola and the Juventus defence lawyers re-affirmed their belief that the club doctor had acted in the best interests of his players, resorting to a variety of medicinal products only to help the players through a 70-match football season that stretched their physical strength and powers of recovery to the limit. Everything had been done above board, all of the contested 'substances' had been declared prior to routine post-match dope tests and, what is more, such practices were commonplace in professional sport. Dr Agricola's recorded testimony on 10 July 2003 reads:

> The issue of pathological exhaustion has to be seen as one
> of the most important aspects of high-level sport, that is,
> a so-called sickness or pathology related to elite sport …
> For example, one of the main symptoms of this so-called
> pathological exhaustion … is a sudden change in mood,
> another is having difficulty getting to sleep even though
> the athlete is very tired. Another symptom is the inability
> to recover from one training session prior to the next in
> the way that physiologically should be possible …
> Certainly, if players are asked to play three times a week
> … and play as well for their national teams, then they run
> the risk of pathological exhaustion.[12]

On more than one occasion, the players themselves appeared to be reluctant witnesses. On 21 July 2003, five Juventus players were called to testify: Alessandro Birindelli, Alessio Tacchinardi, Gianluca Pessotto, Alessandro Del Piero and Antonio Conte.

Frustrated by the apparent evasion, loss of memory and lack of co-operation from the players, Judge Casalbore exclaimed in court: 'The problem here is that we need answers to questions. If all of you come here and sort of talk and then don't talk at all, it's all the more alarming. You don't really think that when you tell us you don't know what your team-mates are doing in the dressing room, we're going to blindly believe you? Come on, you've been together for ten years ...'

In his *motivazioni* (explanation of the verdict, released in February 2005), Casalbore made reference to the players' testimony, calling them 'all inadequate and unreliable' and adding that the State attorney might decide to look into them, presumably with a view to perjury. The Judge describes Del Piero as a 'highly reticent' witness whose testimony was 'highly unlikely'. He calls Gianluca Vialli's testimony 'obscure', adding that Vialli had been 'highly unconvincing about the quantities of creatine' used by Juventus players. He is bitterly ironic about Birindelli, concluding from the player's lack of information about his team-mates' habits that he 'clearly lives a solitary life', adding that all the other players had the same problem.

There were moments, too, of near farce. On 19 December 2003, the club's Uruguayan defender Paolo Montero was called to give evidence. At first, Montero seemed sure of himself, even venturing to say '*Ciao, Dottore*' to Dr Agricola during his testimony, prompting the Judge to reprimand him: 'You will answer to me, Montero. This isn't some sort of happy little get-together.'

Later in that same session, however, Montero seemed in difficulty, eventually telling the Judge that he could not remember anything and that he had been upset by all the people gathered in the courtroom. Eventually, Judge Casalbore agreed to hear Montero's evidence another day, adding 'or otherwise I would have to conclude that you are refusing to answer'.

At the heart of the prosecution's case against Giraudo and

Agricola were two fundamental accusations – the use of perform-ance-enhancing drugs, such as EPO, and the 'off-label' use of other drugs to make them performance-enhancing. 'Off label' use refers to the dispensing of specialised medical products such as Samyr (an anti-depressant), Neoton (used for heart patients) and Liposom Forte (used, among other things, for patients recovering from operations such as brain surgery). Why give such medicines to the Juventus players, who, presumably, were not depressed and had not undergone recent heart or brain surgery? Were they not administered in order to have a performance-enhancing effect? In the conclusions to his *motivazioni* Judge Casalbore gave his answers:

> … With regard to EPO and to all the other medicines and substances already mentioned, there is the proof in the judicial acts that the defendant used them in a fraudulent way in order to modify the players' athletic performance and consequently the result of the sporting competition …
>
> Dr Agricola has dispensed medicines and substances – some of them, as we have seen, freely usable, others to be used only in certain circumstances and others again totally prohibited – not for therapeutic reasons, nor because they were necessary for the players' health, but because in this way, and only in this way, could he achieve the result of fraudulently, and not physiologically, improving the players' athletic performances … There is the full and certain proof that EPO was administered to the players.[13]

Earlier, the Judge had examined the question of EPO in detail, commenting: '… Professor D'Onofrio's investigation has led to the discovery of a, so to speak, chronic use of EPO based on infor-mation relative to all or nearly all of the players in consideration.'

For the record, 'the players in consideration' were Antonio Conte, Didier Deschamps, Angelo Di Livio, Ciro Ferrara, Gianluca Pessotto, Alessio Tacchinardi, Moreno Torricelli, Michele Padovano, Fabio Pecchia, Angelo Peruzzi, Dimas, Mark Iuliano, Paolo Montero, Gianluca Vialli and Zinedine Zidane.

With regard to the 'vitamin' pills taken by the players prior to the Champions League final of 1998 and discussed by Del Piero in his testimony, Judge Casalbore links them to two people: the Dutchman Henk Kraajenhof and Spanish-based Argentine doctor Guillermo Laich, both professional collaborators with Juventus for a brief period in 1998. The Judge notes that Dr Laich had in the past been linked to 'episodes involving Diego Maradona', adding that he was best known for his ability to dispense 'stimulants that could not be traced in routine dope tests'.

With regard to the use of Esafosfina, admitted by Vialli in his testimony, Judge Casalbore concludes by quoting Professor Muller's analysis: 'The only reason for administering Esafosfina, generally given before a game and exclusively by an intravenous drip, was to achieve "a co-related effect in the biogenic role which the fruit sugar 1.6 dyo-phosphate plays in the process of releasing energy usable for motor movement".'

The Judge found Agricola guilty, but managing director Giraudo was acquitted because, wrote Casalbore, 'of the lack of full and direct proof against him'. Casalbore did, however, write that it was hard to believe Dr Agricola had acted on his own, adding that in a club where any expenditure of over €50 had to be documented by employees, it was inconceivable that Giraudo was unaware, not just of the sums of money being spent on medicines but also of the use being made of them. (In his summing-up at the Appeal in November 2005, prosecutor Guariniello made the same point when pointing out that expenditure on medical items had risen from approximately €10,000 in 1992 to around €51,000 in 1995.) Casalbore also ruminated on the fact that the Juventus administrative team – Giraudo, Lippi and Agricola – were part of a Juventus 'new wave' that took over in 1994 and which might have felt themselves under huge pressure to deliver results.

Inevitably, immediate reaction to the court's judgement on that November 2004 day was wildly contrasting, with both prosecution and defence claiming a victory of sorts. Both Giraudo and the Juventus legal team immediately expressed their belief that Giraudo's acquittal would lead to the eventual acquittal of Dr Agricola on appeal. Senior defence lawyer Luigi Chiappero put it this way: 'I'm satisfied that Giraudo has been acquitted … but we will continue to fight to clear Dr Agricola's name, certain of our just case … We will now take this to the Court of Appeal where there are three judges, and let's hope that six eyes see better than two. The fact that Giraudo was acquitted underlines the weakness of the prosecution's case because if it was really true that the club has resorted to doping, then it is unthinkable that everyone [in the club] didn't know about it.'

Underlining the Juventus view of the court judgment was the fact that the club confirmed Dr Agricola in his role of club doctor, a position he still holds at the time of going to press.

Investigating magistrate Guariniello, the man who prepared the whole case and who, ironically, considers himself a Juventus supporter, had a rather different interpretation of the sentence: 'The conviction speaks for itself. All you have to do is read the formal charges of which Dr Agricola has been found guilty. The charges speak of, among other things, "the systematic administration of medicines intended to stimulate the eritroproiesis process, i.e. EPO" to the Juventus players. It's absolutely clear, there's nothing to add. If, in the meantime, certain people have lost their sense of reality, well, so be it. The important thing is that the sentence upholds the prosecution's accusations. The law does not exist only on paper but must also be respected and enforced.'

Dr Agricola, inevitably, was highly critical of the verdict, commenting: 'I have been used and sliced up like a human guinea pig ... The writing has been on the wall for three or four years now and it simply wasn't possible, given the protagonism of certain judicial quarters, that I would be acquitted.'

Inevitably, too, FIGC and CONI were cautious. Both bodies immediately issued statements reserving the right to inform the relevant international sports bodies such as UEFA, FIFA, the IOC and WADA (World Anti-Doping Agency) of the court's ruling but only after they had fully evaluated the *motivazioni*. Reading between the lines, though, it was clear that FIGC was reluctant to act while the Juventus case was still going through the State judicial process (as the club had taken the case to the Court of Appeal).

In theory, FIGC's disciplinary body could have intervened immediately, putting Juventus on trial again (in the form of a sports body trial) with the threat of sanctions that could even include not admitting Juventus to the Serie A championship as well as stripping them of the relevant league titles. In practice, FIGC has taken no action so far.

In contrast, CONI did intervene. Having consulted the Lausanne-based CAS (Court of Arbitration for Sport) in April 2005, CONI's anti-doping authority asked for Dr Agricola to be tried before FIGC's disciplinary commission, calling for a two-year suspension. The disciplinary commission, however, preferred to await the outcome of the Appeal before taking any action.

Not everyone was quite so circumspect. Green Party senator Fiorello Cortiana, the man who framed Italy's current anti-doping legislation, commented: 'I hope this conviction calls a halt to the arrogance of those who have opted for a pharmacological shortcut. But I have to say I am also amazed because, unless you are a total hypocrite, it is simply not credible to imagine that Juventus and its club directors did not know about the fraudulent acts of its team doctor ...'

Another outspoken reaction came from Dick Pound, head of WADA, who told *La Repubblica*:

> There are few innocents in this story. The players knew and so too did the club directors ... 281 substances in the medicine cabinet – what was it, a football team or a first aid station? I still believe that whoever plays a sport is in good health ... All of Juventus should be punished. What they did was not accidental, but deliberate and planned. The players didn't know? Who believes that? And don't try and tell me that it was all the fault of a looney doctor. Juventus committed a fraud and they gained by that fraud – in fame, money and publicity ... Not only should they be stripped of their titles, they should hand back the sums of money they won illegally ... I hope that CONI and FIGC are considering sending out a strong signal, a sort of warning ...

Needless to say, there was huge media curiosity as to just how the original whistleblower Zeman would react to the judgment. Three months later, on the day after the *motivazioni* was released, Zeman told *Corriere Della Sera*:

> The Tribunale di Torino, even if this is a first level sentence, has opened up a case that should now go before the sports' judicial authorities. It's obvious that a lot of people, starting with the players, have lied. I feel genuinely sorry for them, they don't know the risks they are taking ... What is the worth of all the things that Juventus won in those four years, 1994 to 1998? When an Olympic champion tests positive, he or she has to hand back the medal. Whoever cheats in football should hand back their titles.

I'd also like to know what the Order of Sports Doctors thinks about Dr Agricola. He gave players EPO, he violated every code going, and yet he's still the Juventus club doctor ...

When Lippi was appointed coach to the Italian national team, I said that if I had been in FIGC's place, I would have waited for this trial to finish before appointing him. All the more so now. I say that someone else should take over from him. I think it would be right if Lippi were to resign.

Marcello Lippi, for his part, had been typically defiant in his defence of his former players and club. In a tense head-to-head on television with Zeman in November 2004, on the Sunday after the original verdict, he told viewers: 'This sentence doesn't change my admiration for and appreciation of all those people, players, directors, medical personnel and others, who worked with me at Juventus. Many of these guys are still at Juventus and they're still winning. Others, players like Di Livio, Torricelli, Ravanelli and Carrera, even when they moved on to other clubs, they were always held up as examples by their coaches as model players, for their serious, professional attitude. That's why my Juventus won a lot, that side had an extraordinary mental and moral strength ...'

That TV confrontation – Lippi in one studio and Zeman (then coach of Lecce) in another – inevitably became heated, with Lippi suggesting that Zeman himself had used substances, such as the restorative creatine, to improve his players' performances. Yes, we did, replied Zeman, at Lazio (one of his former clubs), but only for a month and only at a dosage of three grams per day, not the 20 grams that Juventus used. As the brief televisual exchange concluded, Lippi invited Zeman to 'get out of football' if he wanted to criticise it. No, no, replied Zeman, 'you can be part of the system because you want to improve it, to make it cleaner'.

There is a widely held belief that Zeman's stand on doping and his full-frontal attack on Juventus have cost him dear. When he made that attack, he was coach of one of the country's biggest clubs, AS Roma. Since then, his career has taken him to Fenerbahce, Napoli, Salernitana, Avellino and Lecce (in that order). Of these five clubs, only Fenerbahce in Istanbul (where he remained for only three months) could be described as top flight, whilst of the other four Italian clubs, only Lecce were actually playing in Serie A when Zeman coached them.

In a country where the conspiracy theory is a national obsession, the idea that Zeman's apparent attack on the football 'system' has damaged his career prospects is all too credible. Yet, Serie A players I have talked to, including those who have worked with Zeman and hold him in high esteem, say that this is not the case. If he has not had a big club since his Roma and Lazio days, it is because of his results (or lack of) and not because of anything else.

That may be the case, yet, to my eyes at least, he did a great job with Lecce in the 2004–5 season and still got the heave-ho. There is no doubt that his career took a downward curve from the moment of his infamous 'J'Accuse'. At the time he seemed to be doing a good job at Roma but at the end of the 1998–9 season, to the surprise of many, he and the club parted company. Certainly, Zeman himself appears to believe that his stance has cost him. In *Corriere Della Sera* in December 2005 he was quoted as saying: 'It seems that he [Giraudo] is very keen for me to have plenty of free time. For 30 years, I worked constantly, now I'm no longer coaching, and I think that is much more attributable to his strengths than to my weaknesses.' (Since then, Zeman has, in fact, returned to coaching, having been appointed to Serie B side Brescia in early March 2006).

Another obvious reflection concerns Marcello Lippi, now the Italian national team coach. Tough, talented, intelligent and dynamic, Lippi is clearly one of the outstanding coachs in world football today. Inevitably, such a man will view as a direct personal offence the suggestion that the club he trained owed their success to 'pharmaceutical help'. It must also be pointed out that prior to taking over at Juventus in 1994, Lippi had done well with two much weaker sides, Atalanta and Napoli. Furthermore, since taking over the Italian national team, Lippi has again underlined his considerable abilities by forming a *gruppo* that may lack the quality of some previous Italian teams but which is certainly competitive.

When Juventus won its Appeal in December 2005, the judgment was greeted with relief and jubilation, and not just by the club itself. *Gazzetta Dello Sport* gave it full front-page treatment with a headling declaring: JUVE ARE CLEAN. To be fair to *Gazzetta*, they had given the same treatment to the first 'guilty' verdict, one year earlier. Needless to say, the Juventus reaction was euphoric with managing director Giraudo commenting, 'This is a triumph for justice ... For years we've been offended all over the world because of a theory that has now been destroyed, both in legal terms and for its suppositions. We have suffered very serious damage to our image. Who will ever repay us for that? ... In the meantime, Zeman should go and read this verdict.'

Clearly, only the *motivazioni* (not yet released) can tell us just why Court of Appeal Judge Gustavo Witzel chose to differ so radically with his predecessor, Judge Giuseppe Casalbore. It may well be that he felt the 1989 law on sporting fraud, on which Judge Casalbore's sentence depended, simply does not apply to alleged doping practices. It may be, too, that the Court of Appeal did not accept the evidence of the independent medical expert Professor D'Onofrio, who had claimed it was 'almost certain' and 'very probable' that Juventus had used EPO.

Of course, one person not much impressed by the acquittal was Zeman, who commented in a *Corriere Della Sera* article in December 2005:

> Even the Court of Appeal verdict proves that I was right. In 1998, I said that football had to get out of the pharmacy, and if there is one absolute certainty to come out of both these trials, it is that there has been abuse of pharmaceutical products ... I find it sad that Juventus consider themselves clean with 281 different types of pharmaceutical products in their stocks ...
>
> Of course, this trial should never have ended up in a judicial court. Sports disciplinary bodies, which ought to have moral and ethical guidelines that go far beyond the penal code, ought to have looked into the case, investigating not just Juventus but all Italian football at that time ... Instead, they did nothing.

In between the two Juventus trials, another disturbing incident occurred, which again cast a dark light on Italian football.

The incident in question came via an amateur film, shot by now-Juventus, then-Parma defender Fabio Cannavaro on 11 May 1999, on the eve of Parma's UEFA Cup final against French club Olympique Marseilles (which Parma won 3–0). Somehow, a copy of Cannavaro's 'film' found its way to RAI, which then aired it.

The action takes place in Room 712 of the Grand Hotel Marriott in Moscow. For the occasion, Room 712 has been turned into a physiotherapist's clinic with the Parma team doctor, Luca Montagna, and team physiotherapist, Corrado Gatti, both busy helping various players prepare themselves for the following day's final. All of this we are able to see thanks to Cannavaro, who has walked into Room 712 with his own camcorder in hand, filming all that goes before him and, in this case, all that goes into him.

As Cannavaro lies down on the doctor's couch, we see him being attached to an intravenous drip. Furthermore, as Dr Montagna prepares the medicine that will be administered to Cannavaro, we see that it is called Neoton, a product normally used in the treatment of patients with heart problems and one of those which featured in the Juventus trial.

The Parma team doctor carefully places a needle into Cannavaro's left arm and then attaches it to the drip containing the Neoton. Throughout all of this, Cannavaro keeps up his own tongue-in-cheek commentary. 'This is the final proof that we all stink ... Look at how low we've sunk. I'm 25 years old and they're killing me,' he says, in jest, as he turns the camera onto himself.

Clearly, Cannavaro's four-and-a-half-minute-long 'film' was never intended for public viewing. Clearly, too, his running commentary, while in questionable taste, was meant to be a joke.

None of that, however, stopped the footage from becoming a major source of controversy. Remarkably, however, while one or two commentators pointed an accusatory finger at alleged doping practices in football, the vast majority of Italian coaches argued that the whole thing had been blown out of proportion. Many argued that the Neoton had been used as a restorative for tired players at the end of a busy season and with one more big match to face. Many also suggested that such practices were par for the course.

'You see scenes like that in dressing rooms all over the world,' said Palermo coach Francesco Guidolin.

'All teams and clubs use drips, with the agreement of the player, of course,' said Lazio coach Giorgio Papadopulo.

Under WADA regulations, such drips, although legal in 1999, are now banned.

In contrast, however, Zeman continued to ask a simple question: 'Why do healthy young athletes need medicines normally used for heart patients?'

Remarkably, even that question prompted an intriguing answer from one of his most successful colleagues, AC Milan coach Carlo Ancelotti, who said: 'An athlete is not a healthy person, rather one under huge physical stress. Training and playing matches are genuinely stressful and they leave their mark. The thing that surprises me is that accomplished medics fail to understand this. You cannot draw comparisons between a professional footballer and someone out for a run in the park.'

Current Inter Milan player Argentine Juan Veron, then a team-mate of Cannavaro's at Parma, sounded the same note. Veron, who is visible in Room 712 on the film, explained: 'We had just played in the Italian Cup final a couple of days earlier, and then we had the trip to Russia itself, so some players decided to make use of this [Neoton] ... It is something that is used and has been used ... All the teams use it.'

One of the recurrent points made by the Juventus defence, of course, had been that their medical practices were commonplace at the time. Did the Cannavaro film confirm that claim? After all, Parma appeared to be using one of the very same products used by Juventus.

Another aspect of the Juventus case, too, is the fact that magistrate Guariniello's investigation also led him towards other issues not related to Juventus. For a start, he came across at least 70 suspicious deaths of ex-footballers (nearly all Italian), players who had died from Motor Neurone Disease (MND), leukaemia, as well as liver, thyroid and stomach cancers. Many of these deaths concerned players who had played their football in the 1960s and 1970s, but there was also the more recent case of the former Roma and Genoa player Giuseppe Signorini, who died in November 2002 at the age of 42, killed by Amyotrophic Lateral

Sclerosis (ASL), a form of MND sometimes referred to as Lou Gehrig's Disease.

Had all these players died of natural causes, or had they, as many of their loved ones suspect, died prematurely as a result of the substances administered to them during their playing days? Speaking in Rome in the autumn of 2005, the head of Neurological Science at Turin University, Professor Adriano Chiò, claimed that widespread use of anti-inflammatories could have played its part in these ASL cases, but he did also add that other elements, such as the use of herbicides on the pitches and heading the old, heavy leather ball might have contributed, too.

Allegations of doping practices in modern football are, of course, nothing new. As far back as 1954, questions were asked about substances used by that year's World Cup winning West Germany team, substances which allegedly prompted half the squad to suffer serious illness some months later. In 1978, Scotland's Willie Johnston was thrown out of the World Cup finals in Argentina after a positive dope test.

In 1987, the former West German goalkeeper Harald 'Toni' Schumacher published a highly controversial autobiography called *Anpiff*, which graphically details a vast range of alleged improprieties, including substance abuse, by his generation of German footballers. For his troubles, Schumacher was suspended both from the national team and his club, FC Cologne.

In Italy, one of the biggest post-war doping scandals featured the 1964 title winners Bologna. In March 1964, five Bologna players tested positive after a Serie A home game with Torino. FIGC's disciplinary commission immediately suspended the five players, the club coach and the team doctor, while three points were also deducted from Bologna in the Serie A table. After a second analysis of the players' samples proved negative, however, that harsh disciplinary verdict was removed and Bologna went on to finish the season joint top with Inter, before going on to win

the play-off in Rome on 6 June 1964. (Then as now, goal difference does not count in Italian football, and if two sides finish the
season joint top, then the title contest goes to a play-off.)

In more recent times, in the 2000–1 and 2001–2 seasons,
there was a mini-epidemic of Serie A players testing positive for
the anabolic steroid norandrosterone (nandrolone). Among
those to test positive and subsequently suspended (usually only
for four or five months) were some top-flight players such as
Dutchmen Jaap Stam (then with Lazio) and Edgar Davids (then
with Juventus), as well as the former Barcelona playmaker Pep
Guardiola (then with Brescia), Portuguese defender Fernando
Couto (then Lazio) and the French Under-21 international goalkeeper Jean François Gillet (then with Bari).

These suspensions prompted observers like Sandro Donati,
an ex-member of CONI's anti-doping commission and a long-
time campaigner against drug abuse in sport, to tell me that he
felt 'Zeman has been proved right'. In other words, Donati
believes that today's professional footballers, and not just in
Italy, systematically use a whole range of substances, some legal
and some not, which are essentially intended to be performance-
enhancing.

The nandrolone cases also prompted an intriguing, if indica-
tive, reaction from the sports medical community. Meeting at
FIGC's centre in Coverciano, Florence in April 2001, Serie A
and Serie B club doctors proposed that the permitted level of
nandrolone be raised from two to five nanograms per millilitre, a
proposal at odds with the IOC's guidelines.

One month after Juventus was acquitted, yet another alleged
doping scandal broke in European football, this time in France.
This time former Olympique Marseilles player Jean-Jacques
Eydelie was the whistleblower. In an interview with *L'Equipe*, he
claimed that almost every player on the Olympique Marseilles
team that beat AC Milan 1–0 in the 1993 Champions League

final in Munich had received a mysterious injection shortly before the match:

> Before the final, we were asked to stand in line and receive an injection ... Rudi Voeller was the only one to kick up a fuss. He went on yelling at everyone in the changing room ... I had a dry mouth during the game. My body didn't react like it would normally ... Actually, the stuff inhibited me more than anything else. It was the first and last time I agreed to take something.

The interview had come prior to the publication of Eydelie's autobiography, a book that was destined to cast a grim light on French football. For a start, he claimed that all the clubs he played for (with the single exception of Bastia) engaged in doping practices. Secondly, he claimed that 'cheating had become second nature' for that Olympique Marseilles team and that 'nearly all the players were involved in match-fixing'.

It has to be pointed out that Eydelie was not new to controversy. In 1993, he played a key role in an infamous Valenciennes versus Olympique Marseilles match-fixing affair when he secretly gave money to the wife of a Valenciennes player, Christophe Robert, on the eve of a key league clash between Valenciennes and Olympique Marseilles, just six days before that Munich final against Milan. In the end, Olympique Marseilles beat Valenciennes 1–0 to clinch a fifth consecutive French title.

However, the bribery was subsequently revealed by Valenciennes player Jacques Glassman, prompting the French football federation to strip Olympique Marseilles of their league title and demote them to the second division. Furthermore, UEFA banned Olympique Marseilles from representing Europe in that year's Intercontinental final, replacing them with the beaten finalists, Milan.

In the wake of the Eydelie interview, UEFA opened and quickly closed a brief inquiry, explaining that there was no case to investigate for three reasons. Firstly, more than ten years had passed since the alleged offence and therefore the matter would come under the Statute of Limitations. Secondly, dope tests on the night on Barthez and Di Meco for Olympique Marseilles, and Maldini and Albertini for Milan, had proved negative. Thirdly, UEFA rules do not allow for 'collective' but rather only 'individual' sanctions when it comes to doping offences.

Inevitably, Eydelie's comments also prompted angry reactions from those directly involved. For example, Bernard Tapie, at the time chairman of Olympique Marseilles, threatened to sue both Eydelie and *L'Equipe*, arguing that the unemployed Eydelie was trying to use 'blackmail' in order to raise money. Tapie also pointed out that the post-match tests had all returned negative. The controversial Tapie, a former minister under French President François Mitterrand, had been sentenced to eight months' imprisonment for his part in the Valenciennes affair.

That Olympique Marseilles team, coached by Belgian Raymond Goethals, was packed with talented players, including midfielder Didier Deschamps, defender Marcel Desailly, goalkeeper Fabien Barthez, Croat Alen Boksic, Ghanaian Abedi Pele and German Rudi Voeller. Several of the players contradicted Eydelie's story, calling it 'unbelievable'.

Marcel Desailly also denied the accusations, claiming that OM's win was entirely clean and arguing that Eydelie was obviously launched on a PR mission to sell his forthcoming book. The current Olympique Marseilles coach, Jean Fernandez, who worked alongside Goethals at the club in the early 1990s, pointed out that, with that particularly stong squad, there was no need for either match-fixing or dope to win titles.

Not everyone, however, was convinced. Arsenal manager Arsène Wenger, coach to Monaco in the early 1990s, told

L'Equipe that Eydelie's interview confirmed his worst suspicions: 'These were things that people knew, lots of people knew about them, we're talking about the worst period there has ever been for French football. It was completely corrupted from within by Tapie's methods. The things that Eydelie says are in line with what a lot of people think.'

There had, however, been at least one previous mention of the suspect practices at Olympique Marseilles. Writing in *The Times* in December 2003 in the wake of the Rio Ferdinand affair (Manchester United and England defender Rio Ferdinand was banned for eight months for failing to present himself for a spot dope test), Irish international Tony Cascarino described his experience as a player at Olympique Marseilles in the seasons after the Munich final:

I was repeatedly injected with a substance during my time at Marseilles ... To this day, I don't have a clue what it was. The club doctor would only tell me that it would give me an adrenalin boost, and I never felt inclined to ask the rest. Besides, my chairman at the time, Bernard Tapie, was an imposing man in everything but physical stature. His wishes were not to be disregarded. Whatever the substance was, my performances improved. That didn't make it acceptable. I cling to the sliver of hope that it was legal, though in reality, I'm 99 per cent sure it wasn't.

Certainly, when the dust on the Juventus trials had settled, football was left with many awkward questions. Even if every substance consumed by the Juventus players during the period 1994–8 was legal, restorative and not performance-enhancing, there still emerged a picture of top-level footballers who were almost constantly taking pills, drinking creatine and having intravenous drips either before, during (at half-time) or after matches. Can this be football, and, if it is, is it worth the candle?

Leaving aside the medical debate whereby one man's restorative is another man's performance-enhancing drug, can we really claim to be surprised? The reality of today's football, as every child over the age of five knows, is that the best players in the game are asked to play too much. When Zidane says that intravenous drips are 'useful', adding 'otherwise how would we manage to play 70 games per season', is he not making a valid point?

Are the players, the coaches, even the club doctors not the victims of a football world where commercial demands and pressures decree that ever more football should be played in ever more corners of the earth at an ever greater pace? Or is it time for more football professionals to make a stand?

Foreigners may look on the Juventus trial and conclude that because the country's most famous, most prestigious club has been accused of systematic doping practices, this is itself proof of the sick state of Italian football – even if Juventus was acquitted. That could well be. Yet, as Sandro Donati and others point out, it is simply neither logical nor reasonable to conclude that doping (or pharmaceutical abuse) in contemporary, cosmopolitan, globalised football is restricted to Italy and Serie A. If you have it in Serie A, then you will have it, to some degree at least, in the Premiership, the Primera Liga, the Bundesliga and elsewhere.

Many English football commentators seem to take for granted that players will occasionally test positive for what are happily called 'recreational' drugs. The implication is that there is no harm in it, a bit like going for a pint after the match. Is it? Can we be sure that all so-called recreational drugs do not have a performance-enchancing element, if only through modulation of a player's psyche?

With specific reference to the Juventus case, though, is Zeman not correct when he laments the inaction of football authorities, at national and international levels? Surely, it should be the football authorities and not the State judiciary which keep watch over the underlying moral issues affecting the game? Juventus may well have done absolutely nothing wrong, legally or morally, but did the seriousness of the accusations not merit the attention of sports authorities?

Perhaps the Juventus trial should prompt us to ask the following questions. Have football's governing bodies, FIFA, UEFA, CSF etc., actively pursued policies that would reduce the number of club and country games played per season? No. Is the game being played at a more physically demanding pace? Yes. Does football move ever greater amounts of money via sponsors, endorsements and, above all, TV rights? Yes. Are football's multinational sponsors likely to object if and when issues like doping come along to sully the image of the sport in which they have heavily invested? Yes, again. Does all of this mean that clubs, coaches, players and club doctors are under ever bigger pressures to take a 'pharmaceutical shortcut'? Yes. Does it also mean that football's governing bodies are at best half-hearted in their attempts to deal with the problem of doping? On that last question, the jury is still out.

Sadly, I found the whole Juventus trial process predictable. It fits in with an Italian judicial syndrome whereby we move from initial, media-driven clamour through a complex, often difficult trial, which ultimately ends in acquittal. In some senses, that syndrome has been seen at work in a whole series of post-war Italian trials – Moro, Ali Agca, Andreotti, Berlusconi, Bologna, Piazza Fontana. The list goes on.

Legally, Juventus are in the clear, but morally and ethically? Furthermore, only a fool could argue that the questions raised by the Juventus trial with regard to medical practices do not apply to football clubs worldwide. Every major football club today has an extensive medical cabinet.

TEN
ENDGAME

'What the fuck is happening? What are they doing? They've just gone and scored a goal. They're mad, they've scored a goal by mistake ...' *Francesco Dal Cin, managing director of Venezia.*

'Don't worry. Vicente [the goalscorer] is like that, but there's still time to set things to rights ...' *Mauro Paglioni, agent of the Uruguayan footballer Miguel Vicente, who had had the bad taste to score a goal he was not meant to score.*

'That wasn't the way it was meant to go. We had an agreement...' *Enrico Preziosi, president of Genoa.*

This is a story of match-fixing, Italian style. The match in question was Genoa versus Venezia on 11 June 2005, the last day of the Serie B season, and the above 'quotes' are taken from transcripts of police phone taps. Italian football, like Italian society around it, has its own unwritten code. You could well say the same thing about almost any society, but the difference in Italy is that the code sometimes allows for systematic bending of the rules, if not outright dishonesty.

I remember how, in our first month in Italy, Dindy found herself in a Rome public office trying to secure a *libretto di lavoro*, a document necessary for her job at the British Institute. Dindy had wisely brought along Francesca, an Italian acquaintance, to help out. At a certain point, when things seemed to be moving slowly, Francesca snapped at Dindy: 'Give him something.'

'Something' meant money. Dindy fished a 10,000 lire note out of her handbag and gently laid it on top of her documents. The official on the other side of the desk said not a word but dextrously slipped the note into his own files and then stood up, saying: 'I think we can fix that, Signora.'

Of an arguably more serious nature were the unwritten rules encountered by 'John', a close friend who teaches English in a northern Italian university. John was surprised to discover one day that his English department professor was scheduled to address a forthcoming symposium on contemporary English poetry. Given that the professor had previously manifested neither knowledge nor interest in modern English poetry, John, a specialist in the area, was delighted and surprised. At that very moment, John himself had been overseeing the work of Franca, a postgraduate student in the English department, who was doing a doctoral thesis on modern English poets.

When he subsequently attended the symposium, John was desperately curious to hear just what his professor would have to say. To his astonishment, however, the professor had not got far into his address before John recognised, word for word, nearly everything he was hearing. The professor had simply ripped off Franca's thesis and presented it as his own. (He subsequently went on to publish the thesis under his own name, too.)

Later, an infuriated and disappointed John cornered Franca and asked her what had happened. Franca looked at John as if he were some sort of fool and told him: 'I had to let him do it. That way I get my doctorate and he gets to make his speech. That's the system.'

Franca did indeed get her doctorate and later she got a job back at her old university where she is now John's not very accomplished and much less pleasant boss. That's the system.

When applied to football, the unwritten rules of the system were seen at work in the Genoa match-fixing case. For Genoa, this was an all-or-nothing game, one which they needed to win in order to be secure of promotion back into Serie A. In contrast, Venezia, already relegated, were playing for nothing but their pride and honour – not, mind you, that there was much of either about on this particular evening.

As the curtain rose on the final act of the Serie B season, no fewer than six sides – Ascoli, Genoa, Empoli, Perugia, Torino and Treviso – could all still make it into Serie A, with just three places available. Genoa, however, seemed well positioned since they went into the last day in second place, just one point behind Empoli and two points clear of both Torino and Perugia.

For the home fans, things got off to a bad start when Uruguayan Vicente opened the scoring for the visitors in the thirteenth minute. Genoa's Argentine striker Diego Milito, however, proved himself the hero of the night, not only scoring a vital equaliser just before half-time but going on to score the winner in the sixty-fifth minute for a 3–2 victory that put Italy's oldest club back into Serie A.

For the Genoa fans, it mattered not a jot that Venezia had come to Genoa with a weakened team. Nor were they going to care about the apparent piece of good luck that went their way just before half-time. Venezia's Czech goalkeeper Martin Lejsal, until then the man of the match with a string of excellent saves, had picked up a hand injury, and was replaced by inexperienced 19-year-old Riccardo Pezzato.

Genoa's win prompted a rapturous reception from the home fans, who remained at the Marassi stadium long after the final whistle, applauding the players, coach Serse Cosmi and President

Preziosi, who all came out for laps of honour. After a ten-year absence from Serie A, excitement was at an all-time high. *Gazzetta Dello Sport* wrote in a front-page leader:

> The future takes off on a summer's night, in a stadium resonant with history. The Luigi Ferraris stadium, which we all call the Marassi, applauds. Thirty-four thousand hearts beat drum-like, enraptured by those colours, by that team shirt worn with the pride of a 112-year history. Ten years and a day later, *il grifone* [the vulture, symbol of the club] is flying high again ...

Leaving aside the merits of a prose style that may strike the Anglo-Saxon ear as just a little over the top, *Gazzetta Dello Sport's* reporter was not alone in his positive view. Genoa's promotion was a major item in most TV and radio sports news bulletins as well as a front-page item in most newspapers. The interest in, and affection for, Genoa is more than understandable since the club had a major role in the earliest days of modern Italian football when it won the first Italian championship in 1898.

Not only the media were excited by Genoa's promotion. Club sponsors, the sportswear firm Errea, promised a brand-new team shirt for next season. Club sources suggested that negotiations were already under way to strengthen the squad, with experienced internationals such as AC Milan goalkeeper Christian Abbiati, Inter Milan's Greek midfielder Giorgios Karagounis and Juventus defender Croat Igor Tudor being targeted. Informed sources also claimed that the club had already contacted the former Vicenza, Bologna and Palermo coach Francesco Guidolin, as a replacement for Cosmi. On top of that, the Ligurian regional authority announced a civic reception for the victorious Genoa team.

Yet, within days of the match, the Genoa victory celebrations had turned sour. Newspaper reports were suggesting that the game was 'suspect'. Media suspicion had been aroused when, on the Tuesday following the match, Venezia's general manager, Giuseppe Pagliara, had been stopped at a 'routine' police checkpoint, just minutes after he drove his KIA car out of the headquarters of the toy manufacturing company Giochi Preziosi, owned by the Genoa president and based at Colgiate, near Milan.

In the car, police found a briefcase containing €250,000. Pagliara was unable to explain how he had come by the money or for what purpose it was intended. Subsequently, he explained that the money was part-payment for the transfer to Genoa of Venezia defender Ruben Maldonaldo.

By Friday, 17 June, less than one week after the match, media reports claimed that the Procura di Genova was investigating into possible 'sporting fraud' carried out by the Genoa club and by President Preziosi. One week later, the sports papers were carrying the transcript of various conversations, including one in which Matteo Preziosi, son of Enrico, invited Pagliara to drop round to the Giochi Preziosi headquarters to 'settle things'.

Media speculation then suggested that another of the Serie A promotion candidates, Torino, might be involved. It was reported that the former Torino player and sports director Roberto Cravero (rumoured to be heading for a job with Genoa) had alerted Genoa to the fact that Torino had been in contact with Venezia with a view to encouraging them to give it their all against Genoa. If media reports were to be believed, Venezia were much in demand. Genoa were busy persuading them to lose, while Torino were encouraging them to win.

Clearly, yet another nasty Italian-style football scandal was brewing. Not for the first time, the initiation of this particular investigation owed nothing to the vigilance (or lack of) of the football authorities and everything to the professionalism of two Genoa-based investigating magistrates.

In April 2005, State attorneys Alberto Lari and Giovanni Arena were investigating a credit card fraud, which had already led to the arrest of three people in France, when their authorised police taps accidentally led them into football. One of those involved in the credit card fraud was also a heavy gambler, of the sort who operates in the world of clandestine betting. The two magistrates quickly realised that some skulduggery was afoot in relation to the Genoa versus Venezia game and were given authorisation to tap the phones of both Genoa and Venezia officials as well as to place bugs in the Novotel Hotel, Genoa, where the Venezia team stayed prior to the game. It was the content of these phone taps that prompted the magistrates to open an investigation with a view to charging various Genoa and Venezia officials with 'sporting fraud'.

Within two weeks of the match, General Italo Pappa, head of FIGC's investigations office, paid a visit to the two young magistrates in Genoa. He travelled back to Rome with a weighty dossier containing transcripts of the incriminating conversations. While the State judicial processes would inevitably be lengthy, the sports disciplinary body could not afford to wait. After all, the new Serie A season was only two months away.

One month later, the Lega's disciplinary commission held a three-day hearing into the Genoa affair, concluding that the Venezia match had indeed been fixed. Genoa were demoted from Serie A to Serie C1, while Genoa president Enrico Preziosi, Genoa general nanager Stefano Capozucca, Venezia managing director Francesco Dal Cin and Venezia general manager Pagliara were all given five-year bans. Furthermore, Francesco Dal Cin's son, Michele, received a three-year and one-month ban, two Venezia players, striker Massimo Borgobello and goalkeeper Lejsal, were given bans of five and six months respectively, while the former Torino director Roberto Cravero received a four-month ban.

'This is just so ridiculous that I can't even find the words to offer my opinion … this is the blackest page in Genoa's history,' commented Stefano Capozucca, while Genoa's defence lawyer, Alfredo Biondi, thundered, 'Genoa is the sacrificial victim of an inquisitorial approach to the whole business.'

By the early evening of 27 July, more than a thousand Genoa fans had gathered in the town to express their anger, burning rubbish bins, throwing a smoke bomb at the Genoa police head-quarters and attacking a couple of TV cameramen from Prime Minister Berlusconi's Mediaset group. Nor did the Genoa fans let it rest there. Throughout late July and well into August, they organised a series of protests, some of them attended by more than six thousand fans, during which they blocked access to the city's *autostrada*, attacked the office of the local Genoa news-paper, *Il Secolo XIX*, burned some more rubbish bins and turned over a couple of cars, for good measure. For the Genoa fans, the club was the victim of an ill-defined plot.

Inevitably, too, Genoa contested the 27 July sentences. Unfortunately for them, a FIGC Appeal hearing on 8 August upheld the disciplinary commission's ruling.

At that point, we moved onto a now almost traditional, high-summer Italian farce which saw the league's rulings contested through the State judicial system, threatening to delay the start of the season and leaving fans all over the country, not to mention international broadcasters all over the world, in a total quandary. Judge Alvaro Vigotti, sitting in a Genoa (where else?) regional court in early August, argued that the club was entitled to appeal the ruling and, in the meantime, ordered FIGC not to publish the new season's Serie A fixture list (which at this point clearly did not include Genoa).

FIGC, in turn, took its case to the Lazio regional appeal tribu-nal (Tribunali Amministrativi Regionali – TAR), a body which, under a 2003 law, had been designated as the one and only forum for the resolution of sports litigation, sanctions and disciplinary proceedings. TAR ruled that the Genoa court had no jurisdiction on the matter and not only gave FIGC the go-ahead to publish the fixture list but also sanctioned Genoa's demotion to Serie C1. On 20 August, Judge Vigotti in Genoa conceded the inevitable, ruling that it was indeed TAR and not his court that had jurisdiction in the matter. Genoa were definitively in Serie C1.

To the outsider, this bemusing succession of newspaper leaks, alleged phone conversations, judicial investigations, disciplinary commission sanctions, byzantine conflicts of jurisdiction – all of it punctuated by semi-violent fan protest – might seem faintly amusing, just part of the crazy world of Italian football.

If one takes time, though, to read through the findings of the Lega's disciplinary commission, the Genoa affair emerges as anything but amusing. Just reflect on the opening words of the commission's *motivazioni*:

> The paradoxical element to have emerged from this hearing – an element explained with frankness not only by Enrico Preziosi but also by Francesco Dal Cin and an element which constituted the basis of the defence's case for all those attached to [the club] Genoa – comes from the circumstance that it was and is taken for granted that a team which in the final days of the championship has no particular motivation with regard to the league table or the need to get a result should, when playing against a side which in contrast is driven by precisely that motivation and those needs, play the sort of game and take the sort of attitude that would 'fit in' with the expectations of its very opponent.[14]

Translated into everyday speak, the commission was expressing its consternation at the fact that Messrs Preziosi, Dal Cin et al argued that it was only right and proper for an already relegated side not to try too hard against a team that desperately needed the points to win promotion. Lest anyone fail to get the point, the commission went on to criticise Francesco Dal Cin for the following statement he made during the hearing: 'If the team that has nothing at stake plays with excessive passion against the side that absolutely needs to win, then that is a sports offence.' What Dal Cin is saying here is that not only should an already relegated side lie down and get beaten, but that if such a team dares to offer serious opposition, then it is committing an unlawful act (he uses the term '*illecito sportivo*'). In other words, lads, we all know the score here – we need to win, you lot have nothing to play for, so roll over and get beaten. Even by the grim standards of the modern footbiz world, Dal Cin's attitude strikes a new low in terms of calculating cynicism. With regard to Dal Cin's remarkable statement, the disciplinary commission commented:

> [This] … is an assumption that in an unacceptable manner presumes the 'normality' of not trying too hard and which furthermore prompts the consequent pathology represented by the need to 'make sure' that such 'normality' is respected and that your friend-cum-rival team director is 'looked after' and is 'reassured'…[15] [The punctuation marks are those of the Commission report.]

The commission went on to decry the fact that it was considered only 'normal and fitting, a sort of anticipated, legitimate self-defence' for the Genoa directors to make contact with their Venezia counterparts prior to the game, once they had heard the rumours that Torino might be willing to offer the Venezia players a bonus to win. In order to thwart Torino, commented the commission, '…you react by taking a series of measures designed to guarantee you a bland and non-belligerent attitude on the part of your opponent (Venezia), so as to re-establish their proper and "dutiful" athletic disinterest'.

The accusations filed by FIGC's investigations office stated:

In the days prior to the game, there were a series of meetings between Venezia players and directors which focused on the fact that many of the players were reluctant to play, given that they knew about the agreement reached by the two clubs and in view of the fact that their defeat had already been established.

In particular, the player Lejsal (the Venezia goalkeeper), who was determined not to play, was persuaded to play by both Pagliara and Michele Dal Cin so as to avoid arousing the suspicions of the investigations office. Furthermore, he [Lejsal] was reassured that just as soon as he gave the nod, he would be substituted.[16]

The commission went on to deplore 'the climate of conspiratorial silence' ('*il clima omertoso*') that too often permeates the 'shadowy world' in which many of the defendants, including players, moved. In particular, the commission deplored the fact that Lejsal withdrew some of his evidence during the hearing, in spite of the fact that he had previously given a full and frank testimony to the investigations office inspectors, in the presence of two defence lawyers.

In the end, the commission appeared to have taken into account attenuating circumstances when handing down a relatively modest six-month ban to Lejsal. Arguing that Lejsal's partial retraction in no way altered the value of his original evidence, the commission concluded:

His admissions … offered an important contribution to the reconstruction of the events and the furthering of the investigation, in a climate which, as we have already observed, was one of conspiratorial silence ... In particular, Lejsal related three specific and significant incidents: the fact that Pagliara and Michele Dal Cin insisted that he play, not so much so as to guarantee the team cover in a key role, but rather so as not to arouse the suspicions of the investigations office; the pressure from Genoa, and this was referred to him by Pagliara, that he should not play; and the agreement that he be substituted following an agreed signal ...[17]

With regard to the question of the infamous €250,000 found in Giuseppe Pagliara's car at the police checkpoint, the commission commented that this 'incident' only served to 'worsen the defendants' situation and render their behaviour all the more illegal', adding: 'This incident in which Enrico Preziosi and his collaborators gave money to Pagliara ... they tried (unsuccessfully) to pass it off as part of the process of the negotiations for the transfer to Genoa of Maldonaldo ... a transfer that was revealed to be a mere artifice intended to cover up the illegal agreements between Genoa and Venezia.'

The commission furthermore pointed out that, in the days after the police had seized the briefcase from Pagliara's car, Matteo Preziosi, Francesco Dal Cin and Giuseppe Pagliara were heard (on the phone taps) discussing a whole range of concoctable 'stories' as to the origins of the money. The commission concluded that, given that neither Maldonaldo nor his agent knew anything about a possible transfer to Genoa, clearly the whole story had been fabricated.

In the days immediately after the game (Sunday and Monday), Pagliara made a number of phone calls to Enrico and Matteo Preziosi and to the Genoa general manager, Stefano Capozucca, looking for the 'pay-off'. Becoming impatient, and perhaps suspecting that Genoa were not, after all, going to pay up, Pagliara at one point threatened to spill all the beans, adding that if they didn't pay, he would 'send them straight back down to Serie B'.

The commission also related snippets of (bugged) conversations between goalkeeper Lejsal and Venezia striker Massimo Borgobello which recorded them saying 'the two clubs have reached an agreement'; 'there's money in this but it's not clear who gets it'; and 'Lulu [Venezia's Belgian-Brazilian striker Oliveira Barrosso] said that they've got to lose 3–0'.

The commission, in particular, cited Francesco Dal Cin as the mastermind. He acted as the 'guarantor' for Preziosi, 'assuring him that he could control the Venezia players via his son, Michele Dal Cin, even during the game itself'. Furthermore, in different conversations, Francesco Dal Cin regularly reassured Preziosi, even at one point telling him, 'Keep your cool, everything is OK, we couldn't have done it any better', and then, in relation to the payment made to Pagliara, 'Don't pay up until I'm there.'

Finally, with regard to the main accusation, that of a match-fixing agreement between Genoa and Venezia, the commission had no doubt:

> It needs to be pointed out that the sports felony relative to … the Codice di Giustizia Sportiva [Code of Sports Justice] … relates to acts designed to alter the prosecution or the result of a game so as to assure whomsoever an advantage in the league table. That advantage and that alteration are implicit in the fact that Enrico Preziosi and Francesco Dal Cin agreed and acted so that the sporting performance of the Venezia team would be 'normalised' so as to ensure that the outcome of the game (and, in the process, the fate of the Serie B championship) would be 'as it should be'; a win for Genoa, defeat for Venezia.[18]

There we have it, a splendid case of match-fixing, Italian style. It would be nice to think that this was the first of its kind, but the unwritten rules of 'the system' decree that it happens almost every year when it comes round to last-day promotion/relegation struggles. Players and ex-players tell you these things, but only on agreement that such talk is strictly off the record. Fans simply take it for granted.

Occasionally, a journalist or writer takes up the story. In his informative and entertaining book *The Miracle of Castel Di Sangro*, Joe McGinnis gives a detailed inside-track account of the preparation and execution of just such an alleged, last-day-of-the-season match-fixing when little Castel di Sangro travelled to play Bari. For Castel di Sangro, already certain of avoiding the drop back down to Serie C1, the match meant little or nothing. For Bari, it was an all-or-nothing promotion decider. McGinnis alleges that money changed hands and that the game was fixed from start to finish. In the end, Bari won 3–1 and went up to Serie A.

Not all match-fixing, however, concerns end-of-season promotion and relegation battles. In the spring of 2004, investigators from the Naples branch of the DIA (Direzione Investigativa Antimafia – the anti-Mafia investigative taskforce) accidentally came across one such scam.

On the evening of Friday, 16 April they intercepted phone calls between two players, Siena midfielder Roberto D'Aversa and his ex-team-mate, goalkeeper Generoso Rossi. 'D'Aversa was in the team hotel prior to a match [a 2–1 home defeat to champions elect AC Milan] along with team-mate Nicola Ventola,' wrote the investigators in their subsequent report, adding: 'On the explicit request of the last-mentioned [Ventola], D'Aversa gave Rossi the results of five matches due to be played on Sunday, 18 April.' The five matches in question were: Chievo versus

Reggina (0–0) in Serie A; Ascoli versus Piacenza (0–0) in Serie B; and Lumezzane versus Sassari Torres (0–0), Taranto versus Catanzaro (0–1) and Crotone versus Fermana (3–0), all in Serie C. Remarkably, all Rossi's predictions proved correct.

That intercepted phone call was just one element in a wide-ranging investigation which, in the end, involved twelve clubs: Chievo, Reggina, Lecce and Siena in Serie A; Ascoli and Piacenza in Serie B; and Catanzaro, Crotone, Fermana, Lumezzane, Sassari Torres and Taranto in Serie C1 and C2. The DIA discovered, among other things, that two players, Stefano Bettarini of Sampdoria and Antonio Marasco of Modena, previously teammates at Venezia, had exchanged more than 60 text messages over a five-day period in April 2004 prior to a Modena versus Sampdoria Serie A game. The investigators concluded:

> In the course of the investigation, concrete evidence was acquired re. the existence of a sophisticated organisation which has fixed the results and obviously the league tables of the current Serie A, B, and C championships ... The investigation proves that agreements were regularly made to fix matches, that many different clubs were involved, that the matches were fixed in order to make unlawful gains [i.e. via betting] ... and that also involved with the footballers were persons some of whom are connected with the Camorra.[19]

The following August, the Lega's disciplinary commission punished, in one way or another, five clubs (Como, Pescara, Modena, Sampdoria and Siena), six players from different clubs and two Siena officials for their part in the affair. Most heavily punished among the players involved were Modena's Marasco, who got a three-year ban that effectively ended his playing career, and goalkeeper Rossi, who received a one-year ban. The commission ruled that Marasco was guilty of 'sporting felony' and Rossi of breaking the ban on players betting on football. Furthermore, both sanctions were subsequently upheld in FIGC's Court of Appeal. The most heavily punished club was Modena, which was deducted five points, subsequently reduced to four on appeal.

Most infamous of all Italian match-fixing scandals happened in 1980 when more than 30 players, including Paolo Rossi, then the world's highest-paid player, received bans for involvement in a match-fixing ring. The scandal also cost Milan and Lazio dearly, both sides being relegated to Serie B. Rossi, of course, got back from his suspension only two years later, just in time to inspire Italy to that 1982 World Cup victory, scoring six goals along the way.

It would take a very long book to relate the story of all the various match-fixing scandals of modern times, in Italy and elsewhere. Perhaps the most sensational incident in recent times in Europe was the infamous Valenciennes versus Olympique Marseilles affair in 1993 (see Chapter 9). But the interesting aspect of the Genoa case is the concern of the disciplinary commission that systematic cheating was somehow normal. Certainly, the behaviour, language and attitude of those involved in the match-fixing would imply that they felt they were not doing anything very wrong. Indeed, according to Francesco Dal Cin, the 'wrong' thing would have been for Venezia to have played hard and won.

If this story has a positive dimension, it is that neither club got away with it. One wonders, however, if the Genoa match-fixing would ever have come to light but for the work of the two State attorneys, Alberto Lari and Giovanni Arena.

ELEVEN
FANS

'Come on,' cajoled the referee, Roberto Rosetti, 'stand up and be men.'

Roma captain Francesco Totti and Lazio's Sinisa Mihajlovic, however, were not up for it. They were not going to play. Minutes into what should have been the second half of the Rome derby of March 2004, Rosetti was left with no option but to suspend the game.

It was as if the athletes in an Olympics 100 metres final, at a given signal, stood up from their blocks, shook hands with one another and then walked off the track, leaving the perplexed starter with his pistol poised but redundant.

What had happened? Two minutes into the second half, a couple of smoke flares had been lobbed onto the pitch. Within seconds, much of the Olimpico pitch was shrouded in heavy smoke, making it impossible for play to carry on. Such incidents are not unusual. On countless occasions, referees in Italy delay the start of the second half in order to allow the smoke from flares to clear. This time, however, it was different.

For their own reasons, elements among both the Roma and Lazio fans seem to have decided they wanted the match abandoned. In theory, the fans claimed that they had been outraged by the death of a child, a Roma fan, allegedly run over by a police vehicle during minor skirmishes between the police and fans prior to the game. In practice, no such death had taken place. Yet, the rumour of the child's death apparently caught on like wildfire. Not even seven different denials over the public address system could convince the sceptical fan leaders.

After the smoke flares had cleared, we expected the game to restart. Amidst scenes of total confusion, however, neither set of players seemed in a hurry to get back into action. Then, down at the *curva sud* (the Roma kop), a three-man 'delegation' of *ultras* amazingly found its way onto the Olimpico running track.

Roma captain Totti trotted down to speak to them. What was said between Totti and the fans is still a matter of dispute. What we do know is that the body language was revealing. One of the *ultras* put his arm on Totti's shoulder in a manner that seemed both patronising and menacing. What we also know is that, when he returned to the Roma bench on the halfway line, Totti turned to Roma coach Fabio Capello and shouted, 'If we play on now, they'll kill us.'

I was doing a match commentary for RAI from their Via Teulada studios and Totti's words ('*Se giochiamo addesso, questi ci ammazzono*') came loud and clear over the effects headset. Millions of Italians were also able to lipread his words.

Totti and Roma have always denied that the teams were blackmailed into not playing on. In one sense, the denial matters little, for the two teams subsequently abandoned the game. Totti was seen talking to his team-mates, to the Lazio players and to the referee. It was quite clear that he did not want to play on and he appeared to be launched on a mission to convince everyone else to abandon the match.

At this point, referee Rosetti was in the hot spot. On the one hand, it was plain that a majority of the players and staff from both clubs were unwilling to resume the game. On the other, the Prefetto di Roma (Rome's senior police officer), Achille Serra, also out on the pitch, was adamant that, in the interests of public order, the game should be re-started.

Then Rosetti was handed a mobile phone. On the other end of the line was Adriano Galliani, acting boss at the mighty AC Milan, and, at the time of the derby, president of the Lega. Watched by millions worldwide, Galliani and Rosetti had their little chat. A resigned Rosetti then officially abandoned the match.

And the Prefetto? Surely, law and order considerations would outweigh those of the Lega, the players and the club officials? Was this not a perfect moment to send a clear message to the flare-throwers and the self-appointed fan-ambassadors? What if the suspension of the game led to rioting, mayhem and even death?

The Prefetto's words, however, went unheard. Fan power had won. Fan violence, too, then ensued, as violent elements in both Roma and Lazio camps engaged in a series of running battles with riot police outside the ground. By the end of the night, 60 police and 15 fans had been injured, while 36 fans had been either arrested or summonsed. Given that the Olimpico had been filled to capacity, one has to conclude that such a 'score sheet' represented a pretty good result. At least, a panic and resultant mass stampede had been avoided.

Prefetto Serra was left to rage at his own relative powerlessness when faced with the football 'machine'. He did, however, suggest that the protest was not spontaneous but rather pre-planned. Furthermore, he drew attention to some strange movements amongst the *ultras* at half-time.

For the rest of us, it was enough to see allegedly sworn enemies such as the Lazio and Roma fans agreeing within seconds to wrap up their banners and call for the game to be stopped. That in itself stank to high heaven. Someone, somewhere in the organised ranks of the *ultras* wanted to send a message, making clear the power they wielded.

Driving home that night, I felt gloomy. Now, I thought, we will have a week of banner headlines, TV and radio chat shows, possibly even questions in parliament, all dedicated to the *scandalo* at the Olimpico. Opinionists, football commentators, sociologists, psychiatrists, priests and politicians will all be queuing up to tell us what is wrong with Italian football. Theories will be expounded, remedies proposed, legislation mooted and, in the end, nothing much will happen at all – until the next time, when the whole talk circus will start up again. (At the time of going to press, a judicial investigation into the incident is still ongoing, while the three fans who 'invaded' the Olimpico are subject to a restriction which obliges them to present themselves at a police station and sign a form any time that either Lazio or Roma are playing in Rome.)

I thought about all the ordinary, normal, decent Roma and Lazio fans I come across in my everyday life. Did they deserve this?

There is Simone, who works in my accountant's office and who regularly travels from Trevignano to the Olimpico to support Lazio.

There is Enrico, one of the stewards who runs the Vatican press office, another great Lazio fan.

There are the season-ticket-holders Ivo and his brother Paolo at the bank just up the road from the foreign press club in Rome, both lifelong Roma fans and men with whom every transaction involves a whimsical discussion of the latest development in Roma affairs.

Or there is Marina, mother of a classmate of Róisín's. She is a successful businesswoman, from a wealthy family, who runs two very swanky Rome hotels. She once astonished me by telling me the following joke: 'When you see a Lazio fan throw himself off the top of a 20-storey building, what he is doing? Answer: A good thing.'

Then, too, as a special treat, the parents of several of Róisín's classmates had bought tickets and organised for the kids to attend this particular ill-fated derby. Was it right that they be exposed to such potential danger? What if things had really got out of hand and there had been a stampede?

Certainly, FIGC's subsequent disciplinary ruling, which saw Roma banned from the Olimpico for one match and Lazio fined €51,500, hardly seemed a harsh enough punishment.

In 20 years of covering Italian football, I have come across plenty of different fans, at the stadium and in everyday walks of life. Nearly all of them are genuine enthusiasts with a passionate understanding of their club's most intimate business, on and off the field. None of them, you imagine, wants a match suspended.

Yet, there are clearly other fans, too. What about some of the banners we have seen in recent years at the Olimpico? Perhaps the worst of all was one that appeared during a Rome derby in 1998, directed at the Roma fans and proclaiming 'Auschwitz is Your Country, the Ovens are Your Homes'. Little better was another, again courtesy of Lazio fans, that declared 'Honour to the Name of Arkan', the Serb war criminal wanted for alleged genocide who was subsequently gunned down in a Belgrade hotel. In January 2006, during a Roma versus Livorno Serie A game, we saw an unwelcome return to the Holocaust theme when a section of Roma fans greeted their Livorno counterparts with swastikas and a banner reading 'Lazio and Livorno, Same First Letter, Same Oven'.

It was hard to ignore the banners and harder still to explain to TV audiences worldwide, as well as to various British and Irish radio programmes, the exact genesis of such ugly, mindless ignorance. Primarily, those gestures were again about intimidatory fan power, about the willingness of the *ultras* to pull off even the most outrageous gesture in order to threaten the clubs (and here we are talking not just about Roma and Lazio). For the *ultras*, the pay-off might include free match tickets, travel concessions and, most importantly, the freedom to run their own lucrative merchandising rackets.

The 'Auschwitz' banner, too, clearly reflected a level of staggering ignorance. What did the fans who held that banner actually know or understand about Nazi concentration camps? Indeed, do they know anything about their own history? Yards from where the Roma and Lazio fans stand every Sunday, there are metres and metres of splendid marble mosaics and an imposing obelisk all proclaiming Mussolini 'Dux' (Il Duce), Mussolini the great leader and Mussolini's Roman Empire. If you knew nothing about your history, you would conclude that this old Mussolini guy had simply been another important figure in recent Italian history, just like Garibaldi, Cavour and King Vittorio Emanuele were important figures in the unification of Italy.

Nowhere on the marble mosaics does it say that Mussolini introduced racial laws in 1938, based on those already introduced by Hitler in Nazi Germany, which effectively banned Jews from public office of any kind, excluded them from the medical, legal and teaching professions and even banned them from owning a radio. Nowhere does it say that Mussolini entered into a disastrous pact to go to war alongside Hitler's Germany. Nowhere does it say that the Mussolini regime, directly or indirectly, sent more than 6,800 Italian Jews to their deaths in Nazi concentration camps. Nowhere does it tell the story of the thousands of Italians, opponents of the Mussolini regime, who were imprisoned, tortured or sent into exile.

Nor do the mosaics tell of the 1,200 Italian Fascist war criminals who, by 1945, were wanted in connection with the hundreds of thousands killed (sometimes with mustard gas) by Mussolini's troops in Ethiopia, Libya and the Balkans.

The very existence of the mosaics would seem to underwrite the claims of many latter-day apologists for Mussolini – namely that he was basically a decent auld skin, with Italy's best interests at heart, who perhaps went a bit wrong when entering into an alliance with Hitler. This is the country where Il Duce's granddaughter, Alessandra Mussolini, has carved out a right-wing polit-ical career based on an unashamed use of her famous family name.

Nor do the players always help. Take Lazio's charismatic Paolo Di Canio. On at least three different occasions in 2005, one of them after a Rome derby in January 2005, he saluted the Lazio fans with the infamous straight-arm Fascist salute. Eleven months later, he was at it again, after a 2–1 away defeat by Livorno, a side that has a traditionally strong leftist following. When his repeated gesture prompted a major polemic, the unre-pentant Di Canio merely offered to do it again. Which indeed he did, a week later, after being substituted during Lazio's 1–1 draw with Juventus at the Olympic Stadium in Rome. Di Canio, a man who has the word 'Dux' tattooed on his arm, explained:

> I have huge admiration for a great leader [Mussolini] who, in a particular historical context, if nothing else, was able to restore a sense of national pride...
>
> I cannot stop myself saluting the fans that way ... it's about expressing a sense of belonging to my people. At Livorno, I had to put up with awful insults about me, my mother and my family, but, proud and determined, I still went out and played, and played well ... I'm proud to be part of the Lazio people. When you have true values, you're always in the right ...

To be fair to Di Canio, the Livorno versus Lazio game had been a high-risk encounter, as evidenced by the fact that when the Lazio team bus arrived at the Livorno stadium, it was 'attacked' by a smoke flare which crashed into the side of the bus, causing momentary apprehension but no injury.

In his self-defence, Di Canio pointed out that Italian media coverage of the match had made much of his Fascist salute and he carefully played down the significance of the attack on the

Lazio bus. However, he then appeared to undermine his own defence when offering the following comment in relation to the fact that his salute had prompted protests from Rome's Jewish community: 'If a fine were to be imposed [on me] because one particular community was enraged, that would be very dangerous … If we're now in the hands of the Jewish community, then it's the end. All of which prompted Jewish community leader Amos Luzzatto to comment: 'From bad to worse – what is worse than Di Canio's original gesture is the implication of his comment, namely that the Jewish community has occult powers.'

The Di Canio episode did not escape the eagle eye of FIFA president Sepp Blatter who, while admitting that he did not know the full details, warned that players could be banned for such behaviour. In the end, Di Canio reluctantly saw sense and, as he put it, for the good of the club, opted to renounce 'a gesture that for others, but certainly not for me, is demonic'. Now if Paolo Di Canio holds such unrepentant, pro-Fascist views, then can we be surprised that the Lazio fans express strong right-wing sympathies?

For me, all of this was a long way from the Rome derby as I had once perceived it. For me, the derby was about that special buzz of the big occasion. It was about the endless leg-pulling and jeering between Lazio and Roma fans in Jollo's bar next morning. It was about a sense of Italian football as stylish modern-day pageant, not a recruitment ground for Fascists.

In the days after that suspended derby, Prefetto Serra had suggested that the game might set a precedent. He was right. Six months after that aborted Rome derby, the Olimpico was back in the news for all the wrong reasons.

Half-time had just been blown in Roma's Champions League tie with Dinamo Kiev and I was heading for a coffee at the bar when a major hullabaloo near the entrance down to the dressing rooms caught my attention. Swedish referee Anders Frisk had just been hit by some sort of hard object, probably a coin, and had received a nasty cut to his forehead that subsequently required three stitches.

Like almost everyone else at the Olimpico, I had missed the entire incident and only understood what had happened thanks to the TV replays. The curious thing, however, was that the flight path of the object, as captured by the slow-motion replays, seemed to indicate that it had been thrown from the VIP section of the grandstand, immediately in front of the steps to the dressing rooms. Had a politician, industrial tycoon, sports administrator or TV celebrity opted to become an *ultra* for the night?

Half an hour later, we were still arguing over the incident as we waited for the second half to start. Colleagues informed me that Frisk had gone to hospital for treatment for his cut. One began to fear the worst. For the second time in six months, the curtain was about to come down prematurely.

After about an hour's wait, the public address system confirmed that the referee had indeed suspended the game. While Frisk may have over-reacted in claiming that he feared both for his own safety and that of his colleagues, you could hardly blame him. Had the object hit him a few centimetres lower, he could easily have suffered serious eye damage.

Given that Roma had already been in trouble with UEFA following incidents at a Roma versus Galatasaray Champions League game three seasons earlier, the club feared that UEFA might use a heavy hand when its disciplinary body sat down to examine the incident. In the end, Roma probably got off lightly because, while the win and three points were predictably awarded to Kiev, they were not banned from the Olimpico in Rome but rather forced to play their two remaining group home games behind closed doors.

In essence, UEFA appeared to accept Roma's argument that the club really could not be held responsible for what Roma director Franco Baldini called 'the mad act of one person' (still unidentified, by the way, although it was widely rumoured that the coin had been thrown by a policeman on escort duty to one of the VIPs).

Seven months later, in April 2005, the metal objects were raining down again. Once again it was a Champions League evening, but this time the scene was the Giuseppe Meazza stadium at San Siro, Milan. For the second time in three seasons, the twin prides of the city, Inter Milan and AC Milan, were meeting in Champions League combat, this time in a quarter-final tie.

The spark which lit this particular fan fuse came midway through the second half when German referee Markus Merk disallowed an apparently good goal from Inter's Argentine midfielder Esteban Cambiasso. That decision prompted a furious reaction from the Inter fans behind the AC Milan goal, with hundreds of objects – including flares, cigarette lighters, coins, umbrellas, keys and much else besides – being thrown onto the pitch.

During the 'downpour', AC Milan's Brazilian goalkeeper, Dida, was hit on the shoulder by a flare and ruled out of the rest of the game. (Dida was a lucky man, getting away with little more than a bruise.) Merk was left with little option but to take the teams off the field, in the vain hope that the intemperate fans would calm down. Announcements were then made over the public address system, informing the public that the referee wished to re-start the game but would immediately stop it and abandon it if the object-throwing and terrace violence started up again.

Sure enough, when the match kicked off again after a ten-minute break, the violence flared up immediately, with more objects being thrown onto the pitch. At that point, Merk could do nothing other than abandon the tie. Yet again, fan violence had won out. Yet again, a high-profile match had been suspended. Given that a UEFA Cup tie between Inter and Spanish side Alaves in 2001 had been interrupted by a similar explosion of violence, many of us wondered if Inter were in for a very severe sentence from European football's ruling body, UEFA. One or two even suggested that UEFA might ban them from European competition, at least for a season.

In the end, Inter were handed a €195,000 fine and a ban that forced them to play their first four Champions League ties of the 2005–6 season behind closed doors. UEFA's affable and suave spokesperson, William Gaillard, tried to put a good spin on the judgement, commenting: 'There will be some people who think that it is lenient and others who think that it is harsh ... This is the highest fine in the history of UEFA and the loss of four home games will mean that Inter lose out on revenue of around €8 million. You have to put it in the context of the game. There were no further injuries apart from a very slight one to the goal-keeper, which we absolutely regret ...'

Sure, 'no further injuries' – except to the image of Italian football. Like most of my footballing colleagues, I found myself churning out the grim facts over the next few days. In the 2003–4 season, 335 people were arrested as a result of 231 different violent incidents in and around Italian stadiums. On the Sunday prior to the Inter versus AC Milan Champions League tie, 17 people had been arrested and 85 policemen injured during riots at a variety of league matches. That Sunday's violence had prompted Italian Interior Minister Giuseppe Pisanu to threaten the closure of stadiums that are regularly the scene of violence, while he had also called on local police chiefs to use their powers to cancel matches that – before or during – witness violent or racist fan behaviour. Significantly, too, Minister Pisanu had called on both FIGC and the clubs to put their own houses in order. The following night, by way of answer to his appeal, came the shameful violence at the San Siro.

A couple of months before that game, FIGC's president Franco Carraro had come to meet the resident foreign media at the foreign press club in Rome. Did he feel that the fan violence in Italy was getting worse, season by season? I asked him.

'Yes, things are getting worse,' he replied. 'There are four major reasons for our fan problems. Firstly, the stadia are not good enough. Secondly, from the organisational viewpoint with regard to ticket sales, we're still behind. In both these areas in Italy we need to make a lot of improvement. Thirdly, in some cases the relationship between clubs and fans are not good. Some clubs handle their fans very well, others not ... Some clubs maybe don't talk enough to their fans, some maybe get the run-around from their fans. We've got to work on these three fronts.

'The fourth point, however, is another matter, a legal point, regarding the certainty of punishment. In England, a fan who misbehaves will be apprehended and punished. In Italy, it is not so clear. A fan who misbehaves in Palermo might get banned for three years while a fan who does the same thing at Udine, for example, may get off with a caution thanks to a legal technicality ...

'The Anglo-Saxon legal system is simpler, more direct and provides greater certainty that the person who does something wrong will be immediately punished for that ... And I say that, despite the fact that [the Italian] parliament has passed a series of laws to deal with fan violence. The guy who knifed and killed the Genoa fan [Vincenzo Spagnolo, 29 January 1995, killed prior to a Genoa versus AC Milan game] was out of prison after eleven months ... We live in Italy, with all its strengths and weaknesses ...'

One small but remarkable aspect of the violence seen at the San Siro during the Inter versus Milan Champions League tie subsequently underlined Carraro's point. Police experts watching closed-circuit TV footage of the riot were amazed to see Matteo Saronni amongst the troublemakers. From the village of Isola di Fondra, in the valleys around Bergamo, near Milan, Matteo is a die-hard Inter fan. Four years previously, in May 2001, during an Inter versus Atalanta game, he had pulled off a truly mad and dangerous stunt. Before the match, he stole a moped belonging to an Atalanta fan. He then dragged the vehicle all the way to the top of the stand – for anyone who does not know the stadium, this is no small achievement – then, after the final whistle, he threw the moped over the rails and down to the next level of the grandstand below. By the grace of God, the moped-missile crashed onto the concrete steps below without killing anyone.

Although he was given a suspended 14-month sentence for that stunt, Matteo did not seem to learn from the experience. One year later, during an Inter versus Juventus game at the San Siro, he was again arrested, this time for throwing 'objects' onto the pitch. Subsequently, he was given a five-month suspended sentence and banned from football stadia for six months.

Yet again, the learning process appears to have bypassed Matteo because there he was again on the night of the Inter versus Milan Champions League game at the heart of the *ultras* making his contribution to the downpour of objects that rained down on the AC Milan goal.

By the end of the 2004–5 season, it was hard not to acknowledge that Italian football's violence problem was on the increase. To me, that Inter versus AC Milan Champions League match seemed far removed from a derby I had attended in March 1990. Inter, led by the Germans Lothar Matthäus and Andreas Brehme, had beaten Arrigo Sacchi's Dutch-style Milan team of Frank Rijkaard and Marco Van Basten (Ruud Gullit was out through injury). It was a preview of what was to happen when later that summer West Germany beat the Netherlands 2–1 in a World Cup second-round tie played in the same San Siro stadium.

One of the most vivid impressions of the afternoon, though, had not been left by any of these famous players. What I most recall about that day was travelling on the Milan underground to the game in a train packed with both Inter and AC Milan fans who, cheerfully, swapped insults and jokes in an atmosphere of good-natured banter.

Having travelled in some fear and trepidation on the London underground in the late 1970s and early 1980s after Spurs versus Arsenal and other London derbies, I was struck by the different atmosphere. This was what I expected of Italian football. Rowdy but well-behaved fans, most of them neatly ironed, smelling of Armani aftershave and many of them accompanied by wives and girlfriends.

Inside the Meazza stadium, too, the atmosphere was different that day. Even the most superficial glance down the main grandstand with its rows of suntanned faces, manicured hands, Gucci shoes and mink fur coats made it clear that this was the place to be that Sunday afternoon in Milan. This was far from the land of hooligans, thuggery and 'Com'on Iiingggeeelllland!'

In a very real sense, that was one of the attractions of Italy, a land where the game's subtle skills commanded respect and knowledgeable admiration and where you could watch football in some style. This was not why I had come to Italy but it was certainly a major plus factor.

This was a world where Inter and Milan fans, their ears pressed up against little 'transistor' radios, could still travel together on the same train and watch their derby without crowd problems of any kind. That was the age of Maradona and Platini, a time when there were only 16 teams in Serie A, when the entire programme was played at three o'clock on a Sunday afternoon, when teams had only two foreigners per side and when, if you wanted to see anything other than five minutes of edited highlights, you had to go to the stadium. We have moved on from there, but it is hard to feel, in Italy at least, that things have got better.

TWELVE
AUTUMN

It is November 2005. The winter is setting in, the first cold winds are blowing across the lake. The olives have long since been harvested, while the oranges on the tree at my studio door will shortly be good, if not for eating, then certainly for squeezing. You don't get a more freshly squeezed orange than the one you go out in the morning in your dressing gown to pick.

This morning's edition of the *International Herald Tribune* contains reading matter fit for the winter mood. The Italian comic Beppe Grillo has taken out a full-page advertisement, under the title 'Clean Up Parliament!':

This page has been financed by thousands of Italian citizens to find out whether there is another State in some part of the world in which 23 members of parliament have been convicted of a variety of crimes and yet are allowed to sit in parliament and represent their citizens. If a country like this exists, we Italians would like to propose a 'twinning'.

If there is no such State or country, we ask the world to help us understand why the 23 Italian parliamentarians, already convicted of crimes by the Italian judicial system … sit in the Italian and European parliaments.

Among the crimes for which the parliamentarians, many of them national figures, have received convictions are: bribery, perjury, income tax evasion, taking kick-backs, illegal party financing and various forms of corruption. These convictions are not undergoing the appeal process, and yet those convicted continue to sit in parliament, at the citizens' expense.

Grillo's sense of outrage is commendable. In the era of Berlusconi-dominated media, his voice has long since disappeared off the airwaves. These days, he has to use his blog, the *International Herald Tribune* and his travelling roadshow to make himself heard. Effectively, he has been censored for years now.

Perusal of the newspapers in recent days has offered the usual mixed bag of grim stories about Italy, large and small. There is, for example, a small item in *La Repubblica*'s Rome section, reporting the findings of 'Servizio Roxanne', a social project run by Rome City Council: 'There are 2,500 to 3,000 people, 85 per cent of them women, involved in prostitution on the streets of Rome. We don't have precise figures since the girls are always being changed. The phenomenon is rooted in the entire urban area, by night and by day, depending on the streets ...'

Indeed it is. Drive down any of the huge traffic arteries – the Casalina, the Prenestino, the Tiburtina, the Salaria, the Aurelia – which take you out of Rome, and, at literally any time of day, you will see young women, often clad in little more than bra and knickers, standing brazenly on the side of the road touting for 'work' as the commuters make their way home.

Even as far out as Trevignano, more than 50 kilometres from the centre of Rome, we often have the problem on our roads. When Róisín was smaller, she used to ask us what those poor women were doing standing like that by the side of the road. They are about to have a picnic, we would reply.

On television, too, there have been interesting developments. Adriano Celentano, a talented singer, has up to twelve million viewers tuned into his primetime show just because he has had the nerve to invite on comics critical of Prime Minister Berlusconi. Until Celentano, it had been forbidden to criticise, jeer or poke fun at the Great Communicator himself. Celentano has thumbed his nose at the censorship and in the process caused a major political rumpus by pointing out, among other things, that the Freedom House organisation places Italy at number 77, labelling it 'partly free' in its 'Global Press Freedom Rankings'.

(For the record, accompanying Italy at number 77 are Bolivia, Bulgaria, Mongolia and the Philippines. Cape Verde is ranked number 76, while behind them come Croatia, Senegal and Tonga at number 82. The country with the world's least free press is North Korea at number 194, while three countries share top spot at number one: Finland, Iceland and Sweden. The United States weighs in at number 24, along with Barbados, Canada, Dominica, Estonia and Latvia, while the United Kingdom is next in line at number 30 with Australia, Lithuania, Malta and Micronesia.)

Another interesting little tale from the papers these days concerns the hideout of Mafia godfather, so-called 'Boss of Bosses', Totò Riina, arrested in Palermo, Sicily on 15 January 1993. As I write, a trial is ongoing into how and why Riina's hideout, a villa in Palermo, was not thoroughly searched imme- diately after his arrest.

On the day of his arrest, the public prosecutor's office wanted to move in immediately, obviously in the hope of finding docu- ments, papers and anything else that might throw further light on Riina's criminal activities. Curiously, the ROS (Raggrupamento Operativo Speciale *carabinieri*), the special operations department which had Riina's house under observation, asked for some time, just so that they might observe who went in and out of the place. For reasons not yet clear, the ROS then abandoned their surveil- lance of Riina's hideout on the very day that he was arrested.

It was only 19 days later that a furious Giancarlo Caselli, at the time chief public prosecutor in Palermo, discovered that the hideout had been left totally unguarded. In the meantime – surprise, surprise – the hideout had been cleaned out. This is how mafioso Gioacchino La Barbera, one of those who killed Mafia investigator Giovanni Falcone in 1992, described the clean-up operation years later:

> They wiped out everything. They took the hoover to the place, took away documents, clothes and anything important. They even took out the wall safes, walled up the hole and then repainted the walls so that you could find no trace of anything ... Bricklayers were brought in to change the whole shape of the villa, walls were knocked down and new ones put up in a different place.

In a court hearing on 18 November 2005, witness Giusy Vitale, brother of a mafioso from the Partinico family, told the court: 'My brother told me that in the villa there were documents that would have blown the State apart ... If the forces of law and order had got their hands on those documents, it would have been the end of the world.'

Doubtless this case will join the long, unedifying line of Italian mysteries. What about the June 1980 'Ustica' crash in which an Itavia DC9 passenger plane on an internal flight from Bologna to Palermo was blown out of the air, resulting in the deaths of 81 people? As of today, there is no official explanation, and no one has been brought to court or charged in relation to this disaster, which investigators and independent observers alike have always seen as anything but an accident. The list of such unexplained incidents could go on and on, and might include the Bologna train station bombing of 1980, the Red Brigade killing of Aldo Moro in 1978, and

Mehmet Ali Agca's 1981 assassination attempt on Pope John Paul II.

The point is this: is it reasonable to expect that a society which has allowed such tragic events either to go unpunished or less than fully investigated to be unduly worried about the socio-economic problems facing its football industry? Can you be surprised that such a country – apparently happy with 23 convicted persons sitting in its parliament, whose capital city offers the spectacle of roadside whoreshops in broad daylight – can sometimes struggle to establish law and order in the running of its national game?

There is no denying Italian football's problems. They range from financial meltdown, to doping allegations, a lopsided distribution of TV rights, match-fixing, racism and fan violence. The quality of football played in Serie A is often still very good but the overall 'package' can sometimes look wretched. For example, the country's most successful club, Juventus, plays week after week in a stadium that is two-thirds empty and often on a lousy pitch that has been re-laid so often it looks like a parquet floor. (Admittedly, the pitches at the San Siro in Milan and the Bentegodi in Verona are regularly worse – no mean feat.)

In recent seasons, too, Italian football has done its international image no favours by enforced delays to the start of the Serie A season, prompted by legal wranglings about TV rights and promotion/relegation issues. Being forced to change your fixture list even before the season begins does little for your credibility.

Many would argue that Italian football's senior administrators are a big part of the problem. They are the ones who have overseen the boom years of the 1990s without seriously tackling fundamental problems.

Take the two most important jobs in the administration of Italian football, the presidencies of FIGC and the Lega.

FIGC president Carraro, born in 1940, is a member of that very Italian tribe of long-term political survivors. A former skiing world champion, and a member of the IOC, Carraro was already president of AC Milan at 27 years of age. Since then, he has served as Minister for Tourism as well as Mayor of Rome, while prior to taking over the FIGC presidency in December 2001 he had served as president of the Lega from February 1997.

The Lega president is the dynamic Adriano Galliani, one of Berlusconi's closest and most trusted advisers and the acting boss of AC Milan. Galliani's tenure of the Lega presidency represents a 'conflict of interests within the conflict of interests' embodied by his wealthy political *padrone*. How, for example, can Galliani adjudicate the allocation of TV rights when one of the two contenders is owned by his boss?

That same allocation of TV rights seems destined to remain a source of controversy for some time to come, given that, in the absence of collective bargaining between the clubs and the TV companies (RAI, Mediaset and Sky Italia), the 'cake' of TV money seems very unevenly divided. In the 2005–6 season, Juventus, AC Milan and Inter earned €78.5, €72.9 and €68.8 million respectively from TV rights while Ascoli, Treviso and Siena earned €10.9, €10.8 and €12 million.[20]

The bottom line, here, is that in a context where the clubs are legally entitled to bargain on an individual basis in the wake of 1999 legislation, the most famous and successful names (Juve, AC Milan and Inter) will immediately command the largest fees. What about sharing the TV wealth around in the manner of English, French and German leagues, with a collective bargaining system? Does that financial imbalance not risk turning the Serie A title contest into a three-horse race (Juventus, Inter and AC Milan) in which the other clubs merely make up the numbers?

Leaving aside the TV rights issue, critics also argue that Carraro, Galliani and others paid little attention to the financial mismanagement of Italian football, highlighted not only by the spectacular crashes of clubs like Fiorentina and Napoli but also by a mismanagement which became front-page news in March 2004 when the Guardia di Finanza, Italy's tax and finance police, staged 53 raids on the administrative offices of all Serie A, Serie B and some Serie C sides as well as on those of FIGC and the Lega.

Among the factors that had prompted this unprecedented action was a dossier presented to the finance police by Giuseppe Gazzoni Frascara, owner of the then Serie A side Bologna. Put simply, he argued that Italian football is not being played on a level playing field for the good reason that some clubs pay their taxes and their players punctually, and file correctly audited balance sheets, while others do not. Those who 'fiddle the books', claim the Bologna boss, have an unfair advantage on their league rivals since their tax evasion, irregular player wage payment and fraudulent bookkeeping leaves them with greater resources to spend on buying the best players.

'Creative accountancy', claimed Gazzoni Frascara, abounds in Italian football. In particular, clubs do one another favours by putting a false value on players so as to beef up their books. Take the case of the two Milan clubs, which for years now have regularly sold players to one another. Francesco Coco, Clarence Seedorf, Andreas Guglielminpietro, Dario Simic and Christian Vieri are merely the first that come to mind. They were all top-class internationals, of course, and it was only normal that their transfers moved serious sums of money. But what about the following players: goalkeeper Paolo Ginestra, striker Matteo Bogani, midfielder Davide Cordone, midfielder Marco Bonura, and defenders Andrea Polizzano and Fabio Di Sauro?

Between 1999 and 2002, these players were all involved in

cross-town Milan transfers which yielded the clubs, on paper at least, €3.5 million each time. All fine, except that none of us has ever seen these million-euro footballers play in Serie A, given that they ended up with lower-level clubs Sassuolo, Olbia, Prato, Avellino and Catania.

Then there was the Serie A club which sold 26 players one week and then mysteriously bought them back shortly afterwards. Certainly, for at least a week or two, the club's books were looking good. Another regular trick concerns the registering of transfers. Often transfer sales are written into the balance sheet immediately while transfer purchases are not written in until the following season.

For at least one club – namely, heavily indebted Roma – the timing of the finance police raids in March 2004 could not have been worse. In the very week that the police struck, Roma owner Franco Sensi had appeared on the point of concluding the sale of the club to Nafta Moskva, a Russian petrol conglomerate.

Even if they had their misgivings, Roma fans were already preparing to welcome the Russians, who were reportedly willing to splash out €400 million both to buy the club and wipe out its (then) €239.2 million worth of debt. Unsurprisingly, however, the sale fell through, with the Russians' Italian lawyer Salvatore Trifirò claiming that his clients had been worried by the implications of the police raids. In reality, the men from Nafta Moskva were probably even more worried by the size of Roma's debts. In the week of the tax raids Italian football registered a massive vote of no-confidence, at home and abroad.

By the summer of 2004, the financial crisis facing Italian soccer was so bad that Covisoc, FIGC's financial watchdog and the body to which all professional clubs are required to present audited accounts each summer, was being forced to cut some corners. In theory, the clubs are required to guarantee not only that their accounts are in order but also that they have the necessary financial cover to meet the forthcoming season's expenses. Yet, by the summer of 2004, Covisoc was reluctantly agreeing to settle for accounts which showed that the club had paid seven out of the last twelve months of wages owed to their players. As for the other five months, the clubs were given until December to pay them. So widespread is the practice of late payments that Covisoc presumably felt it had no option but to extend this leeway rather than demote the transgressors. At this same time, and off the record, one senior, now retired Covisoc member told me that throughout the second half of the 1990s, a blind eye was turned to a variety of serious financial irregularities and shortcomings that were only too evident from even a cursory reading of club books.

Nor do recent financial assessments of Italian football make for reassuring reading. In the 2005 edition of their 'Annual Review of Football Finance', the international accountancy firm Deloitte reported that at the end of the 2003–4 season, the operating losses of Serie A clubs totalled €341 million, meaning cumulative losses of around €1.5 billion since 1995–6.

Furthermore, of the 18 clubs which contested the 2003–4 championship, only two – Reggina and Bologna – returned a seasonal profit, while Lazio lost €86.9 million, Roma €66.8 million, Parma €85.9 million and champions AC Milan €51.5 million. (Player wages accounted for 72 per cent of the clubs' running costs, as compared to 52 per cent in the English Premiership.) On top of that, nearly all the big clubs owe serious sums of money to the Inland Revenue.[21]

Then, there is the poor quality of Italy's stadia, some of which – such as the Stadio delle Alpi – were even built, badly and new, for the Italia '90 World Cup finals. President Carraro, with an eye on Italy's bid to host the 2012 European Championship, insists that brand-new, purpose-designed or modernised stadia are the first important step towards a better future for Italian football. In his briefing at the foreign press club in January 2005 he said: 'There are stadia in Italy which are simply less than decent, where it's difficult even to find the toilets, where from certain parts of the stand you have difficulty seeing the match ... you have got to have comfortable stadia where you see the game really well from every part of the ground. In a lot of cases, that means taking away the athletics track. There has to be a plus factor about going to the stadium'

Many would agree with Carraro and would also point out that Italian clubs have been severely handicapped by the fact that almost none of them own their own grounds, which are usually the property of the local authority. Not for nothing, Juventus has bought the Stadio delle Alpi, where they intend to abolish the running track and reduce the stadium to a 45,000-seater. Not for nothing, too, Claudio Lotito, the industrial cleaning magnate who took over Lazio in July 2004, sees the building of Lazio's own stadium as crucial for the club's future, arguing that it could generate an annual €20 million. At the most recent count, box-office receipts in Italian football account for 16 per cent of total annual club income as opposed to 30 per cent in the English Premiership.

Just to complete the grim picture, there is the decline in match attendances. In the 1991–2 season, *La Repubblica* has reported, Serie A games returned an average attendance of 34,204. By the 2004–5 season that average attendance had dropped to 24,988, while figures for the first six days of the 2005–6 season showed a further alarming drop to 21,154.[22]

Carraro, however, rejected the idea of Italian football in crisis, arguing that its problems are merely the reflection of the problems of Italian society as a whole. 'Football in Italy is a sporting activity with huge social and economic implications,' he said at the foreign press club in January 2005. 'For that reason, it is currently going through all the same difficulties and problems of the country at large, of the Italian economy ...

'It is true, though, Italian football does have its problems.

The clubs spend far too much, that's clear. But it is worth point-ing out that the 132 clubs of Serie A, B, C1 and C2 this year had to come up with €725 million before they could enrol in this year's leagues. The clubs came up with that money ... but what FIGC cannot do is dictate to the clubs as to how they spend their money because they are commercial entities protected by law ...

'In 2003 the comprehensive debt of all the clubs to the Inland Revenue was €500 million; by 2004 it had sunk to €200 million. What is more, clubs that want to enrol for next season's championship will have to have their books in order by 31 March, not only with regard to the payment of players' wages but also with regard to taxes and social security payments. Clubs that are still in debt have to show that they are making regular payments to the Inland Revenue ...'

In fairness to Carraro, the decisions taken in the summer of 2005, whereby sides like Perugia and Torino were denied promotion to Serie A because of financial irregularities, suggest that FIGC is, finally, beginning to take the problem of fiscal recti-tude (or the lack of it) seriously. But why was a blind eye turned for so long?

Another equally contentious issue, already touched on, concerns the suspicion that the so-called '*palazzo*' (the football powers-that-be) is merely a slavish servant of the two most powerful clubs – AC Milan and Juventus. Many are convinced that these two clubs not only regularly benefit from 'friendly refereeing' but also so completely dominate the Italian football scene that they can make life difficult for those who stand in their way. In an interview with *Il Romanista*, a daily paper dedicated to Roma, in October 2004, Gino Corioni, the president of Brescia, who has been involved in running football clubs for the last 30 years, had this to say about the Juventus–Milan cartel:

In Serie A and Serie B, at least half the club directors are relatively inexperienced and therefore easily influenced or intimidated. It was said to me, and I am no youngster and have had plenty of experience, that 'If you try to oppose us, you won't be in football for long. Do you know where Brescia will end up? In amateur football.' I don't give a damn, but the others? ... The problem is that, since 1997, we've had the mastermind running things, a guy whose ideas always suit AC Milan and therefore get the backing of the president of the Lega. The president of FIGC, for his part, doesn't even dare to propose an idea of his own that goes against the mastermind and, in consequence, against Milan ... The mastermind has been deciding on the most important issues in Italian football for years now.

So who is this mastermind? asks the interviewer. Could it be the Juventus managing director, Antonio Giraudo?

You said it, not me ... Giraudo is someone who has worked all his life for Fiat. Before [the late] Umberto Agnelli came back to take over [Fiat], he had been cut out by Gianni Agnelli ... Perhaps Gianni was still much attached to the old school, to the Boniperti era, to that which came to be called the 'Juventus style'. They were still a very powerful club but that power was handled in a different way, with a yesteryear elegance ... Today's Juventus management think only of getting results ... They're the opposite of the 'Juventus style'. They go for the essential, they think money.[23]

Critics often point to the fact that Juventus and Milan between them have won twelve of the 14 Serie A titles contested between

1992 and 2005 as proof of their cynical manipulation of the football system. It has to be remembered, however, that they are
historically strong clubs who have been winning league titles for
the best part of the last hundred years.

Still, one of the most frequently repeated metropolitan myths
about today's Italian football is that it is all 'controlled' by
Luciano Moggi, the Juventus sports director. Most of the time,
people say that sort of thing to you in a conspiratorial and knowing way at the press-room bar at half-time. Rarely does anyone
make such accusations in print. One exception came in February
2005 when the former president of Ancona (now Serie C) gave
an interview to *La Repubblica*. Mr Pieroni is certainly no saint –
he has been charged with fraudulent bankruptcy and has other
charges to answer in seven different cases. Yet, in this interview,
he points a very specific finger at Luciano Moggi, suggesting
that, via the sports agency GEA (in which both his son
Alessandro Moggi and Davide Lippi, son of former Juventus and
current Italy coach Marcello Lippi, have senior management
roles), Moggi '*padre*' exerts undue influence:

> I paid people in cash, I dodged taxes, and for that I did
> 53 days in jail as well as 110 of house arrest. If I have to
> work out who did all this to me, Moggi would be at the
> top of the list. He never forgave me when Perugia beat
> Juventus on 14 May 2000. [Pieroni was the sports direc-
> tor of Perugia at the time and that defeat, after a heavy
> downpour had interrupted the game, cost Juventus the
> title on the last day of the season.]
>
> Through his network, Luciano manages to control
> eight Serie A teams … He has placed sports directors and
> other directors in lots of clubs, even in ones that are
> historically enemies of Juventus. Via GEA, he controls
> two hundred players and many coaches, and that way he

determines results. I've been in football for 40 years and ... the things that I'm saying are well known to people in football.

Moggi, for his part, has totally rejected such accusations many times, often suggesting that they are merely sour grapes in the face of Juve's impressive winning record. In an interview for *Il Mattino* in 2004, he commented:

Pieroni is neither a friend nor an enemy. In football, there are no friends and no enemies, there is only the chance to go places or go nowhere. I've often been attacked but I've never sued anyone. Football is a crazy stage full of madmen, some more, some less. I opted to take part in the game and accept the way it is. The fact is that no one wants to lose and that the loser shouts louder than everyone else, screaming about conspiracies ... But what conspiracy are they talking about? The important thing is to win, and I win.

Nowhere is that sense of conspiracy more prevalent than when it comes to refereeing. The Italian sports media pay as much, sometimes more attention to refereeing appointments as they do to team selections, often highlighting a referee's track record.

Almost every weekend, the conspiracy theorists find grist for their mills. Back in April 1998, however, they had a bonanza time with a match and a decision which still prompts rancour today. This was the Juventus versus Inter Milan game, the fourth last match of that season, a top-of-the-table clash that would effectively settle the title contest. Holders Juventus were being given a real run for their money by Inter, featuring 'new boy' Brazilian Ronaldo and coached by Gigi Simoni.

With the score at 1–0 for Juventus (from a Del Piero first-half goal), referee Piero Ceccarini denied Inter an apparently blatant second-half penalty when Juve defender Mark Iuliano flattened Ronaldo. The ref's decision that day had a major impact on the final result: a 1–0 win for Juve, who went on to win the title. In the meantime, all hell broke loose, the match and the disputed penalty decision even finding their way into parliamentary question time in the following days.

I was at the Stadio delle Alpi that day, and the least one could honestly say is that it was a 'controversial' decision. From the grandstand and on subsequent replays, it looked to me like a clear penalty.

In November 2005, Inter Milan shareholder and Pirelli managing director Marco Tronchetti Provera may have had both Luciano Moggi and that April 1998 game in mind when he commented: 'One of the reasons Inter have not won a league title for so many years is that we've never stooped to get involved in power games.'

To some extent, the conspiracy theories make for amusing reading. There is, however, nothing amusing about the issue of racism in Italian football, and, in this context, it is at least arguable that neither the football governing classes nor the clubs themselves take the problem seriously.

In November 2005, Messina's Ivory Coast defender, 21-year-old Mark Zoro, prompted a major hullabaloo when he threatened to stop a Serie A game because of the racist abuse being directed at him by Inter fans. In the sixty-seventh minute of the game, played in Messina, Zoro picked up the ball and then went across to the referee's assistant to demand that he stop the game because of the racist chants of the Inter fans, aimed at him. Neither the referee nor his assistants, however, were willing to adopt such drastic action. Meanwhile, black opponents in the

Inter team such as Nigerian Obafemi Martins and Brazilian Adriano pleaded with Zoro to stay on the pitch and not force the suspension of the game. In the end, the match resumed and Inter won 2–0. Talking to the press after the game, Zoro explained:

> It's bad enough that I have to put up with fans making monkey noises and calling me a black shit every time Messina play away from home, but it's never happened to me before that I was systematically insulted at my home ground. That's just too much. For a minute or two, that's all I could think of. We've got to stop this game. It's really important that we send a strong message to these people otherwise this shameful behaviour will never end …
>
> The Inter players [Adriano and Martins] were decent about the whole thing because they get the same sort of treatment themselves every Sunday too. The only thing was I got the impression they were more worried about finishing the game rather than having it suspended because, of course, they were winning 2–0 at the time. Yet, in my opinion, a strong gesture like that [abandoning the pitch] would have done good for the whole world of football.

Inevitably, Zoro's gesture did not go unnoticed, the Italian media devoting much space and time to the incident. Typical was this comment from *Gazzetta Dello Sport*: 'The day that players respond to those idiots who shout racist abuse at players by walking off the pitch … will be a great day, and not just for football.' Petrol millionaire Massimo Moratti, the man who can afford to bankroll Inter as an act of sporting faith, expressed his total solidarity with Zoro, who, he said, was, 'terrific. He has the courage and the indignation of a person in the right. He was dead right. I admire him for it.'

FIGC, too, got in on the act, decreeing that the following week's Italian Cup and Serie A games would all start five minutes late, with the players entering the pitch carrying banners which read 'No to Racism'.

It all sounds like a genuinely caring response. Yet, the suspicion remains that Italian football authorities pay lip service to the issue of combating racism in football, without really understanding or wanting to understand the seriousness of the problem. Remember, too, that in recent years there have been many other incidents. In 1996, Verona fans burned a dummy in protest at the club's intention of hiring a black player. In October 2000, Arsenal's Patrick Vieira complained about racist abuse from Serbian Lazio defender Sinisa Mihajlovic, in a much-publicised incident during a Champions League tie. In 2001, Treviso fans booed when Nigerian Omolade came on as a substitute for their own team; the Treviso players responded by painting their faces black for their next home game.

The fact that some Inter fans continued to shout abuse at Zoro three days later when the club played Parma in an Italian Cup tie suggests that not everyone has learned the lesson.

Does all of this – the financial irregularities, the politics, the conspiracies, the racism – mean that Italian football is launched on the path of definitive decline and fall? Frankly, no, and for the good reason that football is too fundamental a component of the Italian DNA. Italian football may no longer be the Hollywood of the world game, it may well have lost much of its economic clout (regarding the attraction of big-name players) and 'product value' in relation to Spanish and English football, but it remains highly competitive.

In this context, too, it is interesting to note that underage football has never been more popular. In 2003, there were

725,000 kids from the ages of six to 16 enrolled with 8,536 recognised sports clubs, playing a staggering 530,000 games in every corner of the country. Even if statistics say that only one in 50,000 of the children who sign a 'baby' contract (at 14 or 15 years of age) will actually make it to Serie A, while one in 5,000 may make it into Serie C, none of this seems to stop the flow.

Unscrupulous agents, keeping their eyes open on behalf of the big professional clubs, make the most of the dreams that motivate a twelve-year-old – as well as his parents. The agent flatters the potentially talented twelve-year-old, persuading him to leave home and try the 'big adventure' with one of the 'satellite' clubs run by the big northern clubs. If and when the kid makes it and signs a 'baby' contract, then the agent takes his percentage. If not, too bad. The agent probably omits to tell his young client's family that even if he is one of the lucky ones and makes it into Serie C, he will not exactly be earning a Beckham-sized salary or leading a similar lifestyle. In Serie C, especially in the south, €25,000 per annum is normal. That is, of course, if you get paid at all.

Football is always intimately linked to a broad swathe of socio-economic, political and cultural considerations. If Italian football seems in crisis, so too does the country itself. Twenty years ago, Italy, led by Socialist Prime Minister Bettino Craxi, was proudly boasting that its economy had become bigger, richer and more affluent (although, significantly, not more influential) than that of Great Britain. Yet, 20 years later, Italy is looking more and more like the sick man of Western Europe, as its once cosily protected, over-politicised economy struggles to survive on the stormy oceans of market-driven commerce. By comparison with the strident Italy of the *sorpasso*, the country now seems in a political, cultural and economic depression.

It is hard not to feel that, in some way, the apparent loss of national self-confidence has been reflected in some recent Italian football performances. Take the last major act of the 2004–5 European club season, that dramatic Champions League final in Istanbul.

Football analysts will assure you that Liverpool came back from 3–0 down to defeat AC Milan in a penalty shootout thanks, above all, to sheer grit, determination and a very British refusal to throw in the towel. That could well be, but the sight of an Italian team 3–0 up at half-time proving itself unable to 'administer' the match from there to the finish defies all logic. Just, indeed, as it defied logic that Italy would let France in for an injury-time equaliser 20 seconds from the final whistle in the Euro 2000 final in Rotterdam.

In simple football terms, you might argue that the problem is merely a tactical one. It is not that *catenaccio*, the traditional defensive game where the first priority is not to concede a goal, no longer works. It is more that Italian teams no longer play it. Rule changes in the last 15 years and the AC Milan revolution (the insistence on attractive, attacking football), pioneered by coach Arrigo Sacchi but sponsored by club owner Berlusconi, have changed things.

Italian teams, these days, are sometimes neither fish nor fowl, neither able to defend as well as they once did nor able to strike on the counter-attack as venomously as in the past. Just as the national economy has had difficulties adapting to a post-protectionist (defensive), single EU market, so too is Italian football having difficulty adapting to a post-*catenaccio* world.

Obviously, this equation does not entirely hold up. Football never lends itself to quite such facile analysis. For a start, whilst the national economy finds it difficult to remain competitive, the best Italian teams continue regularly to turn up in Champions League and other finals. Furthermore, by the time this is read, Italy may well have performed more than well at the Germany

World Cup finals. Nonetheless, a connection of sorts does exist, if only for the obvious reason that the more your economy prospers and grows, the more money there is to be spent on bread, circuses and football teams.

Italian football, like Italy itself, is stuck in a moment and does not know how to get out of it.

Yet, Italian football will always have its very own fascination, in the same way that millions of tourists will always want to travel to see the glories of Rome, Florence, Venice and thousands of other places on the peninsula. Italian resilience, inventiveness and native genius will doubtless keep Italy and Italian football in the front-row seats at the world movie. The cold November winds may be blowing, the lights may be flickering, but they have not, and will not, go out.

CODA

People often tell me that they envy me my job. Watching all that Italian football must be just terrific, they say; I'd love a job like that. Italian football is so good, it has such skill, such quality, they add.

By and large, they are right. Italian football, in some ways, reflects the vital energies of a nation whose sense of style and creative powers make Armani shirts, Valentino suits, Gucci shoes and Ferrari cars much-desired consumer icons.

Yet, if you watch more than 120 Italian league and cup games per season, you tend to see plenty of bad ones, too. Italian football is different, and it is different because, along with skill, comes caution.

I often think that the attitude taken by FIGC to the running of their national cup competition tells its own little tale. Rather than have an open draw, as in France, Germany and (particularly) England, the Italian Cup is largely restricted to the top three divisions, with the Serie A big guns entering the fray only in the final stages. In other words, you can never have the little amateur side from the valleys meeting Manchester United or Paris St Germain or Bayern Munich in an early round, as regularly happens in England, France and Germany. Indeed, for many fans, the enduring attraction of the FA Cup in England is exactly this democracy, which means that, for a day at least, one of the smallest teams in the land gets to play on the same stage as the biggest. In Italy, it seems, we do not want to run that risk. We do not want to watch much-hyped, much-vaunted Inter, Roma or Milan struggle to overcome a good amateur side. That, frankly, would be a very *brutta figura*, and we certainly want to avoid that.

In an ideal world, the Italian game might bring together the creative genius of Da Vinci, the fun of the *carnevale* and the improvisational skills of the sixteenth-century street theatre, the *commedia dell'arte*. Twenty years down the road, I would humbly suggest it brings together the calculating cynicism of Machiavelli, the minimalism of Beckett and the occasional, lightning flash of any Renaissance genius you care to name, from Michelangelo to Raphael.

Put another way, Italian football and Italian footballers almost never 'throw caution to the wind', 'opt to give it a lash', 'put their heads down and charge', and so forth. Italian football, like Italians themselves, is pragmatic, careful, reasoned and aimed at limiting risk-taking to the minimum. For that reason, its greatest tactical contribution to the world game has been to invent a canny, defence-based tactic in which you aim to make the most of the occasional counter-attack. It is a splendid style, in its own way, and one that has proved effective in the past and doubtless will prove effective again in the future. I personally like it, others may not. Yet it is not the sort of anarchic, atavistic spectacle that some might imagine as typically Italian. There again, Italian anarchists nearly always go home to Mama for a plate of pasta after the demonstration.

After 20 years of life in this country, I realise that football has a very special place in Italian society, at that ill-defined cutting edge where politics, power and populism meet. From Mussolini to Berlusconi to the child at the café table beside you, it touches everyone. For that reason, it truly is a major factor in the Italian mindset, whether you are a football fan or otherwise. For that reason, too, the old cliché about the unifying qualities of the Italian national team tends to be true. Italians, by and large, do not have a strong sense of State, but they do have a very strong sense of just how, where, when and with what personnel the national team should play.

That is why I like to see the *azzurri* do well, and it is why I look forward to World Cup and European Championship finals. I just hope, too, that the next time Italy get to such a final and find themselves leading as the game goes into stoppage time, they hold on to win. *Campioni del mondo, campioni del mondo –* that would be one match report I would like to write.

REFERENCES

1. 'Il Terremoto Infinito', *La Repubblica*, 13/12/2004
2. 'Quelle Feste Con I Boss', *La Repubblica*, 15/02/1991
3. 'Il Calcio Dello Cifre Fasulle, Ecco I Trucchi Delle Società', *La Repubblica*, 13/04/2004
   'Sempre Diù Rossi I Conti Del Pallone', *La Repubblica*, 18/11/2004
4. 'Il Soldi Del Diavolo', *La Repubblica*, 10/07/1992
5. *Il Padrione del Diavolo* (Ferrari), Camunia, 1990
6. 'Foot Politics, Tifo Dunque Voto', *Limes*, 2005
7. 'Dimezzate Lo Spalmadebiti', *La Repubblica*, 13/03/2005
8. 'Gli Italiani Nel Pallone', Sondaggio LaPolis, *Limes*, 2005
9. *Rapporto Italia 2004*, EURIPSES, 2004
10. *Indagine Censis-Fondazione BNC*, 2003
11. Testimony from *Tribulane di Torino*, 26/02/2004
12. Testimony from *Tribulane di Torino*, 10/07/2003
13. *Motivazioni, Tribulane di Torino*, released 2005
14,15,16,17,18. Lega Disciplinary Commission, July 2005
19. Lega Disciplinary Commission, August 2005
20. 'La Nuova A A Rischiostrappo', *Gazzetta Dello Sport*, 26/10/2005
21. *Annual Review of Football Finance*, Deloitte
    'Il Calcio Dello Cifre Fasulle, Ecco I Trucchi Delle Società', *La Repubblica*, 13/04/2004
    'Sempre Diù Rossi I Conti Del Pallone', *La Repubblica*, 18/11/2004
22. 'Le Cifre Della Grande Fuga', *La Repubblica*, 05/10/2005
23. 'Il Pallone Non E Rotonda' *Limes*, 2005
    'Il Pallone E Tonde', *L'Ancora de Meditteraneo*, 2005

INDEX